Swallow

Also by Mary Cappello

Night Bloom
Awkward: A Detour
Called Back: My Reply to Cancer, My Return to Life

Swallow

Foreign Bodies, Their Ingestion, Inspiration,
and the Curious Doctor Who Extracted Them

Mary Cappello

THE NEW PRESS

NEW YORK
LONDON

Requests for permission to reproduce selections from this book should be mailed
to: Permissions Department, The New Press, 38 Greene Street, New York, NY
10013.

Published in the United States by The New Press, New York, 2011

Distributed by Perseus Distribution

LIBRARY OF CONGRESS CATALOGING-IN-PUBLICATION DATA

Cappello, Mary.
  Swallow : foreign bodies, their ingestion, inspiration, and the curious doctor
who extracted them / Mary Cappello.
      p. cm.
  Includes bibliographical references and index.
  ISBN 978-1-59558-395-6 (hc)
1. Throat—Foreign bodies.   2. Deglutition.   3. Jackson, Chevalier, 1865–
1958.   I. Title.
  [DNLM: 1. Mütter Museum.   ]
  QP311.C37   2011
  612.3'1—dc22

                                                              2010035608

The New Press was established in 1990 as a not-for-profit alternative to the
large, commercial publishing houses currently dominating the book publishing
industry. The New Press operates in the public interest rather than for private
gain, and is committed to publishing, in innovative ways, works of educational,
cultural, and community value that are often deemed insufficiently profitable.

www.thenewpress.com

Composition by dix!
This book was set in ITC New Baskerville

Printed in the United States of America

10   9   8   7   6   5   4   3   2   1

For Jeannie and Jim,
for Malaga, and for Russell.
I gulp. You gulp.

We are always at, or on, the oral stage wherever else we are.
—ADAM PHILLIPS, *The Beast in the Nursery*

CONTENTS

IV. Mystery Bones and the Unrecovered Boy   235

AUTHOR'S NOTE

I use the following abbreviations throughout this book to refer to texts by Chevalier Jackson that I rely on most frequently: *LCJ* for *The Life of Chevalier Jackson: An Autobiography*; *DAFP* for *Diseases of the Air and Food Passages of Foreign-Body Origin*; *NMP* for "New Mechanical Problems in the Broncho-scopic Extraction of Foreign Bodies from the Lungs and Esophagus"; *B&E* for *Bronchoscopy and Esophagoscopy: A Manual of Peroral Endoscopy and Laryngeal Surgery*. I rely throughout on Jackson's abbreviated coinage "fbdy" to refer to "foreign body." I capitalize the word "thing" when I want it to refer to an object that has undergone a transformation once it has been swallowed, retrieved, studied, and placed in Jackson's collection, or for objects that, by way of over-valuation, exert an auratic charge.

I.

WHO *WAS* THAT MAN?

What was so potent about these protected objects? Was it that my world was
kept out? Or that some imaginary world was kept in? . . . It took very little
time to see that the objects spoke to one another, and to me.
                              —ALLEN KURZWEIL, *The Case of Curiosities*

"Alone on Floor with Pile of Buttons"

This is a book about stowage and retrieval.

A book made of things found in a cabinet—not just *any* cabinet, but
a recess containing a plenitude beyond all human measure. Not just *any*
things, but wondrous, weird, and even sacred things. Many things that had
one thing in common: a strangeness that conjoined them without making them into twins. Common objects turned into mysterious markers because of what they'd been through, where they'd gotten lost, and how they
were later found. Here are capital Things, and so I will capitalize them.
Here are trinkets not reducible to trifles.

The regularity of living (or its pretense) seems at odds with the fabulous specimens in Philadelphia's Mütter Museum, a repository of medical curiosities created to instruct nineteenth-century practitioners. The
building is unprepossessing—it could be an elementary school with its
Aladdin lamp insignia and shoe-buckle window designs, offset by its stately
marble floors; the edifice is small, not grand, made intimate by its adjacent
medicinal garden and cherrywood doors. But does anyone who enters its
hallways afterward forget what he has seen? In 1858, Thomas Dent Mütter, a prominent Philadelphia surgeon who specialized in treating cases
of clubfoot and harelip, endowed the museum and contributed his collection of seventeen hundred anatomic and pathological specimens and
other assorted items to the College of Physicians of Philadelphia. One of
the oldest private medical societies in the country, the college included

Benjamin Rush among its founders; it was at Rush's suggestion that the garden was created to stock doctors' individual medicine chests and to inform a pharmacopoeia-in-the-making.

What's the distance between a face caught in a cornice on an apartment building across the way and the human skulls arranged on shelves inside the Mütter Museum's glass cabinets? Across the street from the museum on Twenty-second Street, there's a facade made of bodiless singing baby heads stuck inside bonnets made from their cut-off arms—or are they the wings of angels into which their heads are nestled, out from which their open mouths protrude? I think they are diminutive gargoyles, hark-the-herald pudge-ims who have forgotten their origins as gargoyles, hewn from *gargouille* (Old French) and *gurgulio* (Old Latin), words that refer to the throat, or to the gurgling sound of water a gargoyle displaces through the spout that is its mouth.

It's impossible to escape a sense of the uncanny here—the sudden recognition of what was once believed, later strenuously forgotten, and now again confirmed, and I wonder how many are tempted to follow a particular item in the museum to an end and a beginning and back again. Toward multiple beginnings, and multiple ends. Even those who haven't been to the Mütter Museum may have heard of its "horned woman" replica, its displays of Siamese twins, its "wall of eyes," or its numerous anatomical figures in wax that so closely approximate human flesh they animate that all-too-narrow threshold between the living and the dead. On the ground floor of the museum, as I round a bend past the skeleton of a "giant," my eyes widen to take in, in adjacent glass cases, an enormous bowel, better suited to a dinosaur than a man but nevertheless extracted from a diseased human body, and the tiny, handsomely articulated bones of a fetal skeleton arranged in perfect rows of white against black. Between the bowel in its waterless aquarium and the baby bones inlaid into velvet like a set of numbered jewels sits an unremarkable oaken girth, a solid piece of furniture that you might have to be bookish to notice at all. In fact, in my fascinated stupor, I had missed it; I was busy examining an ill-lit collection nearby that seemed to contain a cross between seashells and miniature musical instruments but that was actually a gathering of cartilaginous labyrinths and cochleas, the significant bits of bone that govern balance, when my friend called to me: "Get a load of this! Take a look at *this*!"

The case, at the time of this writing, is awkwardly situated beneath a staircase, so if you stand to one side of it, you can hear the patter of other visitors on the stairs; in order properly to view it, you might have to bend so as not to hit your head on the stairway's metal underside. Resembling an old waist-high library card catalog, the cabinet is heavy and windowless but features rows of handles waiting to be pulled. The Mütter Museum isn't, like Philadelphia's children's museum, a "Please Touch" museum, so one might feel wary of the invitation offered by a placard to OPEN the drawers.

Might the slender crypts be filled with slabs or parts of bodies? The crude and unpliable instruments of early medical practice? The scarily heavy shackles used in the eighteenth century to subdue the mad? The jaw tumor of Grover Cleveland? Human placenta? No. These items are all on plain view in other corners of the museum's small rooms and alcoves, whose wooden cabinets loom in chorus as if to echo the seriated arches of the Unitarian church next door. Could the cabinet be the apothecary accompaniment to the medicinal garden? A pullout drawer whirs on its ball-bearing casings to reveal a carefully arrayed collection of small objects mounted inside little squares, numbered, secured in place with a thread or a wire, and framed. But what order of things are these, and who could have been responsible for their steadfast arrangement? What form of wondrous *de*rangement have we here?

The objects in this set of drawers are items that have come into unnatural contact with the human body: not butterflies, moths, or beetles, these are indigestible and undigested *things*, Things that people have swallowed or inhaled. A pioneering laryngologist named Chevalier Jackson and the colleagues whom he trained extracted nonsurgically more than two thousand "foreign bodies" from people's airways and stomachs and then preserved them in this cabinet, and in this way gave back to them a local habitation and a name. (See figure 1.)

A placard perched atop the set of drawers explains that Jackson, who died in 1958 at the age of ninety-three, wished for the collection of "Foreign Bodies Removed from the Air and Food Passageways" to be "accessible to whomever the [Philadelphia] College of Physicians Deemed Proper." "These specimens," he had insisted, "are not mere curiosities."

Feeling mighty curious, eager to open an unexpected drawer, I am clearly not the intended audience for these Things. My eyes swim with delighted interest, not just in the objects themselves and their imagined sojourns, but also in Jackson's dedicated arrangement. Not curiosities, Jackson repeats; "with the accompanying data," these foreign bodies "are, in my opinion, of enormous clinical value to the physician and surgeon."

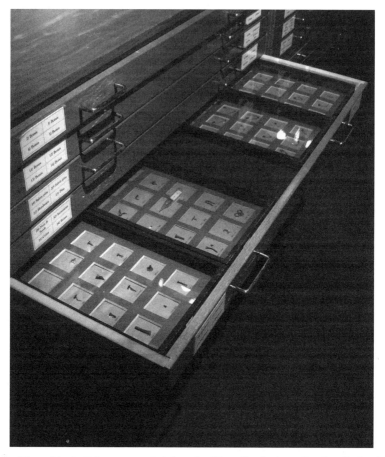

Fig. 1. The cabinet of drawers containing the Chevalier Jackson Foreign Body Collection. Collection of the Mütter Museum, The College of Physicians of Philadelphia.

The data reside in a barely liftable, several-inches-thick Xerox copy of a portion of a book that also sits atop the drawers: *Classified Tabulation of Various Foreign Bodies Endoscopically Removed from the Air and Food Passages with Illustrations of the Foreign Bodies and All Data Pertaining to Their Removal.* Using the text as a cross-reference, a reader can match any of the objects in the drawers with a grid of information that Jackson provides: following each item and drawer number, we can learn the age and sex of the person belonging to the object, the type of foreign body removed, where in the upper torso it was lodged and for how long, the type of anesthetic used (usually none), the type of tube used to extract it, any problems that presented themselves, the type of forceps used, the point of seizure of the object, the result (mostly in bald terms "cured" or "died"), the length of time it took to remove the object, and further remarks about the case.

Lean down toward a drawer and marvel at the categories of lodged and swallowed things:

Coins and other disks
Hardware
Pins and needles
Jewelry
Seeds, nuts and shells
Meat
Bones
Wool and cotton
Buttons
Minerals
Dental and surgical objects
Utensils
Toys

Open a drawer and feel your heart arrested by the shapely particularity of each foreign body and the question heralded of "How?" Here are double-pointed staples, a pair of tooth roots shaped like a tiny pair of pants, the brass foot of an alarm clock, Buffalo-head nickels and Mercury dimes, a half dollar dated 1892. A toy goat, an Audubon Society pin, a tin steering wheel from a toy automobile, a bottle cap, rivets and woodscrews and nails. One toy wristwatch and one real wristwatch; a crucifix with several rosary beads still attached; the metallic letter Z from a toy airplane, one tiddlywink, and a handful of gruesome endogenous objects—substances, like hardened pus, produced by the body itself. Pins, silvery blue, and in each case opened, splayed, an alphabet of angles, upside down or right side up; bones, some slender as a lock of hair. Hairpins and bobbins, hooks and nails, collar buttons, and wire. A two-inch long nail. A padlock. Meat in the form of owl pellets, mosaic indices of onetime food. Jacks the color of their many-pointed shadows on a floor. A radiator key, tiny binoculars (or opera glasses) (see figure 2), a lead-alloy horse, a metallic greyhound, a donkey, a plastic binky doll, the eye of a teddy bear, an umbrella tip, a bundle of string. Numerous peanut kernels—a fraction of which can kill a man. A poker chip, a coffee berry (unroasted), several cockleburs, a carpet

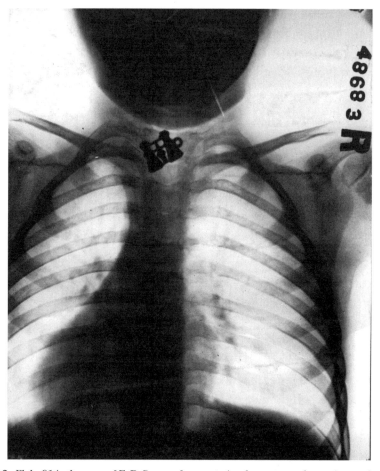

Fig. 2. Fbdy 914, the case of E.R.S., age four, a pair of toy opera glasses in esophagus. Radiologist, Dr. Willis F. Manges (1876–1936). Collection of the Mütter Museum, The College of Physicians of Philadelphia.

tack, a pin (common), a pin (with a white glass head), fragments of egg-shell, a campaign button. A beauty pin and a brooch. A canna seed and a Christmas tree ornament. Orange pulp, a prune seed, the ear from a toy horse. Rubber bands, a burrlike mass, a Job's tear. Birdshot, a shawl pin, a toothbrush bristle, mutton bone, beans, a sixpenny nail, a cambric needle, a toothpaste cap, some oyster shell, a stove bolt, grapeskins, a bullet. A nib of crayon. A glass bead intact. A Perfect Attendance pin (see figure 3).

Each object found its unhappy place in a person's trachea, larynx, bron-chus, esophagus, stomach, pleural cavity, lung tissue, pharynx, or tonsil. No region of the aerodigestive tract was beyond this doctor's ingeniously

Fig. 3. A selection of fbdies from the Chevalier Jackson Foreign Body Collection that includes a Perfect Attendance pin and another inscribed, "B-A-2-WAY Looker says Care Fu Lee." © Rosamond W. Purcell, 2009.

delicate reach. But time played its role in cruelly indelicate ways, because while some removals took four seconds, others took forty minutes, and while some objects had been lodged for a mere four minutes, others lived inside a body for as long as forty years.

What's more marvelous? The fact of swallowing a foreign body? Its nonsurgical extraction by Jackson? Or his inserting it into an arrangement of things? What exactly occasions the collection of objects, as such? Their retrieval by Jackson and subsequent rescue; the acts of unusual swallowing to which they refer; their transformation from quotidian items to aura-laden Things; or the precarious tightrope they perform upon the stuff of indeterminacy, caught as they are between will and accident, between voluntary and involuntary acts?

The Chevalier Jackson collection of foreign bodies confronts us with different orders of the marvelous, competing orders of the strange, each of which draws us into a fascinational field whose foreground seduces us but whose vanishing point is out of reach. While the Jackson collection doesn't exactly share the same kind of jaundiced limelight that most other specimens in the museum do—what Oliver Wendell Holmes called "the pathological sublime"—it does conjure what I'd like to call a "visceral sublime," a combination of fascination and disgust (let us not forget the gustatory in the word *dis-gust*) that is felt . . . well, in the gut! A repulsion and attraction toward, a temptation and a terror around incongruity is what moves us, a boundary exceeded, a physiological rule broken: a battleship caught in a thorax, a jackstone stuck in an esophagus, a padlock not quite at home inside a stomach. We're afraid to think of how those things might have gotten inside a body, we're alarmed by the admixture and more disgusted (or intrigued) by the thought of how they were extracted—and maybe we're bemused or overwhelmed with unnamed wonder by the fact of their arrangement into a cosmology of Things.

Our bodies are implicated as we peer into these drawers; it's a visceral and never merely an intellectual encounter. Most of all, we are reminded of our mouths, the part of our bodies where there is the most going on, our most visible and vulnerable of orifices, the seat of so much that is essential to our staying alive. Jackson's peculiar collection demands that we contemplate the complex physiology of the human swallow (we might even gasp or gulp before his display), but it doesn't end there, because once brought into unseemly contact with the maw by virtue of his maddeningly endless exhibition, we remember the mouth as a site of nurture, breath, aggression, appetite, language, and even knowledge: through our mouths we originally come to know the world and differentiate ourselves from it. Thumb in a mouth, or hair (do you remember the pleasure in chewing on it?), pens and pencils, sweet and sour (when it comes to hard candy, are you a biter or a sucker?). Words—strange, new, or dirty—sometimes piercings, the inability to get things down (have you ever felt as though your heart were in your throat?). Do you talk while you are eating? Do you cover your mouth? What have you never been able to swallow? "There was an old woman who swallowed a fly, / I don't know why she swallowed a fly, / Perhaps she'll die."

What's more freakish? The twists and turns of human deformation, or human beings' scrupulous classification of such? Historian Jan Bondeson tells how, according to one account, the famous Tocci brothers' father had to be institutionalized after first seeing his two-headed boy. The freakish and the sublime have the ability to derange and not just disarm us. But it didn't take long for Mr. Tocci to come to his senses and use his boys to make himself rich (they were first put on display when they were four weeks old). Let us recall that fascination and astonishment, while they seem like states of mind worth courting, take as their point of origin forms of benumbment, shock, and deprivations of sensation, rather than a surfeit of true feeling. Fascination in its original sense is something that witches do to their enemies and animals exert toward their prey. It's a form of paralysis. I wonder what it would mean to fail to "regain one's senses" and not consider that mad? The forms that our returns to normalcy take are always telling.

Meraviglioso. I've always loved the extra syllables in the Italian version of the word "marvelous." The oral gymnastics required to bring the word across, its extension into space. The subtle effort—a push of breath—by which it causes me to linger. So much better than the empty-headed "marvey," by which the marvelous is tamed, or the high-camp "mahvelous," by which it is ironized. There is no question that Chevalier Jackson's foreign body collection is a playground for the imagination, a stimulus for investigation and for art, and Jackson knew this and fought against it. He devoted his life trying to convince fellow doctors that a foreign body in the body is not a rarity, an exception, or a wonder, but a commonplace event: "Of the 1485 cases of foreign bodies that have come to our bronchoscopic clinic during twenty years, there have been over 200 that had been overlooked for periods of from one month to forty years. . . . Foreign bodies have been regarded as curiosities of medicine rather than as routine possibilities for exclusion" (*DAFP*, 43).

In 1952, Louis Clerf, one of Jackson's students, who later worked at the Jefferson University bronchoscopic clinic, delivered the annual Thomas Dent Mütter lecture to the College of Physicians on the subject of foreign bodies. In his address, "Historical Aspects of Foreign Bodies in the Air and Food Passages," Clerf put the case simply: foreign bodies are "always a source of human and dramatic as well as clinical interest." Jackson's struggle to keep the emphasis solely and entirely on the clinical interest of foreign bodies is something I want to understand, all the while knowing he wouldn't want me messing with his things. In a letter dated February 28, 1924 (the year of the bequest), Jackson states the terms of his bequeathing his entire collection of foreign bodies from the air and food passages to the College of Physicians: "The gift would be without any stipulation except that the specimens and accompanying records should be accessible to all reputable graduates in medecine [*sic*] under such regulations as the College of Physicians, or its duly authorized representatives, may deem proper." In one of many radio programs that Jackson appeared on in the 1930s, he repeated to the public, "The specimens and additional data are accessible to reputable members of the medical profession, for study, upon application to the Committee of the Mütter Museum, of which Dr. George H. Fetterolf is chairman."

Long before Jackson bequeathed his collection to the College of Physicians, however, he was in the habit of mounting his objects and kept what newspapermen of his day referred to as a "museum" in his clinic. (Jackson experienced newspapermen as the bane of his existence, especially when they latched onto the sensational aspects of a case and thereby, to his mind, occluded possibilities for prevention and instruction.) One journalist begins his essay, "Dr. Jackson Looked Down Human Wells," with what sounds like a fairy-tale fact: "He had to work hard because people were always swallowing things the wrong way, or swallowing things that shouldn't be swallowed." Then he continues: "At his clinic, Dr. Jackson had a museum of curios taken from human throats. The museum included teaspoons and tablespoons, handsome brooches, gold watches, and other imperishable items" (see figure 4).

"Knickknacks." "Whatnots." That's what another reporter calls them in a January 26, 1924, article for the *Pottstown News* that interestingly foregrounds the fact of Jackson's collection over and against his act of saving a young boy. Titled "Tack Added to Dr. Jackson's Exhibit," the article begins:

> Dr. Chevalier Jackson today added the 1265th specimen to his foreign body exhibit in the bronchoscopic clinic at Jefferson Hospital. It was the carpet tack taken from the lung of eight-months-old Cletus Moore of St. Louis. . . . Mounted on a white card, the tack went to join hundreds of similar exhibits collected at Jefferson Hospital during 30 years. Cletus' tack seemed shiny and new beside the others. It was inside his lung four weeks before Dr. Jackson removed it in an operation that took four and a half minutes.

Jackson was rarely paid by his patients, most of whom were "charity cases"; his only request was that he be allowed to keep what he called the "intruder" or the "fbdy." Trophies, tokens, part-bodies, *petits objets*, Things.

Fig. 4. Chevalier Jackson posed with bronchoscope and foreign bodies. Chevalier Jackson Papers, Archives Center, National Museum of American History, Behring Center, Smithsonian Institution.

Found objects, literally so, and as such, treated by their contemporary interlocutors as just that: tantalizing remainders, to make of what we will.

Chevalier Jackson, the man with a first name that sounds like a last name and vice versa, whose middle initial is Q for Quixote (it's true)—the first time I set eyes on his collection, I pictured a fellow with a top hat, a tight-fitting jacket, a tiny upward-turning moustache, and the whip of a lion tamer.

"The Great Chevalier." So he was hailed by reporters, an appellation that might lead us to place him alongside the Bearded Lady, the World's Tallest Man, and the Tocci Brothers. Chevalier Jackson was as curious as his things are. One reporter (meaning, I think, to describe his skill as "superhuman") used the word "inhuman," as though, unconsciously, she regarded his rare and assiduous practice as lending him an other-than-human excrescence, an unsympathetic mantle, a cruel aversion to the norm. In the course of his lifetime, newspaper accounts called him a "saint," a "wizard," a "magician," and a "modern miracle man," none of which rhymed with the practicality, scientism, and exactitude with which he preferred to ally his practice, if not his preoccupations. (He found such forms of reference to himself "nauseating.") But the fact of the matter is that a great many of the displays in the Mütter Museum, and swallowed objects especially, tread a fine line between the didactic and the entertaining, the spectacular and the edifying, the odd and the commonplace, the freakish and the pathological, the circus and the medical amphitheater. Jackson's curriculum vitae is impressive, awe-inspiring even, and to bring the singular nature of his achievement and gifts to light is part of what drives my own interest in giving his story back to the world. But he was also monomaniacal, oddly ascetic, and extravagant: an eccentric genius, a collector, a maker of a cabinet of curiosities that is also a non-narrative assemblage along the order of a modernist work of art housed in a museum of pathological specimens.

Probably no one would like to admit that medicine's earliest endoscopists learned techniques from Barnum & Bailey sword swallowers, but in the annals of medical history, we find discussions of how German professors Alfred Kirstein and Gustav Killian, whose lectures Jackson observed before developing his esophagoscope and his bronchoscope, derived their methods from sword swallowers, and that Jackson "perfected [in others] the circus sword-swallowers' technique of throwing back the head so far, that the mouth, throat and windpipe or gullet form a straight channel through which a straight metal tube can be slipped" ("Bronchoscopist," *Time*, June 1, 1936). Clerf confirmed the link in his 1952 address: "Passage of a tube into the esophagus or stomach was inspired by the sword swallowers."

Where slipping a sword into the gullet is concerned, some people like to watch, some like to do it, and others like to imitate it in the form of science. The connection was never lost on Jackson, and he exploited the circus as metaphor in startling and macabre ways. In a 1922 article for the *Annals of Surgery*, "New Mechanical Problems in the Bronchoscopic Extraction of Foreign Bodies from the Lungs and Oesophagus," he conjured a delightful link when he wrote, "The forceps are, mechanically speaking, a prolongation of the fingers. Their necessarily great length makes their use somewhat in the nature of walking on stilts. Special practice is necessary to acquire perfect control." In one of his numerous textbooks, *Diseases of the Nose, Throat and Ear*, he explained how he taught children whose throats had closed from the ingestion of lye to swallow a tube so that the esophagus, in time, might expand again. (Lye burns the esophagus and the scar tissue that follows can cause it to narrow.) The enticement toward cure was achieved by encouraging the children to feel that they were circus performers. "The stricture has to develop a lumen of normal size again," he explained;

> a patient of this age (five) can then be taught to swallow a stomach tube of about this size. He is cautioned against pushing on the tube. He must be led to be proud of this "sword swallowing act," which inspires awe in other children witnessing it. Doing this once a week will keep the lumen open, so that anything can be swallowed, and the lumen of the stricture gets larger and larger as the child grows. The normal segment yields and enlarges until the cicatricial segment becomes a scar on the sidewall. Although a five-year-old patient has been taken for illustration, children as young as two years can be taught the swallowing act.

And yet. The admission of play, of beauty, or of the imagination, the acknowledgment of desire or indulgence of appetite, is the exception rather than the rule in the life and work of our exquisite cabinet-maker. "In medical matters as in all affairs of life, I am an <u>actualist</u>." He underscored the final word in his notebook and paraphrased himself for a commencement address: "I never read fiction. I never could get interested in a story that originated in the writer's brain. In medicine I want <u>clinical facts</u> not theories."

Jackson was a self-pronounced abstainer—from cigarettes, from alcohol, even from food. His particular formulation of "prevention" came nearer to self-protection than self-care. Denial became his trademark; anti-risk, his brand. To eat a peanut kernel is to expose yourself to the threat of sudden death; to cheer your team on at a football game is a form of willful self-harm because it damages the larynx (on this score, Jackson admitted he might be perceived as a "wet blanket"). Accidental ingestion of foreign bodies is within our control, according to Jackson—if only we would be more vigilant, damn it. Just as he could not admit a degree of reverie or daydream into the etiology of swallowed things, so he was loath to let the objects he retrieved from bodies be afterward promiscuous. The objects in Jackson's collection mustn't be allowed any waywardness; one senses that he needed for them to do the right kind of work—to serve as utilitarian prototypes for practitioners and exert a disciplinary force for viewers. The collection must be definitive rather than suggestive.

Like so many *Kunstkammers*, or cabinets of curiosity, Jackson's treasure trove is accompanied by a catalog meant to help it make a kind of sense.

First, collect: if every Thing is gathered, nothing can be missing. This is what it means to hoard.

Then, catalog: if every Thing is identified, then nothing is *not* accounted for.

But this is not the case. No drawer is bounded on all sides. The introduction of a drawer invites the idea of other drawers nestled within it, the secreted inside the secret, the letter inside the word inside the envelope.

Jackson's cabinet is so full and so scrupulously documented, held in place with an encyclopedic girth of information, and yet so much is left out of his account: the bodies the objects once inhabited; the lives of their onetime owners; the things he knows about the cases that he doesn't tell, especially if the story isn't one of accident but of aggression. Violence. Ingestions, willful or forced. A new category for the circus to consider: the freak accident, when accidents within our normal range of comprehension gain an uncanny protuberance, when the laws of nature are upturned, when sequence is interrupted by confluence. There is an illogical fatefulness with which so many of these objects are imbued.

In 2007, an eighty-three-year-old woman named Margaret Derryberry inquired at the Mütter Museum about the pin she aspirated when she was nine years old. Why, we might ask, would she want it, and what would be the draw of the pin to a person reaching the end of her life? A fbdy, once lodged, is part body, is it not? Each enjoyed an intimate, itinerant strangeness with its host. An in-animacy inhering, adhering, and afterward removed—but not forgotten or so easily dispensed with or disposed of. I don't think we can assume that their victims didn't afterward want their Things, that they wouldn't have wished to keep the souvenirs of their near-deaths, that an unspoken tension doesn't undergird the collection: between Jackson's relation to these objects and those to whom they, in another sense, belonged.

The story of medicine is a story of patients as well as physician-operators: what Jackson left out of his grid was a matter of personal predilection—what his particular personality would not allow itself (especially the desire of the other, the human appetite)—and a matter of what medical discourse cannot afford to admit, what refuses to be contained, what is rife with multiple beginnings and unpredictable endings: the narratives, even stranger than the fiction that Jackson eschews, of psyche and soma, of sociology and place, of a nearly infinite set of any being's conditions of possibility and the terms of its crisis. Foreign bodies are haunted bodies. Memento mori, half-finished tombstones missing their owner's names. Dead-live matter. Does every human being have one of these things to show for himself in his life's hereafter? As if to say, here is what is left of me, what's left of me is that-which-was-once-within-me.

It has been said of collections generally that the whole overpowers the narratives accompanying each object in the singular. The Chevalier Jackson Collection of swallowed and aspirated things doesn't exactly erase or supplant such stories—stories that are, in every sense, original—but hints evocatively at their absence. If the collection is haunted, then to restore the collection's missing parts, to call after its ghosts and allow them to materialize, is not to *complete* the collection but to open it. What might happen to the collection if we let narrative and desire back in? We might begin to choke if we think too much about the precarious proximity of trachea to esophagus, the airway and the foodway, in humans. We might start to notice that certain flowers have throats, and be glad that, unlike squid, our esophagi aren't collapsed inside of our brains. We might have to ask why we say we swallow our pride and not our envy, anger, or greed. We might be drawn inside a psychic bottleneck that holds that swallowing is just another name for incorporation or come to terms with our own indigestible thoughts. We might want to consider the consequences of our imaginations, like our mouths, being open to preemptive intrusion from the day we are born. We might want to contemplate our own fascination with found objects, the object world, objects lost and found, and to remember that "puzzle" can, as a verb, mean both to confuse and to solve. We might pause to note that "scarf down," "wolf down," and "inhale" are synonyms for a certain kind of consumption in which eating is reduced to swallowing.

Consider the physiology by which a body swallows. Swallowing is an only partly voluntary and, by any estimation, a highly complex activity reliant on a series of interdependencies and even blockages. In order for food and drink, for example, not to go into the trachea, the vocal cords actually close over it to temporarily seal it off. (It is no doubt for this reason that one is advised not to try to eat and talk at the same time). Simultaneously, the larynx rises up to help direct the material toward the esophagus. Last but not least, a flap of cartilage, the epiglottis, closes over the trachea to further shield the airway.

Consider the stomach's lesser or greater curvature in embryo; imagine that moment at which it rotates therein. Is there anything more tympanic, more like a concerto, than the combination of involuntary contractions and transport, rising and falling, protection, and preparation that is eating? Or how about the interplay of complementary movements by which inhibition, elevation, approximation, and deflection make it possible to breathe, to eat? There's a poetry to the language of the swallow implicit in the names for things. The stomach is misnamed—the "proper" name is "ventricle." Or tummy. Belly. Bread basket. A swallow is a deep hole opening in the earth, a yawning gulf, a capacity, an inclination. It's a river losing itself in another. Gobbling. It's to take completely into oneself. The stomach could steal the place of the heart as a seat of affection so that it's not I heart you, but I stomach you. I feel you inside me. I love you, I carry you. "Bronchi" doesn't really mean breathing tubes. Or trees. The word derives from the word for *shower* or *wet* or *pour*, because originally it was believed that the bronchi carried liquids to the stomach. How is one thing brought to another? Wherefore this dipping, this swooping from place to place? How do we get there? Sphincters above and below play significant roles in the human swallow. The upper esophageal sphincter, it is thought, contracts during inhalation to prevent air from entering the foodway. When we're nervous, it can contract too much. Does the brain efface the body's built-in protective mechanism? The lower esophageal sphincter prevents stomach acids from moving upward into the esophagus and marring it. It too can malfunction when we're beset by mental gripping. Afferent fibers motivate the brain's swallow center. The lips prevent drooling.

"Right now he's practicing swallowing," my friend who is eight months pregnant confidently reports, "and he opened his eyes at twenty-eight weeks." She read about this more or less consistent trajectory in one of many guidebooks that was walking her through the mysteries of her first pregnancy and, by extension, through the labyrinth that was the heart of "human development." While she was moved by the thought of the moment at which the eyes first glide open—and I, too, was fascinated by the thought of sight sans cognition—I couldn't help but be equally intrigued by what it meant to say the fetus was "practicing swallowing" without being able to put food into its mouth. Was this ur-contraction of an as-yet-to-be-formed digestive system a prelude to the sucking that would coax him toward nourishment, that was a preamble to biting, which was a prefigurer of speech? Or was the earliest swallow all about the tongue as an eagerly developing muscle detached from licks and tastes? We practice swallowing without a tutor inside the womb; once out, we learn to use our tongues in practical ways so as to take in food and nourishment, to swallow and to eat. During our earliest years, we reserve sticking out our tongues for protest and invective.

In his 1989 essay "The Anatomy and Physiology of Dysphagia" (difficulty swallowing), the contemporary gastroenterologist Dr. Peter J. Kahrilas begins by noting how essential swallowing is to the human organism: "Swallowing is an extremely primitive behavior, so basic to our existence that we barely take note of it." "Basic" must not be confused with "simple," however, and if a bodily process escapes our notice, this doesn't mean that it is easily comprehended. Dr. Kahrilas understands the baffling intricacies of the human swallow response and its attendant dysfunctions better than most of us, but I am moved by his reminder that we each remain humble in their midst: "In the process of analyzing the sequence of events that allows for ingested material to be transferred from the oral cavity to the stomach," he writes, "it becomes clear that there are significant gaps in our understanding of many of the steps, and what seems on the surface a simple action is actually one of almost unlimited complexity."

One of the many things that makes swallowing such a singularly complex activity is the "intimate association of the airway with the food path." Contiguous, enmeshed, interdependent: where swallowing exists, breathing can't be far behind. Respiration subtends and supports swallowing even as our airway is suspended (temporarily sealed) each time the esophagus opens to receive a bit of (hopefully well-masticated) food. Of course there is a literal difference between a fbdy inspirated into the windpipe and down into a bronchus (an aspirated foreign body) and one that's made its way into the throat, esophagus, or stomach (an ingested foreign body). And what might jar us laymen most is the knowledge that a fbdy can obstruct but not entirely cut off an airway. In fact, fbdies can enjoy a silent interval or symptomless period for days, months, and years, what Chevalier Jackson was apt to call a period of "delusional calm."

What becomes curiouser and curiouser with each plumbing of a Chevalier Jackson foreign body drawer is the always immanent conflation of airway and foodway, ingestion and aspiration. "Tracheo-bronchial symptoms are present in almost all cases of obstructive foreign bodies in the esophagus," Jackson explains in his 1925 "Discussion on Overlooked Cases of Foreign Body in the Air and Food Passages." An aspirated foreign body can manifest in difficulty swallowing, and an ingested foreign body can mask its locale by presenting as labored breathing. Because the esophagus and airway share a party wall, a fbdy sometimes erodes from one site into the other. If the lodged object distends the esophagus, it can cause an airway obstruction, and diagnosing a fbdy is always complicated by the fact that the symptoms of aspiration and ingestion are identical or referred. Choking, gagging, coughing, and wheezing, Jackson remarks, may occur regardless of the fbdy's residence: lung, stomach, or throat.

In the course of each day, one puts one's faith in the "unerring passage of the bolus" (the medical term for chewed-up food), to use doctor-writer Dr. Sherwin Nuland's felicitous phrase from "Voyage Through the Gut," but all it takes to disrupt a swallow's smooth functioning is a cough or a sudden inspiration. The process is easily disrupted, and yet, at the same time, a fbdy, in order to enter the wrong orifice, must "run the gauntlet," as Jackson suggestively puts it, "of the epiglottis, the upper laryngeal orifice, the ventricular bands, the vocal cords, and bechic blast"—a fancy phrase for the blast of air that enables and accompanies a cough (*DAFP*, 20). A fbdy makes its way past and in when the body's normal protective mechanisms fail or relax or malfunction or are distracted from their watchful purpose by a laugh, say, or a sob. "Swallowing is elicited by a peculiar combination of conscious and subconscious cues," notes Kahrilas, and I begin to imagine the idiosyncrasies of your laugh or my cry, at which point fbdy ingestion seems peculiarly tied to personality. "Laughter, sobbing, and crying," Jackson writes, "in addition to the altered inspiratory rhythm, bring into play other movements"—buccal (of or relating to the cheeks or mouth cavity), pharyngeal (implicating the small tube into which food passes before it enters the esophagus), and laryngeal (relative to the voice box)—"and also extraordinary respiratory movements of a special and unusual character" (*DAFP*, 22). Sometimes the body's efforts to resist or repel a foreign body are self-sabotaging, since an outward exhaling push requires a sequential, even deeper intake of breath, and the next thing a person knows in her attempt to prevent the swallowing of a fbdy, she has accidentally inhaled it instead.

Swallowing's and breathing's intersections seem to prompt Jackson to make quirky observations, collect anomalous statistics, and draw strange differences. For example, "it may be cited that certain foreign bodies of relatively frequent occurrence in the air passages have never lodged in the normal esophagus" (*DAFP*, 17), but he doesn't say which those are.

Though more watermelon seeds are swallowed than inhaled in the course of a year, more get *stuck* in the airway than the foodway (*DAFP*, 32), and "more fishbones have become lodged in the tonsil than in any other portion of the anatomy" (*DAFP*, 32). Most foreign bodies, if they are going to enter an airway, tend toward the right lower lobe bronchus because of the greater diameter of its opening—medically speaking, its wider lumen—and the fact that it doesn't deviate much from the tracheal axis. But individual anatomy, posture, and gravity play a part as well.

If Chevalier Jackson waxes poetical about a fbdy, it is likely to be an umbrella-headed tack, inviting us to stroll an imaginary pathway of the marvelous as he figures the body's upper cavities as a windswept terrain.

> This preponderance of incidence of the umbrella-headed tack may be due partly to its shape. The umbrella-shaped head with the weighty stem for ballast certainly is well constructed for being drawn in by the inspiratory blast, like a parachute on a rising wind, and the convexly rounded shape of the advancing head offers a favorable form for entering through the glottic chink. This shape, as well as the point, resists bechic expulsion unless the tack is overturned; we all know the pull of an umbrella when the wind gets under it. (*DAFP*, 35)

In spite of Chevalier Jackson's asceticism, he could lavish attention on a pencil. The Eldorado 5B was a favorite. That's not a rosary he's saying in the photograph in which he bends forward attentively, emanating quiet joy (see figure 5). That is, according to its caption in his autobiography, "a characteristic attitude studying a duplicate foreign body." Jackson studies the object as an afterimage, an aftereffect: the Thing mastered. Here there is benediction and an eerie inhabitance of an in-between space, the space between what the Thing was and what the Thing now is in Jackson's hands. Rather than look at the camera, Jackson looks into the Thing until the photo seems not to be of him at all but of a constellation of relative items: a round-topped wooden table, a Legion of Honor boutonnière, a pair of spectacles.

Every collection is a verge in the sense that it wishes to postpone or defer the inevitable. Do we tremble together on the threshold of the archive or take refuge in the bottomless cabinet we can return to at the end of the day, our computers and our iPods in which everything is stored and

Fig. 5. Chevalier Jackson "in a characteristic attitude studying a duplicate foreign body." Chevalier Jackson Papers, 1890–1964, MS C 292, Modern Manuscripts Collection, History of Medicine Division, National Library of Medicine, Bethesda, Maryland.

nothing is not known? Nothing is curious about those collections and everything inside them is safely out of reach. The archive is another kind of catalog in which things are arranged and ordered and stowed, but archival pages can also plummet, soar, and turn, winged matter ascending from an open drawer.

In the archives of the National Library of Medicine, I turn brittle pages with people's case histories and trace the life and lines of photographs of Jackson embodied. I think about his having lived once—his contribution, superhuman—and thus the nearly unbelievable sense that he has really died.

In the archive, I move from awe to investigation and back to awe with various forms of awfulness emerging in between.

On a piece of letterhead, Jackson scribbled: "Death is an irreversible process; imminent asphyxia is not."

Tucked inside a litany of conclusions, a boldface fact: "Death often lurks under an overhanging epiglottis."

In the John Quincy Adams Library of Otolaryngology, the boxes with Jackson's illustrations are so heavy they practically pull me to the ground. I wish I didn't have a body. I wish I didn't have to break for lunch. I hold the heft of his small wallet and wonder how it came to be here. I learn from the archivist that the fastidious doctor, preoccupied with control, carried a four-leaf clover in his purse. Is this a personal effect or an aftereffect? I turn the pages of small Naugahyde-covered three-ring notebooks, the many fbdy diaries, and the daybooks filled with the details of each case; wallet-size photographs of objects; photographs of X-rays; a photograph of fingers splayed, abstracted, illustrative of the "clubbing" that results from a foreign body lodged in the lungs too long, a photograph that could match the formalist masterpieces of Man Ray; the hand-hewn illustrations; and occasionally a return to the language of his maternal ancestors, which makes the objects, sinister, seem like bonbons, badly taken, *mal prise,* or well taken, *bonne prise*: *chataigne* (chestnut), *noix de coco* (coconut), *pince à cheveux* (hairclip), *les bijoux* (jewelry), *sifflet* (whistle), *un clou* (nail), *broquettes* (tacks).

Boxes, cartons, means of preservation; crates with reinforced edges, indestructible, maybe even fireproof; cardboard, white, the lumen of the stomach salmon-colored; and silence, hours of quiet in the room shared by me, the archivist, and a librarian.

In the Jefferson University Archives, I begin to feel the moments of Jackson's early training, the grain of his day, a tone of voice, his peculiar third-person address, a sliver of paper with his scribblings in an ink not yet dry. Is it possible the ink of Jackson's letters to his mother is still fresh?

Feb. 7, 1921

Just had a tooth cap in the lung that they could not get out at Johns Hopkins. "My Chevie"—he did it. Lady was brought in on a stretcher, bad heart disease. Poor old Lady was badly used up by the long bronchoscope under ether at Hopkins. My Chevie he took it out with only a little <u>local</u> anaesthetic. Nice old Lady—kissed my hand and prayed long and fervently for me. Guess I need it. But they wanted to cut out some ribs and go in through the outside chest wall. She never would have survived.

Love, Chevie

Feb. 16 1921

Dear Mother—

On my way to University for the removal of bone from a woman's lung—

All well

Hope you are too

Love, Chevie

Undated

Sent you a few <u>French</u> sardines. Box looked like ones Mark Mitchell used to get at the rooms and drink the oil after eating the 'dines.

. . . You know me—neither rest nor let anybody else rest.

. . . Have so many little children that I am able to help. I save many lives.

The Mütter Museum's curator, Anna Dhody, turns a wheel and I expect the earth beneath the two of us to move or a sail to flap open, but instead the walls move, walls made of drawers interlocking, beyond the reach of a ladder, velvet-lined cases with bronchoscopes and distal lights and a plaster cast of Jackson's hand. I'm Alice to her Mad Hatter—she resides here while I just have happened to fall in. Her realm is anything but glamorous: the archive is in the basement, the building's bowels, where it's all low ceilings, fake wood paneling, and exposed pipes; they're currently working on maintaining a street-level window. She opens drawers for me and lets me linger, but the sesame is in the opening of an internal door that offers immediate access to the main galleries. I expected the door was an exit onto a Philadelphia street, but instead it opens onto a promontory, like a seascape hidden behind a dune. The galleries now seem false, and the archive true; the galleries a show, the archive the machinery; the galleries, a public palace, the archive the place for private moles.

In all of these archives, in the drawers within drawers, there are lists. Endless lists. Lists upon lists, and indexes. The tome-like grid that appears with the fbdy collection in the Mütter Museum is only one of numerous kinds of catalogs that Jackson devised for the Things. As though in search of the ideal form for the things, or the form that would make the collection most useful, he sometimes relied on chronology and sometimes didn't. Sometimes the lists are alphabetical, and other times they are arranged numerically. Now they read top to bottom; now they read right to left. Sometimes the record is scattershot; other times it is stacked, bi-columned or tri-columned; sometimes it is devoid of description and other times briefly descriptive, but each and every object and case is recorded in mind-bogglingly multiple ways.

Even lists, seemingly meaningless place markers, speak; they intone a presence, documentary and mythological at once. They fail to stay in their place as mere data. When the names appear detached from the detailed account of a case, they have the effect of a roll call of untoward swallowers, an incantation of contact with the indigestible, a queer sort of club. And when the names, only the names, appear together this way, with or without their objects and their dates and places of treatment, they are so many and so familiar that you begin at first to find people you know there, you become convinced that all the world's people appear here, you stand at the ready for your own name's appearance. Yes, you must have at one time in your life swallowed a piece of the object world and been treated to a Jacksonian extraction along with Victor Moulton, Elizabeth Fielder, James Fox, Maude Smith, Reverend Lamuel Blair, Eleonor Slocum, John Walton, Martin Mosley, Kate Shapiro, John Jones, Charles Malloy, Barton Cunningham, Mattie Thompson, Anna Solt, Mildred Strong, Wilmer Ditzer, Marian McCleary, Daisy Dietrich, Rita Barecca, Emma White, Roy Stinson, Moe Jacobs, John White, Minnie Rankins, Patricia North, Salvatore Sabatino, Lolita Waller, Peter Ford, and Harold Mintzmyer, who had fragments of paper stuck in his left lower bronchus while others were beset by three pieces of squirrel bone, a fifty-cent piece, a gold locket, a meat bolus, and a portion of a Christmas tree ball.

The lists charm when you think you've hit upon the most spectacular example but keep finding others that outdo the last. Which is more outlandish: Ezra King's swallowed padlock from 1929, Robert Hall's swallowed belt buckle from 1941, or Laura Kragler's shoe buckles (yes, in the plural) from 1942? I can't for the life of me decide which is more extraordinary, but I begin to feel the tug of narrative. We have entered—let's admit it—a form of literature and not of science, a philosophical treatise, a dramatis personae for a theater of the absurd, a medieval passion play when the names inside the catalogs inside the archives begin to match their Things. John Winhorn had a metal whistle in his esophagus, and Richard Stangle had a piece of glass in his trachea at the carina. And what to make of entire families being treated for the ingestion of foreign bodies, as in Frank Babb, who was treated for a peanut kernel in his bronchus, Edwin Babb, for whom a tack had lodged in his; and Arnold Babb, whose meat bolus stuck in his throat? Then there's Doris Key, who in September 1930 came to the clinic with a pork bone in her lower left bronchus, only to be followed—and I might add, outdone—by a Rose Key who presented with an earring in her foodway nearly one year later.

When objects gain a name by way of archives, the effect isn't always to make the cases more real, but novelistic in a truth-is-stranger-than-fiction sort of way. Is it me, or do these names seem fabricated? Could you match each of these names with its literary mate or author? Rat Crancer (probably a gumshoe). Powder D. Coulter. Weymouth Crumpler (longtime friend of Little Miss Muffett). Pansy Hines. Donald Dumbleton (wouldn't you know, he had a timothy-head screwdriver in his esophagus). Alice Dalrymple. Zadie Smallwood. Mrs. L. Stretch. Myrtle Yonders (sister of Thistle Near). Anna Skeen (I think she appears in Gertrude Stein's *Three Lives*). Florabelle Sledge (an oxymoronish personage). Sister Mary Octave. Waldo Intermill. Evelyn Marie Loveless. Irma Erben (William Wilson's cousin and Humbert Humbert's wife). Linnwood Wheeloff (hadn't Henry James made a place for him in *The Americans*?), and the incomparably unbelievable Sister Mary Pica—"pica" being the DSM-IV descriptor for disordered swallowing.

Found objects yield found poetry in one version of a grid with offerings of "how." There is something confluential here, and something pure, purely true, something kooky and something sad, and suggestively incomplete, much like personality, much like desire, much like life:

Child alone in room found hairpin under pillow

Nickel and half dollar in a glass of water, child pretended to drink

Was playing on school ground, afraid of loosing 50 ct piece put it in her mouth

Eating mashed potatoes, patient remembered that while mashing potatoes, small piece of enamel came off the pan, meant to throw potatoes away but forgot

Playing around "wicker chair"

Safety pin in mouth, suddenly stepped on dog's foot

Put toy in his mouth to hide it from sister

Patient playing with tin cup containing a white pearl button. Child threw cup up, patient's mouth was open and button fell in.

Eating clam chowder

Eating grape fruit

Suffering of melancholy
Alone on floor with pile of buttons

Every object in Chevalier Jackson's collection is the product of a trajectory; each fbdy has gone from a thing in the world to a thing in the body, to a thing in Chevalier Jackson's grasp, to a thing inlaid by Chevalier Jackson into a secular tabernacle. Each has been put through a particular system of meaning; it's been made, by Jackson, to serve not exactly an epistemological inquiry nor a philosophical inquiry, but something like a physiological inquiry, an inquiry into corporeality. How can you wrest one body from another? In what sense does the precariousness of foreign-body ingestion point up the human body's foreignness to the world of which it is a part, and the world of objects that it has, itself, produced?

To each collection, a life of its own that it is said to "take on"; to each collection, an irrevocable attachment to its collector. What is the nature of this to-and-fro reciprocity that the fbdy collection ignites, a seesaw of identifications whereby its owner projects himself onto his arrangement at the same time that he takes on the qualities of the objects therein? Here's Jackson: a forager for the stuff of life, for a heightened kind of "real," tucked inside recalcitrant folds and intolerant viscera. There's Jackson: enshrined inside his collection but not exactly caught, instead retreating into amplitude beyond all gustatory or esophageal measure. See the objects recede into their cabinet as body double, impervious and wide. Glimpse the outside, explore the inside; turn the inside out and the outside in.

Who *was* that man, Chevalier Jackson? What *are* these things? How does someone swallow *that*? No matter our differences, these are the questions everyone seems to ask in the pauses between craning to catch a look inside the drawers of what just might be the most popular exhibit in the museum of pathological specimens in Philadelphia: Jackson's swallowed objects.

The questions are as simple as the human swallow is complex.

I would like to risk some answers.

Remembering Forward: The Idea of a Legacy

The mass of knowledge we know as medical science is built of the activities of forgotten men. The structure is parallel in a figurative sense to the coral island that is built of the carcasses of obliterated lives. . . . What difference

will it make to the next generation whether it was Jackson, Johnson, Smith,
or Jones who discovered bronchially lodged peanuts as potentially fatal to
children? The important thing is for the disciples to expound the gospel of
education of mothers as to the dangers of peanuts and nut candies to the
baby without molars.

—*The Life of Chevalier Jackson: An Autobiography*

The tissues of the air passages are quite tolerant of vulcanite.

—CHEVALIER JACKSON,
Diseases of the Air and Food Passages of Foreign-Body Origin

Each of us has our identity themes, motifs that we return to as we attempt to give shape and color to our lives, receding docks of departure to
which we return when we want to feel moored. Our commitments might
change, our passions may wax and wane, our focus might shift either by
will or accident to such an extent that we no longer recognize ourselves,
but our identity themes remain steadfast, us to them and them to us, like a
regressive assignment and an agreeable consignment.

Two images perpetually surface in Chevalier Jackson's life's work; two
distillations of an idea of a self recur: Jackson as housepainter and Jackson
as lighthouse keeper. According to the first, he's working his way through
the rooms of a house or applying pigment to an exterior facade, "hurrying
to get through before his paint should give out"; according to the second,
he'd like nothing so much as to be a "lighthouse tender where the supply boat came only every three months," affording him "enough uninter-
rupted time to get something done" (*LCJ*, 4).

The president of the Section of Laryngology of the Royal Society of
Medicine, Frank A. Rose, tapped a fork against a glass before ascending
the podium at a dinner in 1930 to honor Chevalier Jackson. As master of
ceremonies, Rose speculated about what Jackson would be remembered
for by future generations—not his success in operating on the larynx for
carcinoma or for his dexterity in removing foreign bodies. No. Rose imagined Jackson's legacy to be comparable to the act that made Elias Howe
famous for the sewing machine. The *British Medical Journal* recorded part
of his speech:

Howe showed the world that the eye of a needle ought to be at its point;
similarly Chevalier Jackson would perhaps be remembered longest as the
man who taught the world to place the light of a bronchoscope at its tip.

It might be that when the memory of his other achievements had grown
dim, as they merged into the ever-growing stream of medical knowledge,
Chevalier Jackson would for all time be known by his bronchoscope.

In an interview for Energine Newsreel that Jackson gave in 1936, he described the ingenious device of the bronchoscope as "a thin-walled, brass
tube with a tiny electric light, smaller than a grain of rice, at the far end,
about the size of a canary seed. This tube is inserted, through the mouth,
into the bronchi; looking through the tube we can see the interior of the
bronchi brilliantly lighted up; and through it under guidance of the eye,
we can insert the many other accessory instruments, such as slender forceps, hooks, safety pin closers, or whatever is needed for the solution of
the particular problem" (see figure 6). Jackson's incorporation of the distal light was a major advance in the perfecting of the instrument that he
also designed, but he got the idea for the placement of the light, the idea
of *entering* the body with a light inserted into the tube rather than trying
to light the interior of the body from without ("proximal illumination"),
from Max Einhorn, who, Jackson writes, in 1902 "made the excellent suggestion that a light carrier, then recently patented by a soulless mechanic
for use on a cystoscope, be used on an esophagoscope" (*LCJ*, 106). Clerf
concurs that Einhorn "introduced the idea of the auxiliary tube in the

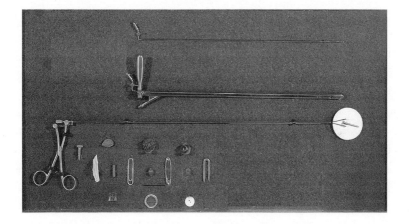

*Fig. 6. Part of an "action exhibit" mounted at Philadelphia's Franklin Institute in 1938
that featured a breathing mannequin complete with inserted bronchoscope through
which museumgoers could view and grasp (with forceps) an inspirited nail. Top to
bottom: distal light, bronchoscope, forceps, fbdies. The Historical and Interpretive Collections of The Franklin Institute, Inc., Philadelphia, Pennsylvania.*

wall of the esophagoscope as the light carrier," thus marking the "first employment of a distally illuminated tube." Some historians would no doubt
beg to differ with both Jackson and Clerf by naming the urologist whom
Jackson dismisses as "soulless"—Maximilian Nitze—as well as surgeon Johann von Mikulicz and instrument maker Josef Leiter as the first to use
the distally placed light. In a 1934 essay on the history of the stomach tube,
Ralph Major puts the problem of attribution succinctly, at the same time
that he understates the case: "Questions of priority are always vexing and
troublesome, difficult to decide with full justice to those concerned and
always certain to provoke bitter controversy and even more bitter recrimi-
nations." Perhaps what Rose meant to say was that Jackson would be remembered for making direct observation of regions of the upper torso
possible, thus making direct-vision diagnosis of otherwise hidden parts of
the breathing and alimentary canals indispensable to doctors the world
over. He will come down to us as one of the earliest explorers of—and one
of the first to set eyes upon—the *living* body's otherwise dark interior: its
speech center, its esophageal folds, its breathing tree.

I could remember otherwise: I could say Chevalier Jackson will be remembered to this day as the person who dared to specialize in diseases of
the throat—laryngology—in an era when specialization of any sort within
the medical profession was affiliated with quackery. That his reputation for
performing emergency tracheotomies using a technique that almost entirely prevented complications from diphtheria is what will endure. Or that
he made his peers what one of his assistants called "foreign body conscious."

His construction of the bronchoscope in 1899 (it was not the first, but
it came to be considered one of the best) was a major advance, as was his
development of techniques for its safe passing and his proof of its harm-
lessness, if carefully applied, to living tissue. But prior to designing his
bronchoscope, in 1890, Jackson conceived of, built, and brought into his
practice an esophagoscope. After graduating from Jefferson Medical College in 1886, he raised enough money to travel abroad and visit clinics in
Vienna, Berlin, Paris, and finally London, where he met and learned from
Sir Morell Mackenzie, whose lack of a practical device for examining the
esophagus inspired Jackson to develop one. The very first foreign bodies
to constitute Jackson's collection were a tooth plate that he had removed
from the esophagus of an adult and a coin he removed from the esophagus
of a child. Before Jackson's instruments and techniques, only two patients
out of one hundred might successfully cough up, regurgitate, or excrete a

foreign body, and surgery resulted in death in 98 percent of all cases. In the course of his career, Jackson developed over five thousand instruments and saved as many lives; his students went on to save half a million more.

Here's a remembered chronology: he began working with wood and sharp tools at the age of four and was never without a workshop thereafter; he established his first medical practice in what had originally been a tailor's shop in Pittsburgh at twenty-two; by the time he was thirty-five years old, in an era when medical professorships were reserved for practitioners at the end of their careers, he held the chair of laryngology at Western Pennsylvania University (now the University of Pittsburgh) and had been elected to staff positions at fourteen different hospitals. By then, he was considered an authority on the larynx. In 1916, when he was fifty-three years old, he and his family—wife, Alice; sister-in-law, Jo; and son, Chevalier L.—moved to Philadelphia so that Jackson could accept the professorship of laryngology at Jefferson Medical College. The position carried no stipend, was not endowed, and was, practically speaking, without precedent, but Jackson saw in it the opportunity to train more students, establish more clinics, and bring to full flower the medical specialty whose technical method he had recently devised.

In 1911, 1913, and 1917, Jackson suffered three separate bouts of pulmonary tuberculosis. He spent a great deal of his recuperative time writing in bed from dawn to dusk or painting "endoscopic views." Two years after moving to Philadelphia, Alice found the perfect place for them to live: a miller's house and accompanying grist and sawmill that they restored; in the old water mill, Jackson rigged a machine shop that he called his "experimental laboratory," a place for designing and producing instrument prototypes. The machine works were struck from various woods that Jackson recognized: hickory cog wheels, oaken gear shifts, and pine shafts. The home he came to call Old Sunrise Mills wasn't convenient to the clinics where he worked or the classrooms in which he taught, but he experienced home as a recuperative sanctuary and didn't seem to mind the seventy-eight-mile round-trip drive in his motorcar from Schwenksville to Philadelphia and back.

By the age of ninety-three, this prodigious writer had produced 238 single-authored articles, 473 co-authored articles, 12 textbooks, and 6 monographs. Trained as a visual artist, he was known during his lifetime as much for his "chalk talks"—lively lectures accompanied by the visual aid of colorful illustrative sketches that he would make on the spot—as for fbdy removal. Copies of the sketches became coveted collectors' items among his students. In 1938, at age seventy-three, he composed an auto-biography that was an instant bestseller, *The Life of Chevalier Jackson*. His textbook *Bronchoscopy and Esophagoscopy* (1922) was considered the bronchoscopist's bible. His first book, *Peroral Endoscopy* (1915), inaugurated the age of diagnosis by direct inspection of the upper torso.

Vision and visual apparati were the new order of the day, and Jackson played a major role in their ascendancy in the medical domain—yet he still relied just as heavily on his ears and even more so on his touch. He might listen for the "asthmatoid wheeze" but then challenge acoustical protocol by instructing that "all that wheezes is not asthma" (an axiom so often repeated by Jackson, it is to this day an adage common among pulmonologists). He listened for "whiskey throat" and "grog blossom"—qualities of voice that signaled dilation of the capillaries of the mucous membrane that lined the larynx, which was indicative of too much drink. He tipped an ear or sometimes brought a stethoscope bell to an open mouth as though listening in on a concert played with broken musical instruments as he tried to sense "percussion notes," "audible slap," "tympany," "cracked-pot note," or "Wintrich's change of tone." He applied his palpating fingers like a tuning fork and, with an incomparably gentle and exacting touch, he felt his way with instruments that were extensions of his hands inside a network of seemingly impassable and blind passageways, inside a ligature and webbing so delicate that one wrong move could prove fatal, as it did in the ghastly record of gruesome acts that preceded Jackson's refinement of the field: cases in which the patient was left not only with a foreign body impacted but with crudely designed instruments—metallic hooks, curved forceps, or pieces of wire—tightly wedged alongside or atop the Thing inside an orifice. The patient would in this attitude spend the last days of his life before succumbing.

By his own account, Jackson never was a "medicine-giving doctor," but one who had the utmost faith in his eyes and fingers (*LCJ*, 203). He worked a form of healing that was a particular (and literal) kind of laying on of hands and eyes. Essentially, he was a craftsman, a mechanic, an engineer who enjoyed an education of his senses—especially touch—from a very young age, and whose training at a lathe and "aching void for making things" out of wood or metal became almost an aesthetic in his medical practice, an attitude toward the body that was tantamount to an artistic style (*LCJ*, 197). He loved the odor of wood and could tell the type of tree by its fragrance in the woodshop. He could identify a tree by sight "even when leafless," recognizing it by the "grain, and feel, and color" of its wood (*LCJ*, 196). We could remember him this way: as the doctor whose wood crafting made him highly attuned at the level of skin on skin.

If Jackson could tell us how he wished to be remembered, I'm certain he would do so by assemblage, or meaningful collage, the way he had pieced together a gavel for the otolaryngology section of the College of Physicians: its head was derived from a scrap of dogwood from his home in Idlewood, Pennsylvania, that he had kept since he was a boy; the handle he crafted from the hickory handle of a hammer he'd used in his shop for years; the box he made from a Rambo apple tree planted by his maternal grandfather, Jean Morange, in 1828 on his country place near Pittsburgh. Morange was, in Jackson's words, "a harbinger of the present mechanical age," and the figure from whom he imagined having inherited his own mechanical gifts (*LCJ*, 196).

Wizard. Magician. Miracle man. Stilts-walker. Humanitarian—Jackson's treatment of Pittsburgh's urban poor in the late nineteenth and early twentieth century, his lifelong tendency to prioritize the care of others over remuneration for his work, his refusal to patent the instruments in his armamentarium, and his seminal role in the creation and passage of the Federal Caustic Act of 1927 mandating that poisonous substances like household lye be labeled as such earned him this distinction. But what drove Jackson's bronchoscopic quest—the pioneering work he did that would forever influence diagnostic and treatment methods of diseases of the upper torso—was not initially or implicitly an interest in saving lives. What drove his work was a capacious curiosity, an appetite for the unknown, the courting of impossibility—and a love of color. Saving lives was a happy by-product of his odd-because-uncommon preoccupations, his imaginative drift.

"How did you come to undertake this strange study of bronchoscopy?" a radio interviewer asked Jackson in 1938. And he replied:

It is a pleasure, sir, to answer that question as to myself, but this does not imply that I was alone in the development of bronchoscopy. The mystery of the unknown was attractive to me. Many times I had looked at the larynx with the ordinary throat mirror. Beyond the range of vision, in the mirror, lay a great, unknown, unexplored field. It was parallel to an explorer at the edge of a jungle that had never been seen by human eye. Then came the intrigue of the impossible. It had always been regarded as impossible to explore the air passages. All my life, the most fascinating problems have been those that were deemed impossible of solution. Another factor was the never-ending, awe-inspiring sights, in the depths of the bronchi; one seems to be in the midst of life's machinery. Still another fascination was the play of colors, so beautiful to paint for illustrations and so interesting to draw with chalk for demonstration to the students.

In one of his earliest essays on gastroscopy, he encouraged his peers in the profession by arguing that the misgivings and challenges of inserting a rigid tube into a human esophagus would be repaid by the visual display it afforded the operator: "Thorough and systematic search of the explorable area by introducing the tube into one fold after another, missing none, demands something of experience and more of patience, but these will very readily be yielded by the enthusiasm of one who has for the first time perceived a beautiful picture of the living membrane as obtained at the first introduction of the tube." In his autobiography, he reserved a special place for color as pure perceptual pleasure: "the colors of mucous membranes, especially of the bronchi as seen through the bronchoscope, in health and disease, have always been interesting to me, entirely apart from their medical significance" (*LCJ*, 199).

If I could piece together a telling of the *color* of his days, three hues would dominate: the gray black of Pittsburgh's nineteenth-century skies; the cold green of his operating room; and the blue-brown waters of the mill pond alongside his house outside of Philadelphia where he sat in a boat to write.

At first the sun is absent: he was born in Pittsburgh on a "dark, dreary November day" in 1865, the year that ended the Civil War (*LCJ*, 1). He remembered the sun always receding before he had a chance to play. At the age of nine, following a major financial reversal for his father, he moved with his family to Idlewood, a few miles west of Pittsburgh, where they perched precariously on the edge of bituminous coal districts and not far from oil-producing territory. In the 1880s, his "white-marble-step college days in the then anthracite-burning Philadelphia" impressed him with a before-and-after, black-and-white contrast that stuck (*LCJ*, 96). When he returned to Pittsburgh to establish his practice, he experienced the lack of light there as nightmarish: on the four days in winter when the sun was visible through the layers of soot and grime that filled the air, it appeared like a full moon, white against black. When he came to make his sketches of the interior of the human body, he always worked from a striking black background, as though remembering Pittsburgh's colorless skies.

At the center of his black canvases, he mounted a tondo, a lambent perfect circle; in lieu of an obscured constellation, he drew an orb rimmed in ocher or a brighter shade of gold inside of which throbbed the color made possible by an endoscopic view. If his environment was without natural light, he would seek out light by turning inward, he would insist a light into the unlit recesses of the human body. Did you know that the throat is a bat-shaped cavern bisected by a white V for vocal cords? (See figure 7.) Or that the brownish-pink lumen that is the overture to the normal stomach lodges inside the darkness like a half-shut eye?

The brown clots and white striations of primary pernicious anemia rage like an eye looking back on itself, lopsided inside its socket. A white-and-pink pinwheel radiates out from a disease cluster's exuberant growths, abundant as caviar: they will encroach, occlude, and fatally seal

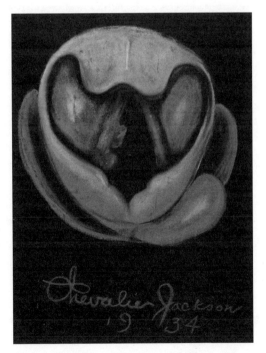

Fig. 7. Chevalier Jackson chalk/pastel drawing of a diseased larynx as seen through his scope. Donated to the Mütter Museum by Arlene Maloney. Collection of the Mütter Museum, The College of Physicians of Philadelphia.

up an entryway if not removed. Is that an egg floating sunny side up across the night sky? His drawing (see figure 8) insists it's the protruding head of a collar button caught inside the puckered fold of an inner alleyway—the mouth inside a mouth inside a mouth that is the human body.

Remember Chevalier Jackson? He's the person who considered a golf links a perfect place for sketching cloud patterns and the bright spots of colored sports clothes but not for playing golf. Chevalier Jackson? He's the guy responsible for something as simple and persistent as replacing the customary white linens with green in the operating room, a color chosen for the fact that it doesn't reflect glare.

Three hues dominate his life's initial course: the gray pallor of diphtheria, the black-and-blue of violence, the blood on the matted fur of abused animals. There was a childhood hiding place for fleeing from bullies— a cemetery where cherry trees admitted little daylight and overhung the tumbled tombstones. Amid old bones in dark corners, he hid out, longing for licorice and imagining the cherry trees having sprung from the cherry

Fig. 8. Chevalier Jackson chalk/pastel drawing of a collar button stuck in the esophagus. Donated to the Mütter Museum by Arlene Maloney. Collection of the Mütter Museum, The College of Physicians of Philadelphia.

pits swallowed by the once-living inmates: "My conception was that the trees grew from sprouting of cherry stones swallowed before death" (*LCJ*, 28). There were ineffective red rubber wheels on a pair of skates replaced with sleek nutmeg-colored rollers made of dogwood. Later, there was a green tin tubular box purchased for a dollar, a flute to hold his medical diploma.

The suddenness of vermilion, his own blood, coughed into a handkerchief at a medical meeting that he didn't feel comfortable at in the first place and didn't enjoy going to, with or without TB: this is how he experienced his second tubercular attack.

Dainty azure blue: the color of the cuffs and lapel that distinguish his compulsory white lab coat.

A judicious choice of parchment: yellow manila paper if he was writing indoors; green-tinted paper outdoors, again to lessen the glare.

What was common practice for him was regarded as highly unusual by others in his profession: an emphasis on teamwork in the operating theater; a habit of treating nurses as his equals; advocating for women physicians; and his generosity toward his assistants, a trait he was excoriated for at length by his peers. Jackson said that what distinguished his treatment of assistants from that of the other leading medical men of his day was that he considered them as his pupils, whereas other doctors thought of them as aides. He was training them to become bronchoscopists in their own right rather than conscripting them to the diminutive role of helper. Time and again, he would publicly credit an assistant with the design of an instrument that was his own. When a student would present the results of Jackson's research as though the student was its author, Jackson claimed to have succeeded. Plagiarism, he said, was the highest form of flattery. Whether he really believed this is questionable—in the National Library of Medicine, an entire folder is given over to articles that Jackson angrily marked as plagiarized from him. He appears to have struggled with the idea of a personal versus a communal legacy to such an extent that his self-effacement sometimes seemed simply a cover for its flip side, self-aggrandizement. Laboring under the desire to be remembered—and who doesn't want to be remembered, to exceed one's lifespan on the planet, to endure?—he seems to have deflected what would otherwise feel like narcissism onto the idea of a greater good, a higher purpose, a cause of evangelical proportion.

Either he exerted a humility that was laced with egotism of the highest order, or he wished to be not simply a memorable sort of practitioner but a founder of a discourse, like Jesus or Freud. This is nowhere more apparent than in what came famously to be known as the Five Chairs—the positions at five different medical schools in Philadelphia that Jackson held more or less simultaneously. He puts the case powerfully in his *Life*: "No one anywhere in the world has ever before created, nor simultaneously filled, nor given away, five medical collegiate chairs" (*LCJ*, 207). After successfully establishing a clinic at Jefferson Hospital, he opened one at the University of Pennsylvania, then another at Graduate Hospital. Following this, he established a clinic at Temple University and later at the Woman's Medical College, where he also served as president from 1935 to 1941. The institutions he was affiliated with wanted him strictly for themselves, so he remained affiliated with each even when he left it for yet another place. He was an iconoclast who didn't think a child should die if she wasn't able to find the sole clinic where bronchoscopy was practiced, nor did he think a student should be bound to a particular institution in order to learn a specialty; he believed no one institution should have a monopoly on the field. But the language he used to explain his five chairs did make him sound just a little nutty: a self-described "evangelist," he needed to spread "the gospel of safe bronchoscopy," and he regarded future practitioners as "disciples." He referred to the talk he would regularly give his patients to relax them as the "sermon on relaxation" (*DAFP*, 184).

I am not a follower of Chevalier Jackson, but in writing this book I sort of feel like his channeler, his chronicler, his poet friend and scribe. Still, over and against my inscriptions, the most enduring memorial to his person and to his work is the memory box he made of swallowed things. A labor of love and a form of resplendent monomania, a sign of an at-once demonic and deeply caring relationship to the world.

It requires only that one read one of his lengthy essays, often painstakingly illustrated with his detailed drawings, to understand that Jackson studied down to each infinitesimal detail the nature of the nooks and crannies that constitute the tissue in our throats and chest, and then he studied, even more meticulously, the peculiarity of each and every type of object that might get caught. He would chart and map and attempt to distinguish the types of metals a body could consume and speculate about the differing effects on the body of an ingested item made of iron—cast, wrought, or malleable; copper—pure (practically) or alloyed with tin or lead; gold—solid or filled; brass—lacquered or nickel plated; steel; tin; or antimony (*DAFP*, 80). An early and curious discovery of his bronchoscopic practice was the observation he made in an interview for Energine Newsreel in 1936 "that a sharp, jaggy tack or pin, in a bronchus, cannot be felt by the patient; it produces no sensation whatever, and for a time, very little disturbance. Whereas a peanut kernel, a bean, pea, grain of corn, a head of grass, a watermelon seed, orange pit, or any other vegetal substance sets up quickly a violent reaction, and a severe, acute illness."

Each and every new foreign body posed a unique engineering problem to him, and this is really where his pioneering work becomes awesome and mind-boggling. He went at each bit of peanut kernel stuck in a trachea, each safety pin in a stomach, each jack in a thorax, as a newly challenging Gordian knot, each solution carefully described in the many books and articles he wrote in the course of his very long life. But what constituted a solution? Nothing as simple as "turn left, then right, then pull." Each foreign body posed a unique mechanical problem, and one in which a human life was a stake.

Did Jackson's fastidious and studious techniques become "common practice" among endoscopists? I don't think so. I think there was only one Chevalier Jackson, only one man who studied each particle of the material world, each of the world's bite-size objects down to its constituent parts, its tendencies in interacting with human tissue, and the mechanical movements of multiple instruments—tiny forceps inserted through a narrow tube into the mouth—required by each situation of a foreign body lodged, every one unique. When three-year-old Kelvin Arthur Rogers traveled nine thousand miles from Australia to Philadelphia in 1936 to have Chevalier Jackson remove a nail from his lung with the aid of a bronchoscope, two readers wrote the *Philadelphia Bulletin* to ask: " 'Why isn't there more than one bronchoscope in the world to take pins out of children?' The answer: there are thousands of bronchoscopes, straight, hollow metal tubes with a light at the tip for looking down gullets, windpipes and lungs. There are nearly 2,000 physicians trained personally by Dr. Jackson in use of the bronchoscope. And there's Chevalier Jackson."

In the corner of a life's work that can never be completed, each of us records a signature, read or not, legible or not, notable. Jackson's signature, a trace worth returning to again and again, is the seriously beautiful, breathtaking description, recounted in numerous places, of the initial feeling of "going inside," first with the esophagoscope, and eventually with the bronchoscope. How many doctors or even poets can find a language for the body out of bounds, our invisible interiors, distinct from a clinical vocabulary of Greek or Latin? The act of endoscopy is a little more profound than feeling with a finger for a pulse, and he recounts the act with reverence for the passage of sensation from one body to another, the passage of a rigid instrument into intolerant viscera, the passage of removal of a fbdy across a dangerously delicate crevasse:

> All of this system of working had been developed with the esophagoscope. It remained, however, to adapt methods to the anatomically and physiologically different passages. The esophagus is a soft, elastic, collapsed, baglike tube full of wrinkles and folds; the tracheobronchial tree stands open by reason of its rings of cartilage. The bronchi enlarge and elongate at each inspiration, diminish and shorten during expiration. The heart at each beat dinges in the bronchial wall or pushes the whole bronchial tube sidewise; the thumping is transmitted to the fingers holding the inserted bronchoscope. One gets the impression of being in the midst of the machinery of life itself. In a baby the obvious delicacy of life's constantly moving machinery is appalling. To work in such surroundings through a tube not much larger than a straw to manipulate a safety-pin, for example, is daunting to the utmost degree. Fully to comprehend this, it must be realized that "safety" of such pins applies only to location in clothing and even then only when closed. In the bronchi, they are usually open, the sharp point is upward and being forced by the spring into the bronchial wall. Moreover that delicate wall is beset with catchy ridges. (*LCJ*, 118)

How long is memory? Even and especially a bronchoscope has its limits, it cannot reach and reach and reach, it has to know where it begins and the body ends. We could remember Jackson for his aphorisms, pithy one-liners, like slogans that incorporate him, or recall him with each articulation of the eponyms that survive him, like Jackson's position (the position of the head for intubation), Jackson's safety triangle (a precisely defined anatomical area bounded by the lower end of the thyroid cartilage), Jackson's sign (a particular wheeze that can be heard in cases of foreign body in the trachea or bronchus), and the Jackson tube.

What shall we remember him for?

For having designed special peanut forceps and for solving "the problem of the thumb tack?" (See figure 9.)

What's more important: what the man did or what the man collected?

A bird lands on a piece of china. Its plump head, its green and yellow body, hover above dogwood blossoms and rose blooms in a setting too exotic to be real. Jackson subsisted at numerous points in his early life by decorating china and painting lampshades. Imagine someone somewhere lifting one of his teacups to their mouths, not knowing that his hand had graced it, not being able to imagine the distance traversed between teacup and life's work, the import of this hand-painted object as a means to an end. Picture someone raising the cup to her lips and swallowing.

Fbdy #C804, Case #3268, X-rays #48451C and #48460C: The Case of Andrew C.

Chevalier Jackson's extraordinary skill and the humble respect he had for the lives of his patients are something that's timeless, and needs to be remembered. . . . The legacy of a physician can be measured by the recollection of his patients.

—V. ALIN BOTOMAN, MD, FACG, FACP

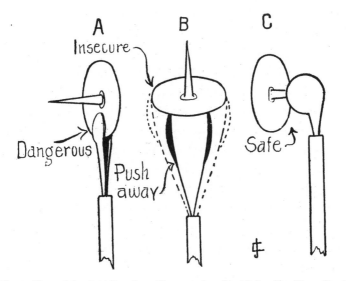

Fig. 9. The problem of the thumb tack as illustrated and explained in Chevalier Jackson's "New Mechanical Problems in the Bronchoscopic Extraction of Foreign Bodies from the Lungs and Esophagus," Transactions of the American Laryngological, Rhinological, and Otolaryngological Society *27 (1921). Courtesy of Thomas Jefferson University, Archives and Special Collections.*

It's possible to *feel* the past in a way that we can never know the present. Time ripens inside objects: scents don't dissipate but penetrate more deeply into the folds of a hundred-year-old letter. A patch of time gains a voice and a step inside the archive. No magnifier is needed; in fact, from the distance of my present turned in the direction of Jackson's past, each seemingly inconsequential and mundane detail writes itself as the center upon which a life depended, the object around which verbs and adjectives cluster, the boisterous kernel of what remains.

In a daybook calendar devoid of annotations, a phrase suddenly appears on March 28, 1886: "impatient but confident." It's his way of containing what he knows about himself but doesn't dare announce in public: that he has done what he needed to pass all of his exams. He's really still a boy writing letters to his family about a rare day off from schoolwork. He goes to the zoo alone and imagines the large seal he sees there to be the same he saw with his father when he was small: "it is very tame, came upon the bank and slept. The Beavers were very amused swimming after apples, the prairie dogs come up and eat out of your hand." He goes to Fairmount Park and tries to bring his family with him to the glens and shady springs that tempt this boy who is otherwise always driven, always moving, to linger. With his sentences as conveyance, he takes them to its river with the unpronounceable name: Schuylkill. He eats catfish and waffles at Strawberry Mansion, coffee, steamed oysters, crackers, and pickled cabbage. "Whoops. Is that the way you spell it?" he asks in a letter from 1886. "I cannot find the word 'pariphernalia' in the dictionary," he notes in a letter for 1884. He is anxious about the skull he has asked one of his brothers to send him through the mail—once dirtied, it can never be cleaned, and he wants to be certain of its proper handling. He attends and even enjoys a Spiritualist performance. "In the evening we went to hear Frank Baxter lecture at the spiritualist Hall corner of 8 and Spring Garden. He gave names and tests which were recognized by the audience it was very gratifying to see some old men and woman speak out and corroborate what spirit said. They sang some beautiful gospel songs 'We shall Meet by the River.' 'We come with the Roses.'"

Another bundle of letters in the Thomas Jefferson University archive shows him hoping and expecting his family to travel to Philadelphia to attend his medical school graduation. The rise and fall of enthusiasm, finally checked by a stoic rationalization, is sad to watch, and all the more poignant in light of what he will go on to achieve: "Am just as well satisfied that no one is coming on as the commencement amounts to little more than red tape. To come all the way for it alone would not be a very good investment." Instead of their company, he will ask his father to send a twenty-six-inch valise, a suitcase big enough to accommodate the length of the tube that contains his diploma as he looks toward embarking, though penniless, for England, Germany, and France.

In 1916, on the horizon of the reopening of his career in Philadelphia, he receives fifteen quail from the father of a patient in North Carolina. He sends his brother maps of the night sky; Alice fulfills her mother-in-law's requests for essence of peppermint and wintergreen. It's impossible to speed through an archive, partly because handwriting slows an eye down, but by the time I arrive at the 1930s, I'm struck by how the ethic of medicine remains marked by what feels like an even more distant past: imagine doctors writing their patients five-page single-spaced letters detailing their assessment of the state of the patient's health, letters complete with recipes, like "lay the potatoes and cabbage atop the onions to simmer," saying that this will help to soothe what's wrong.

The archivist's name is Michael Angelo. (My name if I were to translate it into English is Mary Hat.) Michael Angelo introduces me to a gastroenterologist named Dr. Botoman, who is also carrying out research on Chevalier Jackson, inspired by an encounter with a man who had been treated by Jackson as a child in 1935. I don't fabricate the names of people who enter and exit a Jacksonian theater space. I'm writing nonfiction, for god's sake. Michael Angelo. V. Alin Botoman. Mary Hat. The names are real, and I love them at the same time for how they de-realize us by making us players in a drama none of us can author, in which a Renaissance artist supplies materials for a Victorian Sherlock Holmes and his inimitable sidekick. Botoman tells me that he removes foreign bodies from people's stomachs and has never had the desire to "keep" the object. But he does recall counting the change he retrieved from one person's gullet: exactly $7.25.

For sixty years, a patient named Andrew C. suffered from chronic dysphagia (difficulty swallowing). In 1995, his wife, seeing that it would take him between one and two hours to finish a meal, urged him to visit a doctor. That doctor was Botoman, who identified a congenital esophageal stricture that had gone untreated all of his life and that Botoman endoscopically dilated, effecting an essential cure. While taking his history, Botoman learned that C., who now lived in Fort Lauderdale, Florida, had been treated by Chevalier Jackson at Jefferson when he was nine years old.

It was 1935, and he had gone to the clinic after swallowing a peanut that had become impacted in his esophagus just above the stricture. Andrew C.'s unusual stricture was something he had been born with, Dr. Botoman explained to me, and though Jackson often treated more pronounced forms of stricture in children who had accidentally swallowed lye, the technology available to Jackson would not have enabled him to treat this particular narrowing even if it had been noted. Fascinated by the link to the great predecessor, Botoman asked Mr. C. if he would be willing to record what he remembered, if anything, about his childhood experience in Jackson's care.

C. delivered the following written account:

> To the best of my recollection, I was Christmas shopping in downtown Philadelphia with my mother. It was evening and she bought me a bag of salted peanuts. For some reason, one of the peanuts became lodged in my throat. I could breathe but could not swallow anything liquid or solid. We tried cocoa and water but nothing worked. Mom took me to the Jefferson Hospital Emergency Room. They tried to dislodge the nut with no results. I was admitted for an overnight. They tried different things but to no avail. I was admitted for an overnight stay.
>
> The next morning I was taken to the operating room. They anesthetized me and when I woke up the peanut was gone. I remember the nurse saying how lucky I was that Dr Chevrolet Jackson was available to remove the peanut otherwise I might have had a more complicated surgery. I have never forgotten his name.

Andrew C.'s narrative supplies the otherwise mute fbdy—something so unremarkable as a peanut kernel—with an aura. It's the detail of eating salted peanuts at Christmastime on an evening in the city with his mother that accords a life to the object. It marks it as a genre of trauma that most of us are familiar with—call it holiday catastrophe, the accident that is overlaid with extra pathos and a sense of injustice because you should have been having a good time. We agree to suspend routine for a day and let a spot of time become remarkable, so when harm befalls us on such days, we feel betrayed by our desire to have it otherwise. For Jackson, there's his own father's death one Christmas Day that would mark every Christmas thereafter.

So there's holiday mishap here, but also charm, because you can't not love Mr. C.'s mis-transcription of Jackson's name as Chevrolet rather than Chevalier, followed by his poignant misassumption, "I have never forgotten his name." Is this a mistake on C.'s part? Not really. I want to say he *did and did not* misremember his name because Jackson, by 1935, was as constant as a trademark, and his practice easily conflated with a metallic shiny object—not a fender, but a scope. He was as famous as a Chevy—why not? He *was* a kind of Chevrolet offering a new purchase not on the American landscape but on the American body. "Maybe I did forget the details," Andrew C. might say, "but I never forgot that something unforgettable happened to me. I was saved by an unforgettable man."

When I find Andrew C.'s case history in the National Library of Medicine (which is a little like finding a needle in a haystack, however neatly organized), I'm both moved and stumped. I'm moved by a peanut kernel—I'll admit it—because its postage-stamp-size photograph seems so large, because it makes the culprit voluble, because it resembles the sharp tip of a weapon struck off or a piece of shrapnel, and it is accompanied by a horror: the report of the child's total inability to swallow. The date of the accident was December 18, 1935; the date of the examination was December 19, 1935; and C. was ten years old, not nine. The record is shorthand: "when eating peanuts—tried to swallow a handful—some difficulty—unable to swallow." If it were up to Jackson, parents who fed peanuts to children without molars would be drawn and quartered, the manufacture and sale of peanut candy to children of any age would be considered a willful act of violence against the young, and peanuts would only be made available to adults with a special masticatory license, so often did he remove this particular foodstuff from the bodies of adults and children alike.

But Jackson is nowhere to be found in this case report—and that's what stumped me, even if C.'s case is listed in one of Jackson's foreign-body diaries. According to the scantly detailed case history, Dr. Louis H. Clerf was the endoscopist in Andrew C.'s case, and he was assisted by a Dr. Baker. Chevalier Jackson, who often appears as a consultant even when he didn't perform the operation, is nowhere mentioned here. My guess is that he wasn't even in the room.

I suspect that a postoperative mantra came to be part of the ritual of being treated in any of Jackson's clinics: I imagine the nurses were instructed to tell survivors of endoscopic procedures that Chevalier Jackson was responsible for saving their lives. It was a way of anointing every patient with a sense of medical history being made on the spot. Maybe Jackson wasn't exactly available to Andrew C., but the very fact that the doctor once lived is what he could be thankful for. In this way, Andrew C. was and was not treated by Chevalier Jackson, Jackson was and was not present.

In a presentation made for the American College of Gastroenterology's Seventieth Annual Scientific Meeting titled "First Endoscopic Dilation of a Documented 60 Year Old Stricture: The Legacy of Chevalier Jackson," Dr. Botoman said: "We measure the greatness of this man by his extraordinarily vivid impression he made on a then nine-year-old frightened patient in 1935. . . . Our patient's uncanny recollection of this great man brought him to life for us, and helped us learn and understand Jackson's many accomplishments in early endoscopy. Chevalier Jackson should be remembered not just as America's first otolaryngologist but also as American's first endoscopist."

Even without the good fortune to meet and help Andrew C. so many years after his treatment in one of Jackson's clinics, Dr. Botoman would have been inspired to find a collegial spirit worth emulating in the life of Chevalier Jackson. When I contact Dr. Botoman to discuss the details of this case, he warmly shares a territory he could rightly call his. Botoman explains that in a profession now defined (at least in the United States) by insurance strangleholds and bureaucratic red tape, overladen with medicolegal and regulatory issues that take up a good part of any doctor's day, to say nothing of his spirit, he wants to learn how to keep front and center the humble respect Jackson had for his patients.

What makes Andrew C.'s recollection rich and also uncanny is its necessarily being laced with paradox, gaps, a sense of something momentous having occurred that is beyond the reach of memory but not of the imagination. "They anaestheticized me and when I woke up the peanut was gone." According to his account, Andrew C. doesn't remember the procedure because he was asleep for it, but children were rarely given general anesthesia in Jackson's clinics, and the record shows that he was treated with a local anesthetic of 10 percent cocaine, a spray that would act as a numbing agent but not knock him out. Asleep or not asleep, asleep *and* awake: what *is* that place where we reside psychically when our body is being invaded in the name of cure? What is its time? Insouciant twilight during which part of you leaves while another part stays in the room?

As a glorious afterthought, as though he weren't sure that his account gave quite enough credit to Jackson as hero, with no room left on his page,

Andrew C. added a sentence that runs like a ticker tape up the margin of his remembered case history: "Note. Dr. Jackson is the 'Babe Ruth of Throat Doctors.' " In which case, Dr. Jackson comes into an arena in which everyone is eating peanuts and makes them forget they are eating them by his spectacular acts. In which case, Dr. Jackson is himself a candy bar made almost entirely out of peanuts.

Jackson was and was not present; all that I have described here did and did not happen; Andrew was asleep and was not asleep when he was scoped. An archive is a dreamspace, full of evidence, brimming.

A Peculiar Chap

He was a teetotaler, attended no social functions if he could possibly avoid them, was considered "cold" even by many of his admirers, and conceded that he had no friends in the usual meaning of the word.
   —from "Chevalier Jackson: A Notable Centenary,"
   Eye, Ear, Nose, and Throat Monthly, November 1965

The footfall of a deer is intercepted by a crash, light as a bundle of balsa wood muffling the bright edges of a frozen pond. Birds skitter, unalarmed, and a plume of cloud dabs the sky like a lock of the boy's hair peeking down his hatted forehead, mute witness to his quiet trial as he pushes and falls, reaches and topples, braces himself and buckles, flies and meets the ice face down. Snow collects in corners, and the blunt edge of a skate keeps the boy looking down as he tries to circle and listen to a made-up voice preaching the cardinal rules of skating principles. He talks about nothing, to no one. He is pure thought, glistening, careful as ice, on ice. He recollects his body, he collects himself, because unlike the next boy, he records the number of his falls in the hope of coming home with something other than bruises: fifty-nine in the first hour. At first the pond is the notebook that he scores with statistics; later, as he pulls the skates after him on level ground, his own mind fills with number as with song. Does he have fire and dash, is he enterprising? No. This boy is meticulous, methodical, his own accompanist in record keeping; with no one looking, he pushes a barn door open and tests a pair of roller skates on the hayloft floor. He's teaching himself to walk again, but this time with a burdensome apparatus that promises flight. He leaves and records, exits and notes, turns and is struck down, studying himself; after so many trials on the ice and on the wood floor, he becomes a kind of engine that stops at nothing and whose product is a lesson, the moral to a parable that greases the gears and tells him to try again.

There was this solitude, noble as the red slash across a woodpecker's crown, moody as birch bark, not always wanted but craved. There were these small boy's fingers nimble with numbers that he sculpted, engraved loops and lines, hands that couldn't have known they would someday write with immense control, with indifference bordering on pluck, of surgical nicks, slanted cuts, torn walls and incisings: "with one sweep of the scalpel an incision is made from Adam's apple to the suprasternal notch." He begins in furtive solitude making himself up out of sums. He appears alone but with another boy in abeyance, like an imaginary friend whom he turns to with the thought of finding himself in his story.

Jean Morange. Lemon meringue. Orange tanager. Mother's father.

Kitty Clyde: a name for a ship. Fairbanks: the name of a captain. Bordeaux: the name of a place so far from the pond and from Penn's *sylvania*, latitude and longitude lost in smoke clouds. Captain Fairbanks's promise (the year is 1804): to return the ten-year-old boy, Jean, to his mother after four years of service on the *Kitty Clyde*. But oceans take years to cross; the captain is tired and settles in Dedham, Massachusetts. Jean Morange never sees his mother or France again. Young Chevalier keeps the idea of his grandfather near, the unfulfilled promise handed down in perpetuity. And a key. And a crockpot. And a machine shop. The boat is rolling, but that doesn't stop the crew from drinking, thus supplying Jean with a chance for distinction: Fairbanks entrusts him with the key to the liquor cabinet, and Chevalier imagines that he's inherited the key. From his grandfather, he'll find himself in abstinence—this is what he tells himself. Was it any wonder that he also built cabinets and confiscated keys? That he became a keeper and a warden of lost Things? From his grandfather, he decides, he has inherited a love of cooking (even if he's not too fond of eating), "not merely the broiling of a steak or the melting of a rarebit, or the mixing of a salad, but the grand art of soups, entremets, rotis, hors d'oeuvres, galantines, casseroles, salmis" (*LCJ*, 194). He'll take after Jean Morange for mechanical ingenuity as he's come to believe that, without his grandfather being called to Pittsburgh to work as a machinist and an engineer, nails would never have been mass-produced but would have been forever hand-forged. I am never entirely alone, the boy on the eve of a century, on the edge of discovery, on the slantwise plank of becoming, tells himself and forges types of columns: "roller skates: first hour: seventeen falls."

As objects, personal effects are different from bequeathings. In one case, objects as a hasp without a hinge. Dead matter. Still life with watch, wallet, sunglasses, cell phone, keys. In the other case, the illusion of enduring in a trace. Both of these are different from the things marked PERSONAL, like the envelopes now stowed in an archive in which Chevalier Jackson kept "violets that Alice gave me"; the clovers folded inside a fold inside a fold inside a fold of tissue paper; the "leaf that Alice gave me," grainy and shriveled as a once-living heart; and the list for every year of love, "31 years of love to Alice, 32 years of love to Alice, 33 years of love to Alice," followed by "Love to Alice forever." Personal: those objects that cannot be shared, contraverted, or traversed. Those Things that can't be found.

Some things we'll just never know—like how Chevalier Jackson came to court and marry Alice White. The chapter in his autobiography devoted to "Marriage" only takes up half a page, though it refers to a relationship that lasts for over fifty years. There are novels waiting to be written about romances that begin in medical consulting rooms, but Jackson never wrote one, nor told of how exactly he and Alice came to fall in love. His description of the meeting makes it sound as though he married her entire family, and in a way he did, since they all lived together after Jackson's marriage: "A patient, Josephine W. White, when coming for treatment brought her sister Alice and their mother with her. They were all charming people. I married Alice" (*LCJ*, 114). The End.

Jackson wrote his *Life of Chevalier Jackson* in direct response to so many people wanting to know something about who he *was*. People were fascinated, so he agreed in 1938 at seventy-three years of age to give them a full-fledged descriptive narrative and lavishly illustrated account that included color reproductions of his oil paintings, some of his drypoint etchings in black and white, documentary and home photography, and delicate line drawings in miniature with which he whimsically closed particular chapters. It's not as though Jackson had made no autobiographical forays before then: the object collection itself can be understood as a record of his life (a kind of "foreign body" diary), and his showpiece of a textbook, *Diseases of the Air and Food Passages of Foreign-Body Origin* sketches the life's course of Jackson the obsessed collector in its meticulous documentation of the foreign bodies he secured.

This act of self-documentation would, however, be different. It would fill in gaps and explain intentions. It would reckon with what others saw in him, and try to understand how he came to be the person who he was. As a backward glance, it would attempt to compensate for all that lingers, unresolved. It would collect things—eccentricities and peculiarities—that, in making Jackson into a curio, could still keep him (unintentionally) at a distance. It would reveal things—the powerful undertow of childhood trauma in particular—and this troubled him. In spite of a lifelong tendency toward reticence and withdrawal from something like "the social body," he invited contact with the intimate details of his childhood in *Life of Chevalier Jackson*. But he also feared its repercussions, citing its composition as the only possible regret of his life: "If I have made any momentous error it is the writing of this book" (216).

Who was that man? According to his 1938 autobiography, Jackson was a man who purposely ordered his clothes oversize. In order to get a tailor to mismeasure him, he arrived wearing three suits of underwear. The result of oversize collars was a head and neck that he happily described as resembling those of a turtle, while "shoes must be large to the point of sloppiness, their length requiring eternal vigilance lest I trip over my own feet" (*LCJ*, 172). It's as though Jackson didn't like for his clothes to hold him or make him feel himself, as though he preferred not to be sheathed, but to be free to slip out of a protective skin at any moment. Clothes necessitated an exertion of vigilance.

By his gloves—"thin grey silk to be taken off at meal time" in summer—you will know a very special set of hands (*LCJ*, 168). The only thing that enabled Jackson not to collapse beneath the undue strain of trying to relieve the suffering of children unable to swallow or breathe, he told us, was an utter trust in his hands. Chevalier Jackson was a man who didn't trust much of anything in the world except his eyes and hands, and he protected his hands with gloves much of the time. "Sealing an envelope, opening a package, or turning the page of a manuscript," he explains, "would cut deep enough to draw blood." By his own account, Jackson is *literally* thin-skinned—the gloves were not, as his colleagues supposed, a protection against scars caused by Roentgen burns.

"Caution is natural and extreme with me," he confessed, " 'take a chance,' has no appeal. I would not take a chance on anything. One day when I said so, Doctor Ellen J. Patterson added, 'nor anybody' " (*LCJ*, 174). Jackson avoided placing his bare hand on a doorknob for fear of infection, thought the "Oriental bow" should replace the "Western handshake" as a polite form of greeting, and believed that gauze should be placed over all telephone receivers to halt the spread of TB. He took the idea of defensive driving to an extreme, feeling that "one should drive a motor car on the principle that every other driver on the highway is deaf, dumb, drunk, or demented" (*LCJ*, 174). He angrily eschewed a trust in Providence: "Trust in Providence: keep powder dry—Providence won't keep powder dry, Providence won't keep insts in order, delicate instruments, delicate bronchus of a child."

If you submit yourself to a regime, anything is possible—from the training of the body to do things it doesn't seem capable of to learning how to insert a rigid instrument into a body's intractable folds. Thus, he took a line from Matthew 6:3 and said that every child should be taught "Let thy left hand know what thy right hand does and how to do it" (*LCJ*, 205). Jackson trained himself to become perfectly ambidextrous. He is quick to remind us that his hands were not the product of a genetic endowment or a natural predilection but the reward for his "total abstinence from alcohol and tobacco" (*LCJ*, 138). (He called alcohol a "diluted poison.") He was proud of the fact that he was the only person he knew capable of not breaking the lead of his very soft pencils (*LCJ*, 169).

He boasted of an ability to eat nothing but "postage stamp" sandwiches for lunch consisting of paper-thin slices of bread with a single lettuce leaf in between. He paints a self-portrait of a man who is proud of his "abstemiousness," his "self-denial," and his ability to "leave the table hungry" (*LCJ*, 171). Some of the most delicious sentences in the *Life*, those infused with the brightest dashes of humor and pleasure, are those in which he described the minimalist diet on which, as a student, he was able to survive:

> A creamless cup of Arbuckle Ariosa coffee and the butterless butt of the previous day's French loaf at four-thirty in the morning started the day's work. . . . At noon an apple from home and two not overclean, much handled, costermonger's pretzels took but a few minutes from the two hours' work in the dissecting room that preceded the first afternoon lecture. . . . Dinner consisted of vegetables boiled with a bone. (*LCJ*, 57)

Going to bed at 9 P.M. and rising at 4:30 A.M. was a habit he maintained throughout his life. The flip side to his abstemiousness (or maybe part and parcel of it)—he was also a pack rat and an inveterate collector of junk.

He was a lover of objects, of course, but he didn't make the connection between this tendency at home and the impulse that drove his life's work, instead lamenting, "If there has been any part of my life misspent, it has been due to the tyranny of chattels" (*LCJ*, 173).

His clinical-sounding description of his diminutive constitution— "slightly undersized but free from physical defect" (*LCJ*, 167)—might explain why he didn't spend his college days on the gridiron. Instead, he carried coal from one room to the other in the house at 925 Walnut Street, where, as a student, he rented an attic room for one dollar a week (see figure 10).

Self-discipline is one thing and a fastidious devotion to the idea of a self in absentia is another. In combination, they provide the essential ingredients for an ontological recipe imbibed by many of the world's mystics. Whether Jackson's sundry quirks of character render him more vivid as a person in the world or more opaque, his practice of detachment seems to have upset many of his colleagues, who hoped to forge an intimacy with him but who ultimately found him impossible to know. He told his father in a letter from 1884: "I do not know nor do I want to know a man in the college except Proffessors [sic]." In his adult life, his peers, even though

Fig. 10. Jackson's pen-and-ink illustration of the attic room he rented at Ninth and Walnut streets while a student at Jefferson Medical College. Smithsonian Institution, National Museum of American History.

they revered him for his work, described him as sadly unknowable, cold, recoiling, socially unavailable, inaccessible, even phobically incapable of company, and cut off from pleasure in the extreme.

Perhaps Chevalier Jackson was a person who didn't let himself be touched, entered, or swallowed. Here is a figure who recoiled from intimacy with most other people but who entered numerous of his fellows on a daily basis, profoundly, through a tube. "If you want me again look for me under your bootsoles." If you want to find me again, look inside the human throat. Jackson might have been paraphrasing Whitman in the way he carved his initials into some of his illustrations. Beautifully cross-hatched, the letters C and J loop and lace inside and atop one another like a perfect Chinese woodcut, but it's odd indeed to find those letters not in the corner of a drawing but inside the throat that he's depicting (see figure 11). It could be a way of saying, I was here, this is mine, here's my flag, but with a twist. Obscuring the anatomy, the letters suggest that we have to see through Jackson to get to the body.

What a peculiar chap, who wanted people to find him in their throats. This is the only place where he could meet you, and the only place where he felt sure.

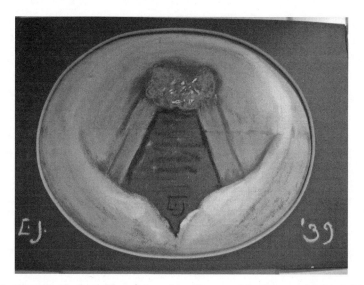

Fig. 11. Chevalier Jackson illustration of carcinoma of the larynx with his initials inlaid. Reprinted with permission of the American Academy of Otolaryngology Head and Neck Surgery Foundation, © 2009. All rights reserved.

The Life of Chevalier Jackson: Early Prototypes of Rescue

I characterize my own soul as a glowing blue orb, about the size of a marble,
in my stomach.
                    —STUDENT BRIAN FORSBERG, "Why Did I Just Say That?"

"At the center of each person," Winnicott writes, "is an incommunicado
element, and this is sacred and most worthy of preservation."
                                        —ADAM PHILLIPS, *Winnicott*

In his autobiography, Jackson tried to narrate the story of his origins
and recover the conditions that made his later peculiar history-making
practice possible by identifying a series of intriguing prototypes of rescue as early harbingers of interest in endoscopic work. The prototypes are
strangely like and unlike each other, and they accumulate in the autobiography like a collection. They can be substituted for each other—they are
metonymic—and are radically distinct from one another. Taken together,
they bifurcate into two distinct types: instances of detached problem-
solving, engineering feats, and uncommon ingenuity that show Jackson
liberating things caught inside (other than bodily) systems; and scenes of
tremendous physical and emotional struggle, life-or-death situations from
which Jackson must extricate himself—as he would foreign bodies in later
life—in order, literally, to survive. The saving of Things—in the sense of
rescuing *and* stowing inside a collection—is linked in the autobiography
with efforts to *save oneself* from the cruelty and torment of others.

When Jackson was twelve years old, his father entered into a business
venture that involved drilling for oil. At a certain point in the excavation, a
number of tools got lost inside the well, leaving the foreman to declare that
the well was bewitched, cancel the job, and suggest they start over. Knowing
that his father was depending on the success of the expedition to get out
of debt (the story starts to take on the existential proportions of De Sica's
Bicycle Thieves), Jackson, still a boy, devised an instrument for retrieving
the tools. He had to visualize the depth, intricate turns, and shape of the
well; the attitude of the tools; and the various pieces of drilling machinery
already at his disposal. Presenting his idea for a multibarbed harpoon to
the local toolsmith, he was told that the plan was sound but its manufacture wasn't possible, so he went home and made a wooden version of what
he had in mind that convinced the craftsman to make the harpoon. To

everyone's overwhelming surprise, the twelve-year-old boy-wonder then used his invention to retrieve the tools lost in the well, and the instrument, though never patented and never yielding income for Jackson, became a standard implement for the fishing industry thereafter.

The retrieval of a cork caught inside one of his mother's olive-oil bottles counts as Jackson's second foreign-body prototype—to everyone's amazement, he fished out the cork in a few minutes with a wire loop. On another occasion, Jackson figured out a way to rescue valuable papers from a planing-mill fire, but the analogy between gullets and architectures, stomachs and landscapes, bodies and machines, physiological arrangements and man-made mechanisms comes fully to light in his description of his work as a plumber's cub at Idlewood, the home–turned–summer hotel run by his father and the family. The gas-driven light and water system would occasionally get clogged by an array of culprits as generically vast as an object stuck in a maw, which Jackson listed: "sand, gravel, rotten wood, leaves, grass, algae, worms, larvae, insects, crayfish, and the like" (*LCJ*, 18). Usually the lines would become obstructed just on the evenings when social events and entertainment were planned for the hotel guests, plunging the entire estate into darkness. Preferring work clothes to evening clothes, Jackson relished the opportunity to feel his way around in the dark—truly pitch dark, before the days of flashlights and without the advantage of firelight, which was too dangerous—while being lowered by a rope into the bowels of the system. This early work with tubes and valves "led to the later discovery that in the bronchial tubes there are vitally important pathologic mechanisms parallel to the stop valves, by-pass valves, and check valves fundamental to pipes, pumps, and plumbing. My whole life's work with the air and food passages seems curiously parallel in its fundamentals to those boyhood days as a plumber's cub" (*LCJ*, 49–50).

These were some of the felicitous facsimiles of his later work as a plumber of physiological depths, a training ground that might seem anomalous for future work with bodies—mightn't Jackson have become an engineer instead?—but the examples enjoy a handsome fit with Jackson's later medical practice, a link more poetic than formulaic, a charming precedent, an enchantingly imaginative correspondence. The conditions of possibility become both affectively darker and more relationally opaque, however, when they involve prototypes of entrapment and rescue that occur at the site of Jackson's own body and that implicate his very being, his psychological and physiological welfare. Among the many persecutions

Jackson suffered at the hands of the bullying boys who were his neighbors in the countryside outside of Pittsburgh was being choked with both
hands around his neck "until unconsciousness approached," "choked into
submission" (*LCJ*, 30). Later on, Jackson would make a life's practice of
only *nearly* cutting off somebody's air supply in order, ultimately, to help
them breathe. En route to the Greentree School, where he was mocked for
being both smaller and smarter than most of his male peers, he was regularly "waylaid, tormented, and tortured" (*LCJ*, 29).

The first of two prototypical episodes involved the boy Jackson's lunch
pail. Some days, it was confiscated altogether; other days, the food was rendered inedible by the sand, coal ashes, or rotten eggs the other boys concealed inside a bread-and-butter sandwich. Sometimes the bullies attached
"the little tin luncheon bucket" to a dog's tail and sent the dog running until the food landed in the mud and the container was lost. In one example,
Jackson revisited the lunch pail as a metaphor for the bodily passages, the
"bread basket" he would later excavate with a tube. The pail had been purposely crushed by a wagon wheel and Jackson's "painful, fruitless efforts
to get [his] little hand into the crimped top and extricate some morsels of
bread" (*LCJ*, 31) delighted his tormentors. When he, "ravenously hungry,"
hit upon the idea to pry the bent top open with a woodman's iron edge,
borrowed from a rail-splitting farmer, he discovered that the sandwich still
could not be eaten because its insides had been "sprinkled with earth"
(*LCJ*, 31). He concluded with a kind of moral: "This was a curious parallel
to hundreds of happenings in the bronchoscopic work of later life, in that
the reward for the solution of a difficult mechanical problem was the satisfaction of achievement, nothing with which to satisfy hunger" (*LCJ*, 31).

The lesson is a peculiar one that recurs in the autobiography—that satisfaction must be had through the solving of a mechanical problem rather
than the satiation of hunger, and it stands as an impetus for Jackson's lifelong asceticism, as though he mastered the fact of forever tainted, inedible
food by fasting: by proving he could live without it. Or by proving that he
could meet his hunger by climbing to a higher level—by cultivating an appetite for achievement rather than for food. He also proves his aggressors
wrong and thwarts their own satisfaction, because in the end he not only
reaches the inedible sandwich (a fbdy in the making) but spends his life
demonstrating that *nothing* is beyond his reach.

Jackson's abuse at the hands of others takes on extreme proportions
in a second episode that lodges like an unforgettable centerpiece to the

entire autobiography. Always there is an extra, over-the-top element of pathos in these scenarios, as if to heighten the abjection: school was dismissed early because of some falling plaster, and Jackson was "elated" with the thought of getting his chores done before dark so he could work in his "little shop" before supper, but he was attacked from behind by a group of boys, blindfolded, bound at feet and hands, and dropped into a coal pit.

Like a living foreign body, a foreign body embodied, he was stuck deep within a mine that apparently had no exit. The darkness was absolute, he was freezing-wet and cold, the ceilings were too low for him to stand upright even after he had untied himself, and the more he groped inside the labyrinth, the more lost he became. Woozy and numb, faint with exhaustion, he dropped to the ground and lapsed into unconsciousness until he was awakened by the feeling of a "rough tongue licking [his] cheek." A "harnessed pit dog" had happened upon him, but, rather than initiate a Disney-style rescue, the scene unfolded into further violence and frustration: the miner who owned the dog called after him and thrashed him brutally for running away while Jackson became overcome by aphonia—he was entirely unable to cry out or to cry out loud enough to be heard (*LCJ*, 34).

The dog was persistent, however, and, escaping his "flogger," returned to Jackson in the mine, finally prompting the miner, whom Jackson describes as a kind of fairy-tale giant, to crawl in. "Welsh Davy, the champion prize-fighter, and champion blasphemer of the whole mining district" lifted Jackson's stunned and stricken body out of the mine. Thereafter he was watched over for weeks by Davy's wife, Jackson's mother, a doctor, and a group of nuns; extremely ill, he lapsed into deliria, crying out to his dog-savior, "Jack, don't leave me. Oh, don't leave me here, Jack. . . . I'm so cold. It's so dark" (*LCJ*, 36). (Does it matter that Jackson's animal savior is his namesake?) Welsh Davy couldn't be properly thanked when the boy recovered because he had been captured by police who were hunting him for a murder committed in another town. Neighbors reported, "It tuck ten officers tuh kill him, 'n six tuh carry him away" (*LCJ*, 37). The image that stays with Jackson of Davy, "indelibly fixed in memory" though Jackson was "dazed and semiconscious," is of a (proximally) illuminated miner: "the vivid picture of the smoking lamp swinging to and fro on Davy's oily cap as he crouched and swung his huge frame along" (*LCJ*, 35).

It's one thing to imagine things stuck in oil wells or bottles as prototypes for foreign bodies that need to be removed from people's airways and stomachs, and quite another to be *oneself* trapped inside the horrific many-mouthed body that is a mine. Perhaps it was this element of his own body as the thing that needed to be solved that took Jackson from plumbing to doctoring. Mining, of course, was the bedrock for his future work, but there's a class element at play. Throughout the autobiography, Jackson presented coal miners as if they were a different species of human than himself—brutish, crude, violent, alcoholic, illiterate, and profoundly not him. He, on the other hand, became a miner who didn't get dirty, a more refined sort of miner who valued work and was a laborer to the end but who distinguished his work as a source of self-cultivation and self-making.

He was a miner who didn't get dirty, who didn't suffocate underground, who mined the body rather than the earth, but sometimes he found himself awash in someone's spittle, and other times he saw through his scope what it looked like for a person to drown in her own secretions, which he then illustrated in oils.

When Jackson was still a medical student, he experienced his own fbdy when the bone of a reedbird he had eaten for dinner lodged in his tonsil. The fbdy was removed without incident at the college, and did not inspire his later work removing foreign bodies, though it did put him off meat (*LCJ*, 59).

Jackson's prototypes of rescue fall neatly into two classes: early experiences rooted in curiosity or in dread. Juxtaposed, they traverse a space between interest and terror, between the experience of being intellectually curious and that of being entirely overwhelmed, between being animated and being paralyzed. Somewhere in the space between these poles of fascination, each of us arrives at our own embodiment as desiring beings in the world, however haunted. The results are never swell or whole or true: like the foreign body collection that it is an answer to, *The Life of Chevalier Jackson* is full of ghosts, and it leaves its readers with images of lingering horror. For me, it is the picture of "a little pit mule blinded with a sharp-pointed coal pick because of the refusal to enter the black darkness of the pit mouth into which it was required to drag the pit cars" (*LCJ*, 15). All of the mules in the pit were blind. It's an image that Jackson himself can't shake, the "shocking cruelty" of innocent creatures punished for their refusal to enter in, carrying the burden of man's progress in the dark. It might be why he lighted passageways.

II.

HOW DOES SOMEONE SWALLOW *THAT*?

If I wish to describe a little child, . . . I must show you something of his oral interests.

—ADAM PHILLIPS, quoting D.W. Winnicott

A button box is a dangerous plaything.

—CHEVALIER JACKSON,
Diseases of the Air and Food Passages of Foreign-Body Origin

Between Carelessness and Desire: Getting Objects Down

Sometimes if I'm reading at the computer, like now, I hold my pen between my teeth, the way a dog holds its bone, but then I might also move it out from my teeth and enjoy the feeling of its cool plastic and rubber parts resting between my lips alone. Chomping gently down, head erect, serene, I read a line from Jackson: "Putting inedible objects in your mouth increases your risk of choking."

"Chew your milk!" Jackson commanded the American public in a 1937 article in *Hygeia*. "Nearly everyone eats too fast for the good of his health. All food should be thoroughly masticated and insalivated. Even milk ought to be 'chewed'; that is, it should be sipped and each sip should be rolled around the mouth so that it is mixed thoroughly with saliva before it is swallowed." Who could take seriously this sort of border-patrolling of the body with its ridiculous injunction? Chewing liquids, I would think, might make a person more likely to choke than not.

But how *does* someone swallow that glass collar button, shawl pin, dental root canal reamer, brass atomizer tip, crucifix, cocklebur? How does a fence staple, rubber eraser, tag fastener, glass bead, shoe button, wristwatch, or pebble end up in someone's stomach? Jackson's answer to the question in his voluminous *Diseases of the Air and Food Passages of*

Foreign-Body Origin is both lengthy and spare. In a word, Jackson explains, *carelessness* is the cause, in most cases, of a thing finding its way into a person's windpipe or down his gullet. Who would have guessed that the "presence of a sharp-pointed piece of wire in a woman's esophagus points to the carelessness of using an old broken egg-beater in making the custard pie, the swallowing of a piece of which constituted the accident in this case"? Then there is the "carelessness of having an inedible, insoluble foreign substance in the mouth" (*DAFP*, 22), or the "filthy method" of using the mouth to hold tools (*DAFP*, 72). Desperate to try to hold these things out of place in place, Jackson moved exasperatedly from unconvincing statistical deductions to an infinite, ungraspable array of causes, at the same time that he remained steadfast that carelessness was the primum mobile of humans' swallowing of things. As a mockery of Jackson's own "Be Careful!" admonitions, one fbdy in his collection stands out: item #2483 is a pin that bears the inscription "B-A-2-Way Looker Says Care Fu Lee" (see figure 3, page 7). If the pin's inclusion here means that someone ate the message rather than heeded it, this could be considered the collection's fbdy par excellence.

"If no one put into his mouth anything but food, foreign body accidents would be rare" (*DAFP*, 72). This simply isn't true, as Jackson's exhaustive documentation of any and everything finding its way into the mouth attests. If carelessness is set aside, perhaps another coherent set of causes can be brought in. Jackson suggested "personal factors, such as age, sex, occupation, and place of residence of the patient; failure of the patient's normal protective mechanism; physical activities, expression of emotion, posture; dental, surgical and medical factors; and properties of the foreign body itself" (*DAFP*, 18). He concluded that "chicken bones are much more frequent as foreign bodies in women," and "foreign bodies occur more frequently in the poor" who don't enjoy the "watchful oversight of the well-to-do class" (*DAFP*, 19).

This analysis hardly amounts to a science and isn't indulged for long before the assumption of carelessness once again creeps in, like a bane laced with responsibility, guilt, and the possibility of prevention; it moves across every page of Jackson's prose until I begin to feel I'm reading a kind of *Moby-Dick* of the source of swallowed things, an insane compendium of postmodern proportions. It's both sad and mildly comic to watch this little word by which Chevalier Jackson would like to contain orality in humans—"carelessness"—morph utterly out of control.

Throat cleared, he began again: "The almost infinite forms of carelessness may be grouped under a few heads" (note the struggle to contain "infinite" with "few"):

1. Carelessness in the preparation of food.
2. Carelessness in eating and drinking.
3. Carelessness in putting inedible substances in the mouth.
4. Carelessness of parents and nurses, and
5. (The wonderfully tautological) "carelessness in play." (*DAFP*, 29)

Moving from the general to the specific case of carelessness, here's a random sample of absurdist prophylactic rules:

It is carelessness to serve food containing fragments of nut shells, egg shell, oyster shells, crab shells, etc.

It is carelessness in the kitchen that permits containers and utensils to contribute fragments of egg-beaters, chips of enamel or chinaware, splinters of wood from flour or sugar barrels, solder from tin cans, etc.

Care should be taken, when cooking or serving food, to see that there are no loose pins or buttons in the waist that could fall into the food.

Hasty eating and insufficient mastication should be avoided as dangerous.

Chewing of pencils, toothpicks, grass, stalks, straw, etc., apart from general objections, is a source of foreign body accidents.

Veering away from carelessness, skirting it with chaotic glee, were the numerous other possible causes that Jackson was compelled to note. A person could ingest a foreign body just by "taking a deep breath to cough or sneeze," which "can relax reflexes that keep things at bay" (*DAFP*, 20). Or by

Recumbency.
Vomiting.
Coughing.
Running and jumping.
Falling.

Anger. Dispute.

Excitement.

Sobbing. Crying.

Laughing and whistling. Note: "The combination of laughing, running and eating peanut candy" could be deadly (*DAFP*, 22).

Stertorous (i.e., heavy, deep, or noisy) breathing.

Drunkenness.

Sleep.

Unconsciousness . . .

. . . and the list goes on.

Watching Jackson try to answer the question of "how"—how did you swallow that, what was that doing in your mouth?—one glimpses a struggle so great that it led him to draw class divisions between the innocent and the guilty because, as it turns out, swallowed objects are *never* due to the carelessness of a doctor or dentist: "It does not appear from our records that an accident was due solely to carelessness on the part of a dentist or oral surgeon" (*DAFP*, 22), and when the spring-catch of a Robertson tonsil forceps is inspirited into a boy's lung during a tonsil operation, "this was not the fault of either Dr. Robertson or the tonsillectomist" but the "fault of the workman who tempered the steel . . . the temper was not drawn to the point where it would bend before breaking" (*DAFP*, 24). Doctors can't be careless because they are presumably full of care. *Diseases of the Air and Food Passages* is marked by exquisite tension between Jackson's strenuous desire to *prevent* foreign-body ingestion and the fact that removal of foreign bodies from the air and food passageways provided him with a distinct and singular pleasure: "there is an indescribable pleasure created by the removal of a foreign body considered quite apart from all the collateral pleasures" (*LCJ*, 201). Without the masses' carelessness, he would be out of a life's *jouissance*. If bodies and their objects could be perfectly protected from one another, then Jackson wouldn't be able to perform his wonders.

Emboldened to scientize the swallowing of objects as if it were a disease, intent on the achievement of a logical answer, Jackson was bound to arrive at zany conclusions when he headed a notebook with the words "Etiology: Race." Having covered gender and class—women seem to swallow chicken bones more than men, the children of the poor are more fbdy-prone than the children of the rich—he ventured into the territory of eugenics and concluded that the Japanese are a superior race in this regard:

It would be to [*sic*] much too [*sic*] say that race, considered entirely apart from environment, is a factor in foreign body etiology; and yet some very interesting observations have been made. The eminent and skillful bronchoscopist, Prof. Ino Kubo tells me that though safety pins are much used in Japan, yet there has never been known a case of safety pin as a foreign body. Anyone who has watched the bright laughing faces of the beautiful children of Japan at play will be glad to know that they are immune to the temptation to put these dangerous things in their mouth; but the explanation is unknown. Possibly Japanese mothers have the good sense to avoid setting a bad example by putting safety pins in their own mouth.

Safety pins, which Jackson enjoyed calling "danger pins," are tempting to the palate of the people of one nation state and not the other: therein lies a tale, but I'm not sure Jackson had the means at his disposal to tell it. So many shapes, sizes, and types of safety pins entered Jackson's clinical domain that he kept a string of prototypical pins in a special place in the clinic. Jackson may not have wanted to be presented with yet another safety pin and the beguiling question of "how" that accompanied it, but as objects they came to take on a fetishistic aura; fellow bronchoscopist Emily van Loon reported that the string was always referred to as the Bronchoscopic Rosary (see figure 12). No doubt it yoked together a group of people by a bronchoscopic creed, dedicated to a higher purpose, who venerated the objects that they also found menacing.

Imagine this scenario: Sigmund Freud seeks out Chevalier Jackson as the best person to treat his throat cancer, and in exchange for his services, Freud helps Jackson with his PTSD—he listens to his dreams and helps him reform nightmares of childhood trauma. It's an encounter that might have been nurturing or instructive in both directions, but the two depth specialists—one of the body, the other of the mind—never crossed paths. Consequently, the invention of the idea of an unconscious seems to have

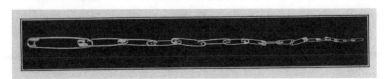

Fig. 12. The Bronchoscopic Rosary, a chain of safety pins representative of the range of prototypes a person might swallow or inhale. Chevalier Jackson Papers, Archives Center, National Museum of American History, Behring Center, Smithsonian Institution.

bypassed Jackson, who found no way to admit human psychology into his accounting of oral acts. Foreign-body ingestion is impossible to prevent not because of carelessness in humans but largely because of factors that Jackson seemed unable to allow into his schema—desire, drive, instinct, hunger, and love. Maybe I swallowed a button because I loved it or loved sucking it, or because it reminded me of a nipple, or maybe it ended up in my mouth accidentally on purpose. Chevalier Jackson could only read the mouth as a site of danger rather than pleasure, of utility rather than appetite. So focused on carelessness as cause, Jackson never considered that poor children might have swallowed objects more frequently not because they were the victims of careless caretakers or lacked self-control but because they were starving.

To be fair to Jackson, it's important to acknowledge that he did at least nod in the direction of "hysterical swallowing," and thus the possible admission of an unconscious, but he treated it as the anomalous instance of "voluntary swallowing" and paired it with "morbid" tendencies and suicide attempts (as in the case of the man who tried to end his life by swallowing a handful of tacks), even though hysterics weren't necessarily trying to take their lives. Hysterics sometimes presented with the phenomenon of "*intentional* inspiration of a foreign body" or, just as often, the highly interesting (if only to an observer) "*imaginary* foreign body" (*DAFP*, 28). Jackson claimed to have experienced such cases but never described how an encounter with a hysterical patient might unfold. I imagine he would be a hysteric's perfect interlocutor because, as Jackson made clear in his textbook, one of the things that distinguished him from his contemporary peers—in addition to his profound gifts, pioneering techniques, and skill—was the fact that he believed in the presence of an ingested foreign body in the first place. Much of *Diseases of the Air and Food Passages of Foreign-Body Origin* is taken up with photographs of emaciated children whose prolonged torment and, in many cases, deaths were caused by doctors' unwillingness to suppose the presence of a foreign body to begin with. Realizing he had to convince people of the presence of an entity that is present though invisible offers another explanation as to why Jackson referred to his textbook as a kind of gospel and to himself as an evangelist.

The hysteric enters the examining room with the complaint of being invaded, of being full, of something being stuck. And Jackson, unlike the rest of the world, believes her because even if the Roentgen ray he'll perform fails to reveal an object, and even if she goes so far as to let herself be invaded again, this time by his scope, there *is* something there, isn't there? Even if it's as simple as something she is trying to say and needs him to hear or something she wants him to acknowledge, if not remove.

Might it have been useful to have recorded the things hysterics claimed to have swallowed? Or really did swallow? Not voluntarily but against their will? Or wished to swallow? These items are hard to identify on Jackson's 636-page grid. The only reference Chevalier Jackson makes to a hysterically fabricated foreign body in *Diseases of the Air and Food Passages of Foreign-Body Origin* appears to belong to a fairy tale of helpless maidens in search of princes in the mouths of toads: "Frogs and toads have been known to be inspirited when being held in the mouth; but all of our supposed cases of this kind proved to be conjurations of hysterical imagination" (*DAFP*, 36). He does cite a case of a woman who came to him with over "500 ordinary pins" in her stomach, and another who had "twenty-six large open safety pins entangled together so that they moved around the stomach as a single mass bristling with points. This massing was favored by a piece of string 4 meters long that the patient had swallowed separately" (*DAFP*, 173). But these cases appear under the heading "symptomatology" in order to make the point that foreign-body ingestion can often be symptomless while the object carries out its silent, destructive work. The woman with the pins in her stomach felt only "discomfort and slight pain." For Jackson, the mystery of how to discern the presence of a symptomless foreign body is more pressing than how to explain its course of entry. No explanation of etiology appears.

People might swallow things as some sort of unconscious psychosocial protest for reasons that are no more evident to themselves than to the physician who attempts to treat their problem. Deliberate fbdy ingestion is considered "hysterical." But people have swallowed all manner of things for sport and spectacle—from frogs and stones to swords and fire—and the annals of medicine are filled with peculiar cases of people swallowing live fish, the creature most apt to find its way into the human mouth, as though the fish felt most at home there. So long as we're not experiencing the impaction of live fish inside our throats ourselves, we might find it freakishly entertaining to imagine one caught inside the body of another, but so long as Jackson is determined to domesticate a phenomenon that has wildly uncontrollable dimensions (i.e., foreign-body ingestion), we will never find discussions of fish-in-throat in his work.

In 1926, one of Jackson's contemporaries documented as many accounts as he could find the world over of live fish stuck inside the human
pharynx or trachea and presented his article to Jackson as a kind of gift.
One can only imagine how Jackson received it. There's not a single mother
to blame in Gudger's article, and Jackson is all about scolding negligent
caretakers. Usually it's the result of a fisherman putting a fish in his mouth
while preparing his hook with bait, or it's the effect of a failure to bite off
the head of a fish as a method of killing it. On more than one occasion, the
fish is found grasping the swallower's uvula in its mouth. Or the fish is entirely stuck in an orifice, and the victim has to wait for it to die in situ, after
which it is brought out in fragments. "On questioning the patient how the
accident occurred, I was told that while he was swimming with his mouth
open, the fish went in, and in an instant he felt something biting in his
mouth." Fish seem to go for the smoothly dark, wet, and cavernous interior
of the human body as if to remind us that we're all so many parts ocean.
You have to picture the precarious human, he to whom things happen
when he's just trying to extend the possibilities of his limited physiology,
such as "Simeon—, a native servant," who, "while fishing in the shallow
waters of the rice fields, attempted to kill with his teeth a fish that he had
caught, and at the same time groping with his left hand to catch another."
In another case, an eel caught in a man's throat could not even be extracted after the man died, and he "was buried with it protruding from his
mouth."

How does a person swallow that? From Jackson's exhaustive lists, we
can draw but one conclusion: that being alive is the cause of foreign-body
ingestion.

Consider (but isn't it obvious?) that the stomach, the mouth, the
lips, and the tongue aren't neutral or even merely physiological entities,
though they may seem no more than mechanical devices by this account.
The words "saliva," "salivate," and "salacious" (lustful) appear to have
something in common. D.W. Winnicott uses the phrase "mouth love" to
describe primitive, ruthless love. One only has to experience even a temporary crush to know that the stomach is the body part most affected by
love and longing. And what of stomachs so full of feeling there is room for
nothing else, not even nourishment?

How do I love thee? Let me mouth the ways. I love you mouth to mouth.
I need to be resuscitated mouth to mouth. Houdini's wife delivered to
him the means of his escape inside a kiss: a key, say, that he would only

partly swallow and then regurgitate, and then set himself impossibly free. We talk about feeling our hearts in our throats, and of being choked up when overcome by emotion. In fairy tales the world over, a woman swallows something—leaves, flowers, almonds, icicles, sparks—and becomes pregnant as a result. Greek mythology has parents devouring their own children, sometimes knowingly, sometimes not.

Once upon a time, a woman who had been without romance for a time fell in love. She was spritelike and eccentric and the man she fell in love with was lithesome and exceedingly fair. The first meal that a lover serves to a beloved is always momentous even if it is entirely ignored, and this was no exception. It was Easter time, so the woman prepared lamb chops and mint jam and played the piano for the man to listen to before they dined. Following a few forkfuls of meat, the swain choked, and the couple spent the rest of the evening at a hospital emergency ward, where they concluded, in the course of an endoscopy, that an entirely unchewed piece of lamb sat on the esophageal shelf that serves as the stomach's antechamber. Everyone joked that the man had choked on "the Lamb of God."

Once upon a time, a girl put things up her nose, repeatedly. Another girl only pretended to have swallowed marbles and required that her parents attend to her complaint, repeatedly. Once upon a time, a professor of Irish literature had a member of the class bake the kind of traditional cake that appears in James Joyce's *Dubliners* for the final day of class. Objects are buried inside each slice of cake, and the object received foretells the recipient's future. The professor, an otherwise respectable and dignified man, slowly pulled a wadded-up "rag" from inside his mouth, at which point the student baker volunteered that it was a square she'd cut out of an old pair of her jeans. The rest of the class, meanwhile, fished inside their slices for an object clue, only to realize there weren't any: all the other tokens, baked in, were made of plastic and had melted into the cake.

Once upon a time, a boy put a raisin up his nose and never told anyone; he often wondered whatever happened to that raisin. Later, he put a pin into the stomach of a stuffed animal and wondered what happened to the pin thereafter. Nobody but he knew that the stuffed animal had been altered, and he enjoyed imagining the pin floating around inside its plush interiors.

Ask your guests at a dinner party to remember some momentous swallow, and even if such a question doesn't seem in the least bit appetizing, each will have her say, because each of us has at least one formative swallow, one out-of-the-ordinary episode at the threshold of the mouth that made us who we are. All acts of swallowing are psychosocial at the core, not just cases of hysterical swallowing, because we don't come into the world self-integrated (our egos perfectly continuous with our bodies, our bodies confluent with our sense of self) but experience the body as a thing to be explored. We test the body by putting things into its orifices, and we test our relations with others by projecting onto the body's surface an idea of those relations to such an extent that the body is never reducible to a con-glomeration of cells and systems, however complex on their own, but is a literal place and a figurative emblem of intrapsychic, interpersonal, and interenvironmental conflict and surprise.

The body is a perfect hiding place: into its folds, bypassing its flaps, melding, the thing you give me or the thing you force upon me or the thing you want from me disappears inside me, and it's anybody's guess whether I can make it rematerialize—but the fact that I think I'm keeping it for you from me, from you for me, is clear. Some people cultivate literal "throat pouches" for carrying contraband, while others experience their mouths simply as the most convenient repository of withholding: if I want to attach to something, I don't just *cling* to it, I *swallow* it. I make it mine by making it me.

Let the record show: Ella May S. of 2942 East Victoria Street in Phila-delphia, aged two and a half on March 19, 1931, was treated at Temple University after she was "given a dime by her mother in order to coax her into taking some cough medicine. The mother turned her back to reach for the medicine and the child put the dime in her mouth." You turn your back, and *unk*. So much for mother-daughter corruption: maybe the baby knew the mother hoped to coax her to swallow something off-the-beaten path and was being dutiful, or maybe she was being defiant by choosing which strange thing should enter her.

On May 25, 1933, here is Beverly W., twenty-two months:

Patient's mother states that yesterday morning, May 24, 1933, she was sweeping the floor when she noticed a small open safety pin. She asked one of the children [the girl's four-year-old sister] to pick the pin up and give it to her. The patient was also near the pin and seized it first and when the mother asked the child for it, she pushed the open pin up the right nos-tril. The mother could see the end of the pin and tried to get it out of the nose but the patient pushed the mother's hand away and then rubbed her nose. When the mother looked again there was no sign of the pin but she could see a slight cut, jagged and bleeding, where the pin had scratched. Patient was taken to the family physician, Dr. Owens, but he could see no evidence of the pin either in the nose or throat. However, he told the parents to take the child immediately to Dr. Buzzard, who is a nose and throat specialist. Dr. Buzzard, upon hearing the history, referred the child to the Mercy Hospital for an X-ray examination. X-ray revealed an open safety pin lodged either at the bifurcation of the bronchi or in the esophagus. When Dr. Buzzard received the X-ray report he referred patient to Dr. Chevalier Jackson at Temple University Hospital—he states: "we are referring this case to you and wish you success."

Of course Jackson succeeded, but so did the patient in taking the pin out of reach of her mother. We can only guess what her next move was in the interplay of give-and-take with Mom.

Ingest. Digest. Gestate. In 1927, Jackson wrote an essay for *American Success Story* listing the twenty-one facts two thousand children had taught him but that mothers the world over had not yet learned. Number nine on the list is that "the idle chewing of pencils while thinking of what to write is a filthy as well as dangerous habit acquired in childhood, and becomes an exceedingly difficult one to break." Yet chewing and thinking seem entirely bound up with one another in humans. Though I personally have trouble thinking, writing, and chewing gum at the same time, rumination applies to mastication as well as to "higher" brain functions like thought; chewing, swallowing, and digesting in humans are understood to be unconscious symbolic analogues to thinking. The ruminative creature is a cud-chewer, munching on stuff regurgitated, and a contemplator. When I worry, I grind my teeth; when you worry, you bite your nails. To think through something, we say we need to "process" it, by which we must mean break down, absorb, assimilate, even if some of our best "processing" happens while we're asleep, while conscious thought is in subsidence but digestion carries on. Still, I can wake up and feel something stuck inside, an indissoluble, lodged, worried object that was there the day before and the day before that and that cannot be gotten rid of with a forceps, and that, even with further "processing," I don't "excrete" but can only hope to transform.

Sometimes orality is just about the contact of skin on skin in which the thing—that pencil in the mouth—figures as a substitute for a maternal body, just as, thumb in mouth, we invent a pacifier. I put something in my mouth quite aside from any nutritive need or gustatory aggression but only for the pleasure of a play of surfaces meeting, the acknowledgment that I am here.

Let's go back to the beginning, to the place where life, in a sense, originates, inside the mouth: the human infant apprehends the physical world at first through the lips, tongue, and mouth. The mouth is an erotogenic zone—Freud suggested that—and, we might want to add, an epistemogenic zone (desire and knowledge are forever linked). Chevalier Jackson admits this, very briefly, at two points in *Diseases of the Food and Air Passages of Foreign-Body Origin*. Infants do test items in their mouths, he conceded, and biting things is an aid to dentition (*DAFP*, 73). Putting things in the mouth is "one of the natural ways for a child to learn the physical character of things," but "some children, natural born research workers, are more prone than others to test with their mouths every object they can handle" (*DAFP*, 31). From Jackson's point of view, rooted in his bronchoscopic clinic, that tendency must be combated and curbed; we must "teach by reproof" (*DAFP*, 73; see figure 13).

From another point of view, the tendency to know the world by putting it into our mouths should not be stopped, checked, or interrupted, but indulged and allowed to evolve. The objects, the *everything* that the baby puts in her mouth is eventually replaced by words (in her mouth). Words not just as mediums to things she once orally bit or sucked or caressed, but as thing substitutes, things in themselves, things that the mouth forms and reforms and emits. "Spit it out," we say when we want someone to talk who is having trouble talking: we understand that they are holding something in their mouths. Most poets, I think, know what it is to hold words fully, tenderly, entirely in the mouth.

Ingestion of foreign bodies, then, is one effect of the human tendency to get to know the world through the mouth—which isn't even about tasting it but about forming judgments about density and shape, weight and elasticity, of gauging the edges of things and the borders between things, me and it, the place where I begin and the world ends, all that stops at me without going through me. I continue not just to represent the world but to learn about its difference from me and me from it, about extension and breadth, porosity and fit, exteriority and interiority, with the advent of language: words taking shape inside my mouth.

Be careful lest you swallow your words: the human larynx initiates a body into the realm of precarious proximities. The descended larynx

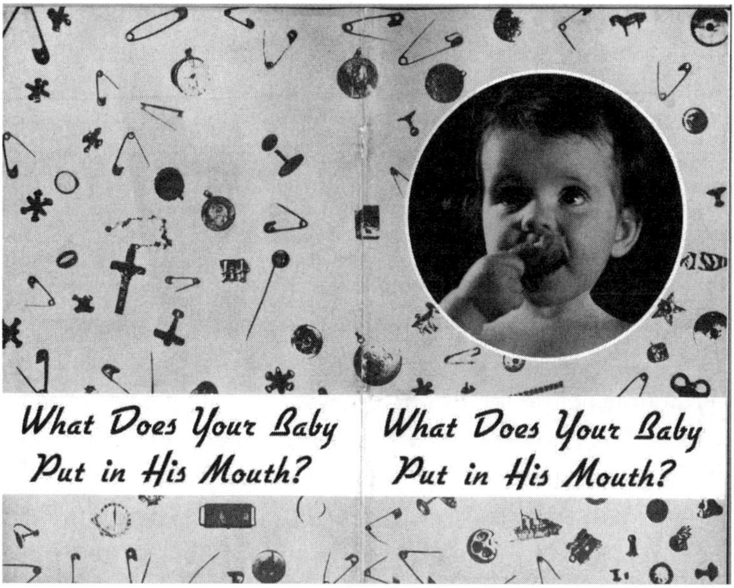

Fig. 13. A baby, bronchoscopically framed, nibbles on a (rather large) piece of toast surrounded by examples of the object world she might, if unchecked, swallow or inhale. Chevalier Jackson, "What Does Your Baby Put in His Mouth?" Hygeia 1, no. 561 (December 1923), reprinted 1937, in the Chevalier Jackson Papers, 1890–1964, National Library of Medicine, Bethesda, Maryland.

distinguishes us from most other animals. It makes possible speech in humans—a necessary vibrating surface inside our throats—at the same time that it makes us one of the only mammals that cannot breathe and swallow at the same time: our sound-in-the-form-of-word-making capacity also seems to be the feature of our physiology that makes it more possible for us to choke. Was it simply evolution that made foreign-body inspiration in humans possible? The larynx forced to descend when we decided six million years ago to stand upright? Did foreign-body ingestion initiate the fall of man? (Think of Eve.) Call me a poet, but what interests me more than the pinning of a first and final cause on fbdies swallowed is the fact that the plural of "larynx" is "larynges," which sounds like "lozenges." That so many words relative to our mouths begin with L-sounds, as if there were a relation between a languid lolling and a lollipop that you lick with your lips loquaciously lapping its liquid. Jackson accompanied his practice with a seemingly nonreferential language, hallucinatory coinages and onomatopoeic thrums, a weird and delightful lexicon for life inside the life of the body, a life athwart, a life beyond our instrumental catch of it, as when he describes a bronchus "lined with exuberant granulations" or records the sound of a "peculiar eolian note," when he listens for an "expiratory rale" or hears "no whispered pectoriloquy." He conjures a language of expedition ("in cases of prolonged sojourn") and of fascination ("chicken bone transfixed in trachea") to approximate a reality outside of observation, requiring a leap of faith.

By the end of *Diseases of the Air and Food Passages of Foreign-Body Origin*, one does come to believe: you become convinced that you must have ingested something, even a filament, some bit of sparkle glue, and it's only a matter of time before it kills you, especially given long periods of symptomlessness. The book convinces a reader of this, and at the same time wants us to believe that artificial ingestion is within our control.

Once inside the book, we experience Jackson's struggle to deny that we are porous. We move across and through space, but we generally don't like to consider ourselves as entities that are also *moved through*. Reading Jackson, there's no getting around the fact that the body consists of orifices, portals, entryways, and exits: "Our records show an infinite variety of foreign bodies that have passed safely through the intestines, coins, nails, tacks, small toys, parts of large toys, wrist watches, chains, all kinds of hardware and jewelry, teeth, natural and artificial, in fact almost every kind of small object found about a dwelling" (*DAFP*, 277).

In an X-ray, an object stops a flow or interrupts a course, bisects a plane, is permeable or seemingly impervious to the X-ray's eye. As in the diaphanous billows and mist-laden hues in which buttons and safety pins float and scatter, dot and tilt, in the X-ray of M.M., just ten days old (see figure 14). At first glance, the image appears to document a case of multiple fbdy ingestion, until it becomes clear that most of the buttons and pins are *outside* the baby and attached to its diaper and clothes. One button rests at the baby's elbow, while two pins turn at unrealistic angles to the right of her lower body in 3-D. Adult hands appear in the X-ray too: they hold the fierce, reluctant arms in place; they've dressed the baby in crinoline or a bridal veil. Only ten days in the world, and to be pinned and buttoned so (this baby is bedecked); only ten days in the world, and to have already been X-rayed with no protective covering; only ten days in the world, and to be forcibly held back and down. What this baby swallowed was a safety pin and a button that then lodged in the upper third of her esophagus. The open safety pin's point—either before or after lodgment—had improbably

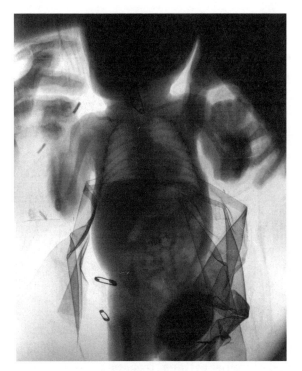

Fig. 14. Fbdy 415, the case of Margaret M., age ten days, June 26, 1915. Dr. G.C. Johnston, radiographer. Collection of the Mütter Museum, The College of Physicians of Philadelphia.

pierced through the hole in the center of the button and left her with a "small areola around the buried point" (*DAFP*, 4).

The floating objects in M.M.'s X-ray, or fbdy #415, converse with the objects that are their more banal counterparts in the realm of the naked eye. Outside the X-ray, they serve a practical function; inside, they play their part in an anomalous collage. Outside the X-ray, hands hold the baby down at its wrists. Inside the world pictured by the X-ray, gravity seems not to exist. There is no inside to the body over and against an outside to the body in X-ray, only an interplay of opacities and transparencies. Until 1918, radiographers were known as "skiagraphers," literally "shadow writers." In an X-ray, because the foreign body dominates, the human body appears to be its swallowed object's shadow. Not "the shadow of your smile when you are gone that will color all my dreams and light the dawn," but the self as shadow of some Thing.

There's not a person among us who isn't invaded. We are creatures bound and beholden to our mouths, and thus ingestion of foreign bodies is one among many of the natural catastrophes of childhood, not because most babies are at the mercy of hopeless bunglers (though that might be one way to describe humankind), but because our mouths are a major mechanism by which we come to know the world and also distinguish ourselves from it. We never stop putting things into it. We never can.

Still, there's a rub, some sense that through sleight of hand or a wave of a bronchoscopic wand, we've been distracted from asking an even more pressing question: not how does someone swallow that, but how does it occur to someone to put a foreign body into the mouths of others? How does it come to be understood as acceptable, allowable, OK to insert a metal instrument into the mouth of another person as an act of human kindness, an act of care? Never carelessly, Jackson would say, always carefully, I put the instrument in. Never accidentally, I might reply, always deliberately. Yes, but not because I really wanted to, he'd say. It wasn't I who did it in the first place. I'm in the clear; my actions are accounted for. You made me have to look you in the mouth and enter in.

Dear C.H.E.V.A.L.I.E.R., aka CJ:

I've retrieved a number of things from within your first name, and shall post them to you forthwith. They include: vale, vile, lever, liver, heir, some rice, some lace, and a chair. Some telling verbs also nest there, including reach, ache, heave, relieve, relive, and care. Hail, revile, and reel. There's much more where these came from. I do not mean to scare you by suggesting that words are magically revelatory. I only mean to say that, like the stomach, they may contain more than at first glance meets the eye. Please inform me of your wishes. Do you want me to keep going? As you know better than anyone, there is always more to plumb.

Your devoted reader,

M.C.C.

Chevalier. Let him revel. Let him see. Let him never be a liar. Let him veer.

Chevalier Jackson's Traumatic "Phases"

It is well also to mention the fact that he may have his breath shut off; but that you know when this happens and you will not keep it shut off too long. . . . The patient, if over 2 years of age, may be alarmed at the inability to speak. He should be assured that this is only because the air leaks out through the cannula, and that in about ten days he can talk as well as ever by putting his finger on the cannula. . . . A child worn out by a prolonged fight for air may fall asleep.

—CHEVALIER JACKSON, "Tracheotomy"

The Chemist laid a few shillings, one by one, in his extended hand. To count them was beyond the boy's knowledge, but he said "one," every time, and avariciously looked at each as it was given, and at the donor. He had no where to put them, out of his hand, but in his mouth; and he put them there.

—CHARLES DICKENS
describing the "ragged orphan" in "The Haunted Man"

A palm thick with calluses grasps a boy's thin ankles, and in a second he is overturned, not knowing which way is up or what to feel for. His face is flushed, scarlet to bursting, his hair seems to change color from its roots to its tip, his ribcage protrudes beneath a tight jacket and shorts, and his shirt falls down toward his face, exposing his spindlyness. Maybe he'll die. He'll never see his mother again. That's what the big-fisted creature who holds him over a quarried chasm, threatening to drop him, says.

Even as a puppy, a white bull terrier can be vicious if mistreated, but with the boy he is gentle, as if learning from an expert teacher how to love. The puppy is a gift from a woman who lost her husband to the mines. One day, the dog, named Billy, goes missing. The boy's father discovers this dog nearly dead on the roadside trying to find its way back to the boy. The father delivers Billy's "limp, tooth-marked, blood-streaked, dead body" to the son: he'd been snatched for a dogfight and fatally wounded (*LCJ*, 8).

An idea comes to the boy (but *where* does it come from?) to make things, to make something out of scraps. Pieces of remnants of jagged, floatable wood. He smooths the wood and shapes it into a small sloop capable of carrying his body and a lunch pail across a pond. He names the boat *Fanny* and joins the boards with leftover tar from the mines. His fellow humans have their own ideas: what the boy intends as a vehicle for passage they see as a container for feeding oats to underfed horses; what he had in mind to cast and rise and fall on subtle waters they turned to mire. It ends up a trough for wallowing hogs.

He takes up the idea again, but who knows why or how? Laced inside winter months, behind windows no bigger than the portholes of a boat, he conceives of a light canoe. Penny by penny by penny, he counts, "one, one, one," Christmas to Christmas his mother and father collect material for a sail, for a skiff, and the paint for careful lettering, his mother's name, K-A-T-H-E-R-I-N-E. The boat is "light, frail, beautiful, but ill-fated." In no time at all, it is reduced to wreckage by a local drunk (*LCJ*, 24; see figure 15).

Still, gliding is a concourse to his imagination—and a means of getting to school in winter months. He's small, so when he chooses the wood for fashioning a sled, it must be elegant, it must be light enough for him to make the uphill climbs easy and the downhill turns a coast. The sled is striking once he's varnished it; gleaming against the coal shed at the Greentree School, it stands out among the "cumbrous sleds built of unsuitable materials, with poor tools, by overgrown boys from farms and coal mines" (*LCJ*, 31). At the end of the school day, having avoided recess, he searches: the sled is gone. And so are all of the boys and their clamor. He rummages, and loses his breath looking. The rope his mother had supplied to pull the sled is wrapped around a bundle of broken pieces. On a dirty piece of paper, two words are smudged: "Kindlin Wud."

•   •   •

Fig. 15. Jackson's pen-and-ink drawing of the boat he had built when a boy, "reduced to wreckage by a local drunk." Smithsonian Institution, National Museum of American History.

On a sheet of dusty blue notepaper bearing the header "Doyle and Bowers Opticians, 113 So 18th Street, Phila, PA" and the none-too-catchy slogan "The Fitting Makes the Difference," Chevalier Jackson expressed himself, in a rare instance, impulsively. Traversing ninety-three years' worth of correspondence, lecture notes, and the occasional personal diary, one rarely encounters out-and-out *anger* as a Jacksonian tone, except in this note that appears to have been addressed to an editor and that has his life story in mind, but who knows if he ever sent it?

> You have no soul. This is all history to me, the history of my life—an incident in the history of my life but if you are not interested, the public would not be either. No man can edit his own writings effectively anymore than a professor can examine his own pupils properly—Legends need revision for what they say as well as for solecisms. Wood—One of life's interests. If public not interested in me, cut out, you know best.

One can feel here the reluctance to hand over his life-in-words to a kind of fellow surgeon; one can gather that he tried to restrain feelings of violation, misunderstanding, ignorance, or lack of sympathy with the wonderful double entendre regarding the impossibility of examining one's own "pupils." It's entirely possible that Jackson as an irreproachable leader in his field wasn't used to receiving suggestions for how to improve his work. An extant, anonymous reader's report makes clear that the editorial quarrel hinged on two significant aspects of Jackson's approach in crafting his autobiography: his resistance to chronology and his erratic use of the third person ("he," "the young doctor," etc.) in describing himself. The editor, whose task it was to anticipate "the general reader's point of view," seems exasperated with Jackson's retention of what he considers a "pretentious" use of the third person even after a first round of revision, and his reliance on a confusing "disregard of chronology," or what he calls a "logical" arrangement over and against a *chrono*-logical arrangement of parts.

It's fascinating to learn that Jackson originally oriented his book around the categories "Physique," "Hobbies," and "Episodes," an approach that may be closer to the truth of being—and whimsical too, because isn't it the case that what life boils down to is a body, a set of interests, and, if we're lucky, things that *happen* to us or because of us, and that these three categories contain a life at the same time that they are strangely unrelated to one another, even generically distinct?

Before the days of what we now call memoir, Jackson's attempt to orient his life-writing thematically rather than adhere to a linear tale shows him to be writing exactly that. Would Jackson be able to construct a narrative that was happily assimilative rather than fragmented? This wasn't exactly the issue at stake: from where Jackson stood, the temporal gaps and reliance on the third person were both symptomatic of unresolved trauma *and* a technique he was trying out, even self-consciously exploring, and were emblematic of an epistemological struggle around cause and effect. At a poignant early moment, Jackson arrives at the insight that "looking backward on this [traumatic] period of my childhood, I always naturally drift into abstract analysis and an outside viewpoint calling for the third person" (*LCJ*, 41). The fractured relationship to time in the book can also be understood as a thwarting of memory by a stunned and damaged ego. But there are enough places in the book where Jackson explicitly, rather than accidentally, introduces gaps or invites a chronological deficit to suggest that he was using his play with form to pursue a problem: he was interested in the question it enabled him to perform.

From where the editor sat, what needed to be foregrounded, with or without Jackson's annoying allegiance to an antichronicle and an impersonal pronoun, was the idea of his life as the all-too-familiar, ever-popular "success story." The book had to have a *yield*, in many senses of the word, and Jackson knew this too—it led him to hide behind the flag of didacticism in much the same way that he had with his collection of foreign bodies: "I have hopes that the book itself will be a powerful factor in the campaign for public welfare," he wrote to his son, Chevalier L., soon after the book was set to appear. "As you know, it was sponsored by the Medical–Public Health Department of the MacMillan Company. It is not a mere autobiography but has a purpose."

The book that emerged from this mix of motives and demands doesn't labor under a need for purposiveness, instructiveness, self-help, success story, or moral example, thank goodness. Instead, it contributes to American letters an aesthetic of impersonality, a barely readable (because extreme) horror story with traces of conventions drawn from African American slave narratives and a scenic, poetically rendered architectonic of time and memory. Time does not yield a clear measure of our days, and Jackson did not force it to; he opted instead to give his remembered experience over to unchronological sliding and overlap. The chapter "A Prophet Honored in His Own Country," for example, is identified as covering the period from 1900 to 1916, but this is followed by the chapter "Building

an International Reputation," whose designated time span begins earlier
and ends later, 1895–1925. Time and experience enjoy an impressionistic
relationship with one another, and chapter titles often fail to identify what
a passage in Jackson's life is really *about.*

As early as the third page of the book (and the second chapter), Jackson addressed his editor's objections via an explanation and a (somewhat
defensive) apology rather than revision. "Many phases of my boyhood days
seem very different from those of the average boy," he wrote,

> and it seems certain that most of these phases had important bearings on
> after life. The phases referred to extended over a number of years, and the
> various yearly groups overlapped in such a way that any attempt at sequen-
> tial chronology would be confusing, inadequate, space-wasting, and at
> best inevitably inaccurate. These phases will be considered under a topical
> arrangement, and the overlapping chronological periods will be indicated
> as accurately as may be possible.

I like to fancy Jackson choosing the word "phase" to describe the ruling unit of his prose because it comes after "pharynx" in the dictionary.
"Phase" is wonderfully ambiguous as a marker of motion and change inside any life. It has the advantage of referring simultaneously to a cyclical
recurrence *and* a temporary stage or pattern that one moves on from: it's
the perfect word for Jackson's circumspect treatment of the idea of a self
or a personality, a life or a career choice as something that *develops* (if we
are prone to repetition, in what sense can we be said to have moved on?).
As if in arch response to his editor's critique, Jackson explained that he
couldn't really be said to have developed; he hasn't ever grown out of one
habit or interest and into another, and if he hasn't developed, then he can't
rely on chronology to represent his life.

The uneasy alliance of cause and effect, the out-of-sync character of
events and traits manifests in mutually contradictory ways as the book advances. The circumstances of his life hardly poised him for future prestige,
nor did they supply a direct route to a life in medicine. He became successful, yes, but he's the first to admit the numerous compelling ways in which
he never entirely succeeded: he failed to access feelings of "bitterness, re-
sentment, or revenge" (*LCJ*, 170) for his mistreatment in early childhood.
These were cut off from him. He never succeeded in feeling at home with
others.

He determines that his aloofness and social reticence—"you are too darned stingy with your personality," a colleague complained—are in part the result of the tortures and torments of early life. That seems to fit. He doesn't understand how he didn't become entirely misanthropic as a result of that early treatment, though. Here the fit fails.

I myself have wondered how he didn't grow up to be a sociopath when the conditions of his early childhood seemed entirely right for such an outcome. He did become a serial bronchoscopist. He did become a slitter of throats and inserter of cold rods—each time he cuts into a throat sans anesthesia, I imagine he's cutting the throat of his onetime aggressors. He controls you now as he first asphyxiates you and then brings you back to life.

"Now we'll show the great Barnum sword swallower": he becomes a victim of a metaphorical force-feeding, as a "long icicle was passed inside collar and undershirt," and he is held until the icicle broke up or melted (*LCJ*, 32). Now he'll make everyone into a sword swallower, with the condition that he controls and inserts the sword.

One day a man came into one of Jackson's clinics threatening to kill "that Doctor Jackson who stole my quarter" (*LCJ*, 100). Jackson claims to have subdued the man with a gentle voice and persuaded him to leave. He never returned the quarter even though the backstory was harsh. A boy had arrived in the clinic having swallowed a quarter. The boy was covered in bruises that smarted to Jackson's touch. The father "ungratefully demanded that the coin be returned to him." Jackson explained that "all foreign bodies removed from the air and food passages were put into a scientific collection where they would be available to physicians working on the problems of relieving little children" (*LCJ*, 100). But surely a quarter is a quarter is a quarter. Do future physicians really need umpteen quarter prototypes in order to get a handle on what they might be dealing with? And didn't Jackson understand that by not returning the quarter, he might be putting the child at further risk? The father "left in a rage," Jackson writes, "taking the child with him." The next day, the boy returned with a broken arm and a bloody lip: the first set of bruises, the boy's sister who now accompanied him explained, were "from a beating by the father as punishment for swallowing the coin"; the second beating was for "refusing to come back and beg for the removed coin" (*LCJ*, 100).

Jackson won't give the angry father the coin even though he knows, firsthand, the kind of violence adults are capable of carrying out against children. He sends the sister home with a fifty-cent piece—as if to show he is magnanimous and not simply overcompensating (the half-dollar was to serve "as reimbursement for the retained scientific specimen and carfare home," *LCJ*, 101). It is at this point that the father returns, "drunk, abusive, and threatening to kill" the thief, Jackson, and reclaim the original coin, which he perhaps understands to be imbued with special value, however perverse. Jackson gives the man his voice, momentarily soothing him. But—astonishingly—the swallowed quarter, the fbdy, must remain his.

Chevalier Jackson was so often ambushed, attacked, and throttled by other boys on his way to school that he sometimes wished that he could willfully drift into the unconsciousness his attackers would inevitably bring on. If he pretended to be dead, his attackers, he supposed, would, frightened, run away. Reticence as a form of self-protection seems obvious enough, but in Jackson's life a more complicated relationship to speech and silence emerged, because it's one thing to fail to speak and another to find oneself unable to speak; it's yet another thing to refuse to speak, and another still to drift toward silence, longingly.

According to the autobiography, the problem of a lifetime for Chevalier Jackson was the one question he was unable to answer: why had he remained silent before his torturers? Why did he not make his mother his confidante? This yields another harder, more unnerving question: why did people with more power than he—the "teachers, directors, parents, neighbors"(and then he adds desperately, "or someone")—not do anything to intervene in the bullying (*LCJ*, 38)? Why did no one notice? Why did everyone, including his beloved mother, appear to be deaf, dumb, and blind to what he was experiencing?

Jackson has three regrets that form a constellation, all of them having to do with silence: silence before his captors and oppressors; silence around the proper use of the esophagoscope; and silence around the need to be paid for his work as a physician. In each case, he admits a kind of paralysis of the vocal cords, usually with the effect of his own further suffering, but in the case of the esophagoscope, with the result of death to others. Jackson initially exhibited the esophagoscope at medical meetings in the late nineteenth century without giving detailed instructions and guidance for its use. In unskilled, unpracticed, untutored hands, the instrument was an extremely dangerous tool, and Jackson dealt with his remorse thereafter by developing elaborate protocols for the use of all of his instruments. Though he does not supply details of the injuries and deaths that were the result of his silence, he explains that, initially, other practitioners' disastrous outcomes with his instrument led to its being condemned. Consequently, "the consensus of opinion was that the instrument was the hobby of an enthusiast, and that others had better let it alone" (*LCJ*, 106). Thereafter, a student in Jackson's charge needed first to demonstrate his ability to use the instrument on cadavers and with rubber tubes that simulated the esophagus. Then he had to remove foreign bodies from the esophagus of an anesthetized dog. Only afterward was he allowed to work on humans, starting with adults. Jackson himself never went right to work on a human subject; he almost always, following location, position, and type of object by X-ray, practiced removing the item from a dummy. In this sense, rarely was a foreign-body case treated as an emergency.

Jackson's operating room was a uniquely silent theater. Most people talked too much for Chevalier Jackson's taste; he came to think of the larynx as an instrument too beautiful and too delicate to be used for the mere creation of chatter. In an era when the taking of an X-ray was referred to as a "séance," rife with the sense of traffic with other worlds beyond the human sensorium, Jackson created capsules of silence in which he carried out his work. Emily van Loon remembered how "Dr. Jackson's strong sense of theater showed in the conduct of his Clinic":

> Nothing was ever casual and nothing was allowed to divert attention from the main issue, which was the patient. A sign over the scrub basins, "No talking except in the interest of scheduled patients," meant exactly that. The patient was brought into the darkened operating room only when everything was ready, the tubes lit, the staff waiting. A sign "Silence" was turned on and only directions to the patient broke that silence. Requests for instruments were made by hand signals and seldom was a word needed. This restraint was carried out also in examining and conference rooms. No words were wasted.

Turn back now as if a dream once dreamt could be entered again, reassembled, however fitfully. He had called it the happiest day of his life, the day of deliverance, the last day of school, but for the boy it was the deliverance from others, not from knowledge, that he longed for. A "Goodbye Session" was arranged at the school in which short, original speeches were to be *delivered* (the word isn't lost on him) by the graduating class. What

Fig. 16. Chevalier Jackson as a pupil at Greentree School, about ten years of age. Chevalier Jackson Papers, 1890–1964, MS C 292, Modern Manuscripts Collection, History of Medicine Division, National Library of Medicine, Bethesda, Maryland.

would the boy choose to speak about? What topic would urge him to rise above a whisper and deliver his certain sense of what he saw? He hit upon it instantly: "Snow." The glass slides of his father's microscope kept the flakes from melting instantly, so he could observe and then depict them. The walk to school was jubilant because he was talking—not to anyone, he didn't talk to someone, but he rehearsed, anticipating an audience for his memorized speech. The schoolhouse was far in the distance—he saw it there—and there the dream stops, and with it the memory, because he never arrived at the schoolroom but instead hallucinated an angel. He never arrived. "It was never known what had happened" (*LCJ*, 40), but the faces, doctors, neighbors, and nurses who tried to understand his words noticed a lump that had risen on the back of his neck, and remarked how, in his delirium, he visualized angels. He doesn't tell them what he knows, he daren't: that he had often seen "Big Bill Drake stun, then kill, trapped rabbits by hitting them on the back of the neck close to the skull with the edge of his massive hand" (*LCJ*, 40).

He does not speak. He does not get to give his speech. But years later, in a letter to his mother, he begs her to remember the roads filled up with Pennsylvanian snow, how deep it always was en route to school, "snow deep, deep white snow—too deep for Chevie's short legs" (see figure 16).

A Catastrophe of Childhood: Gastric Lavage

Endoscopy without anesthesia, general or local, depends largely on the personal equation of the endoscopist, the perfection of his teamwork, and the confidence the patient has in him and his team. A silent, darkened room helps.

—CHEVALIER JACKSON,
Diseases of the Air and Food Passages of Foreign-Body Origin

You're old enough to understand what I'm saying. Will you open it now by yourself or shall we have to open it for you?
—WILLIAM CARLOS WILLIAMS, "The Use of Force"

Without Chevalier Jackson, I probably would never have learned that the medical term for "stomach pumping" is "gastric lavage." I never realized that the evacuating of the contents of a stomach by the pump is afterward followed by the doctor's sending a substance—a saline solution—*back* into the stomach through the hose to, in effect, "clean the stomach out." I certainly couldn't have remembered this detail from my own experience of having my stomach pumped at age four, because all that I can bring back from the episode, bring forth but never up, is a mutated sense of scale.

At the scene of the tube introduced into my mouth, I became infinitesimally small until finally I disappeared (this happened at the point at which the tube touched down into the stomach, then pulled). Meanwhile, a pair of hands became large as the room itself—fat man hands—and the rubber insert, no doubt slender as a drinking straw, morphed to the size of a vacuum cleaner hose, enormous, thick as an elephant's trunk, and black, much too large for my child mouth, wide as the moon but practically no greater than the circumference of a dime. Not black—probably the tube was amber, the color of garden snails my father drowned in amber-colored beer; black was the color of the hose attached to the basement sink that my mother used to wash my hair, a hose attached to the faucet and to the fear of being sucked down the drain.

I remember taking a swig of bubble bath, and I remember that I was sitting on the toilet as I drank. Such a delightful feeling to be in that room of aqueous bubbles and play, to feel something coming in and going down at the same time that something else went out. The bubble bath was called

Soaky, but I always called it Sody, as in soda pop. It was my brothers' bubble bath, the bottle the shape of a fat-bellied sailor whose hat screwed off to access the soap. Such a friendly sailor. I loved his rosy face and knew that it was him I wished to eat. I was thirsty. I uncapped the bottle and drank.

My mother tells me that I'd eaten an enormous lunch of soup and sandwich and more that day—I was ravenous. She'd never seen me so hungry. (There must have been a lot of stuff to pump.) When I came down from the bathroom, bubbles emerged from my mouth. The Poison Control Center was no help because the rotund sailorman bottle with his edible-seeming buttons and his grin, loopy and wide as his girth, bore no words: no ingredients could be found.

And then the day resolved itself into a yellow teacup. My mother gave me milk in it to drink as she carried me, running to the hospital. And it was delightful to my mind, this bobbing yellow teacup, but she was worried and was running with me in her arms.

Objects offer a resolution or a sense of coalescence to a self in disarray. Something collects inside an object, is filled, fulfilled, and held. If a child cannot find himself in the distracted response of a caretaker, he might look instead into the button eye of a doll. When the black irises of a stuffed toy elephant faded entirely to white, I implored my father to paint the black back on. Objects are more sentient to children than they are to adults, as though for those to whom life is more raw, less lived, *everything* is alive. Objects help children to imagine and then experience the real; they play a part in their own feeling real.

Objects hold us and hold our attention. What do you wish this object to do for you? The "transitional object"—for example, the blanket that must accompany the child everywhere—holds a special place in the ego's developing lexicon of self and things, the me and the not-me. "It comes," Winnicott writes, "from without—from our point of view—but not so from the point of view of the baby. Neither does it come from within; it is not an hallucination." This strange thing, held in suspension, holds a baby in a place of becoming, between time. A human subject can concede something to an object, according to Winnicott, and when a baby attempts to bite the head off her doll, she is testing the extent to which the world can withstand her.

In an X-ray of a baby's throat, a jackstone marks the torso's spot like an X in a pirate's map of buried treasure. In a girl's throat, the toy dog detached from a charm bracelet faces the right direction and so seems animated—it's motivated to romp down her throat (see figure 17). The dog that the three-year-old girl had swallowed in case #689 is not really a dog, but Chevalier Jackson is keen to identify the place and position of the object's anatomy: "metal dog, four buried prongs, tail and three legs deeply anchored in esophageal wall; point of seizure, hind leg, tail being covered by tube-mouth during withdrawal" (*DAFP*, 169).

Now I just don't know how one set of humans—adults—forces or coaxes the mouths of another order of humans—children—to open. Doctor-poet William Carlos Williams took on the problem in a story called "The Use of Force" with such a sense of surreal domestic violence—the tortured tourniquet of familial love—you'd think you were reading Kafka. The story uncannily echoes the details from another contemporary modernist's tale, the Russian doctor-writer Mikhail Bulgakov's "The Steel Windpipe." Both stories feature a type of girl-child, idealized (blond ringlets and all), who reminds their narrators of a mass-produced photogravure of femininity, the girl's perfectly round, rosy-cheeked face an advertisement for a

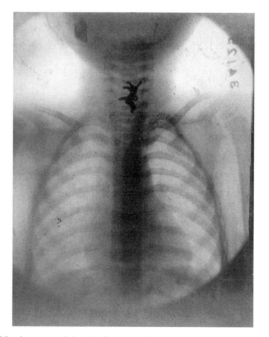

Fig. 17. Fbdy 689, the case of Annie Z., age three, toy dog in esophagus, February 28, 1919. Radiographer, Dr. Willis F. Manges (1876–1936). Collection of the Mütter Museum, The College of Physicians of Philadelphia.

Fig. 18. How do you get a child to open her mouth? Chevalier Jackson Papers, 1890–1964, MS C 292, Modern Manuscripts Collection, History of Medicine Division, National Library of Medicine, Bethesda, Maryland.

chocolate bar or a brand of cocoa (see figure 18). But she only appears this way at first because, in one case, she has a high fever, and in the other case, she's struggling to breathe: in both cases, she's entirely unwell—these girls have contracted diphtheria.

In Williams's story, the doctor needs to see the child's throat in order to confirm his diagnosis, and the narrative, unsentimental as an abstract painting, coolly rehearses the struggle between the child-patient as a withholding runt (in the story's words, a "savage brat") and the exasperated doctor. The child's combination of vulnerability and intractability—to say nothing of her parents' role in figuring the doctor/healer as the enemy—drives the doctor's need to triumph in this battle of knowledge and of wills.

How to get the child to unclench? Longing for her "muscular release," determined to "take a look," he works himself into a blind fury. The girl devours him with her stare; he grinds his teeth. She knocks off his glasses with a catlike swipe—she's as strong as a heifer. At the doctor's command, the father holds the girl's wrists, but no sooner has the doctor slipped the tongue depressor in than she's reduced the stick to splinters. "Burning with the pleasure of attacking the child," determined now to protect the world from her and her family's idiocy, "in a final unceasing assault," the doctor "overpowered the child's neck and jaws," she gags, and he's in.

Reciprocity is out of the question in this visceral contretemps: the doctor wins not only the physical battle but also the child's "secret." She gives it up to him, the telltale "membrane" that reveals her illness—and it's hard not to read it as a substitute hymen (the fact that both Bulgakov's and Williams's girl patients are unusually attractive makes the doctor's conquest all the more suspect; it helps figure doctoring as a form of violation and defilement).

The doctor will make a mess of the girl—that's the sense one has in Bulgakov's gruesome and even raucously comic tale of a bungling, unskilled, unpracticed young country doctor who knows the only way to save his wheezing girl is by cutting into her throat and inserting a steel tube. "You did the operation brilliantly, Doctor!" one of his assistants insists, even though he nearly killed the child. He knows nothing, really, and his medical practice is a sham, but the benighted country folk believe he possesses the knowledge of a wizard (they think he saved his patient by replacing her real throat with a throat made of steel), and his nearly botched tracheotomy earns him a booming practice.

In both stories, the relation of doctor to patient is a strictly adversarial one—no compassion or ethics of care are to be had, and the only difference is that the doctor in Williams's tale seems to hate the child as much as he despises her complicitly stupid parents, whereas Bulgakov's physician appears to loathe the family more.

The girls in these stories of forced entry, of prying in the name of care, lose something to their male doctors, but it's also the case that the girls know something about the doctors that no one else does. "But Lidka [the girl patient] had no wish to speak with me," Bulgakov's story closes, while others sing his praises. She bears the wound, this wound of his that was "quite unlike any [medical] illustration."

Jackson's contemporary doctor-writers figure pediatrics as an arena of ferocity, resistance, marked by a tug of war over ownership of the body, and the question of whether a child can retain bodily integrity and be cured at the same time. Maybe what makes the outcome of these stories as impossible as getting a child to open her mouth is that, while each girl is treated and cured, she also remains fundamentally betrayed.

I still don't know—and I want to know because I seem to need to remember what was done to me—how adults force or coax the mouths of children to open. A friend answers not with words but with a gesture: with her thumb and forefinger she closes her nose, and as she does this, her mouth, of course, opens. I have no memory of how the fat man hands got me to give them entry to my mouth, or even if they did it in a "here comes the train" sort of way. Of course no child is fooled by the train trick but agrees to make his tongue a trestle because he likes the idea of it and would prefer a miniaturized train inside his mouth to a forkful of peas.

Jackson takes a different course:

Inducing a Child to Open His Mouth: The wounding of the child's mouth, gums, lips, in the often inefficacious methods with gags, hemostats, raspatories, etc., is entirely unnecessary. The mouth of any child not unconscious can be opened quickly and without the slightest harm by passing the mouth opener . . . between the clenched jaws back of the molars and down back of the tongue toward the laryngopharynx. This will cause the child to gag, when his mouth invariably opens. (*DAFP*, 191)

What I don't understand is how he gets the lips to part.

This is what my brother, who was seven at the time, remembers from the hospital: "You screamed bloody murder." This is what my mother remembers: that in the emergency room, the nurses and the doctors told her she couldn't come into the room with me. She heard me crying, and afterward, when they put me in her arms, I was a mass of sweat and matted curls. When I collapsed into her arms, crying, she cried too.

I remember—but can't be sure it's true—the command to swallow.

"Swallow."

"Swallow."

"Swallow."

Someone said it more than once and with different intensities each time, different lilts, until my eyes went gooey and the room filled up with birds.

So much afterward would need to be sorted: the forcing of an instrument into the throat is one kind of swallow, and the benighted, greedy, absentminded swallowing of food into an empty gullet or a hollowed-out gorge is another kind of swallow.

Jackson explains that a person about to be entered through the mouth clenches his fists and contracts his forearms, both of which effect a tensing of the neck that makes the mouth hard to open, to say nothing of the throat. The tongue, he reminds us, is a "powerful muscular organ" (*DAFP*, 186), "most persons don't know how to relax," and muscular rigidity can hamper ease of access or a skillful endoscopist's "knack" (*DAFP*, 189). With children, however, "their rigidity does not interfere seriously with the work of the operator who has acquired the essential knack" (*DAFP*, 191).

The "knack" is a complicated, multipart skill. Here he describes it for entry into the mouth and the back of the throat in inspecting the larynx:

The larynx can be directly exposed in any patient whose mouth can be opened, although the ease varies greatly with the type of patient. Failure to expose the epiglottis is usually due to too great haste to enter the speculum all the way down. The spatula should glide slowly along the posterior third of the tongue until it reaches the glosso-epiglottic fossa, while at the same time the tongue is lifted; when this is done the epiglottis will stand out in strong relief. The beginner is apt to insert the speculum too far and expose the hypopharynx rather than the larynx. The elusiveness of the epiglottis and its tendency to retreat downward are readily mastered. The passage of air makes bubbles that assist in finding the glottis; but the patient must be warned; otherwise fear of asphyxia will increase his muscular tension and resistance. Overextension of the patient's head is a frequent cause of difficulty. If the head is held high enough extension is not necessary, and the less the extension the less muscular tension there is in the anterior cervical muscles. Only one arytenoid eminence may be seen. The right and the left look different. Practice will facilitate identification, so that the endoscopist will at once know whether to move the lip of the laryngoscope to the right or the left to expose the interior of the larynx. Excessively wide gagging may increase muscular rigidity and crowd downward the mandible and hyoid tissues onto the laryngeal orifice. Of the difficulties that pertain to the operator himself the greatest is lack of practice. He must learn to recognize the landmarks even though a high degree of muscular contraction be present. The epiglottis and the two rounded eminences corresponding to the arytenoids must be in the mind's eye, for it is only on deep, relaxed inspiration that anything like a typical picture of the larynx will be seen. (*DAFP*, 190)

Most patients can't do what is necessary to enable an instrument to pass into the throat because this would require "relaxing to limpness" (*DAFP*, 184). Most people can't get into a rag-doll state prior to or during a procedure, but what remains of them following forced entry into the mouth is a state more closely resembling a doll's than anything else. Endoscopy brings on "severe fatigue" in a child, "resulting in a deep sleep" (*DAFP*, 200).

Following the pumping of what probably amounted to a teaspoon of mild soap as accompaniment to a heaping lunch, I was undone, spent, finished, beaten, exquisitely fallen, draped. I was self-forgotten, gone, taken, sent. I was leftover—because I know that day I left my body. I was left with obvious aftereffects—an inordinate difficulty throwing my head back for the dentist, for example—and less obvious bodily imprints: to this day, I do not throw up. Not because I don't want to if I need to. I simply don't and can't. It's as though the evacuation of my stomach by force when I was small forever after made me unwilling to give up the contents of my stomach. Or maybe I fear that to "throw up" would be to revisit that feeling of ceasing to exist, of being taken away.

Chevalier Jackson pried into private cavities for minutes that must have felt like years to his subjects. Did they remember him? His face, his hands? Or did they erase him? What is remembered on the other side of entry?

Talking to my brother at a distance of forty years after my stomach pumping episode, I realize that neither of us knows what he was doing home that day, why he wasn't in school. My brother surprises me with a remembered detail that is lost to me but defining for him: he says that he *saw* me drink the bubble bath and "told on me," and has felt guilty about it ever since. As though my getting my stomach pumped were all his fault.

What I remember isn't so much a fact of the matter or an indisputable truth as an atmosphere of deeply pleasurable make-believe. I remember having my own set of wooden table and chairs stenciled with hearts that imitated flowers. In the small basement where my mother washes clothes, I sit at my table coloring, and the room seems to have nothing in it but my table and one toy that lights the room like a skidding sun: a wheeled plastic orange ladybug the size of a small cat with a toggle that I pull it by. I recall a favorite time of day, just after noon, when my brothers, who came home from school for lunch, would come down to the basement, after eating the food that our mother prepared for them, to enjoy another sumptuous meal prepared by me. They knew and I knew that my food was fake and couldn't really be ingested, but I never felt so full as on those days when my brothers agreed to join me in "playing lunch."

The genres of my fake food were mixed—eggs sunny-side up and peas intermingled, pizza made of Play Doh hardened on a plate—and the plastic set of dishware featured items much grander than what we actually used upstairs: a fluted soup tureen and ladle, a serving dish with more than one compartment. My brothers were convincing in their enjoyment of the meal—one wiped his mouth wholeheartedly, while the other exaggerated his munching as though he were chewing gum. All of us were good at pantomiming the act of washing our food down with nonexistent drink.

In those days, around my pretend lunch table, one brother was chubby. Now he's rail thin. My other brother had been twig-like, hands perched on his bottle-thin hips, but now he moves slowly, as if dragging with him a water-balloon body. I had been nimble and neat as a child. Now I habitually spill food on my clothes and have to work against a burgeoning waddle. One brother used to eat to excess and now is obsessed with the latest healthful diet—the most recent requires the vigilance of eating seven small meals throughout the day. The other boy had been picky about his food, and hid parts of his meals inside seat cushions or behind the refrigerator rather than admit that he didn't like the food before him. Now he subsists on 7-Eleven sandwiches and oversize iced teas. I was known for eating flowers and rug fuzz and, one day, bubble bath alongside regular meals. Today, I count myself among the finest cooks I know, and enjoy a widely brimming palate even though, if tense, I fear I won't be able to swallow and might vomit into the dinner party or choke to death out of my body's failure to follow my simple command: *Swallow.* (Flutter.) *Swallow.* (Retch.) *Swallow.* (Eat.)

When my brothers returned to school, I watched TV. Popeye received a number of bullets in his side that he spat *rat-a-tat-tat* out of his mouth. Captain Kangaroo fed a fake bunny a carrot the size of his pinky ring. The face of the woman who hosted *Romper Room* rose up through a cloud of bubbles blown from a pipe, and Schemp of *The Three Stooges* swallowed a harmonica. He played the instrument by pressing himself front and side. Curly threw mints up into the air and caught them in his mouth, but in with the mints was mixed a stolen diamond. A punch to the stomach—*ooomp*—and the object reemerged. The whole gaggle of Stooges put on a play requiring a scene in which they ate cake around a formal table, but a pillow had been accidentally substituted for a layer. They ate the pillow cake and spat out feathers as though their insides were being pumped through a bellows, until the entire stage was filled with coughed-up goose down floating on and falling through the air.

It's no wonder that, with models such as these, I enjoyed throwing Alice in Wonderland faux lunches in which my brothers and I feasted on the *idea* of food, imbibing food facsimiles, because isn't it wonderful to be able to feel the world, ever beyond our reach, reduced to bite-size? I marvel at the magic of a world that imitates the "real" world but in miniature. It might explain what draws me to Chevalier Jackson, his foreign bodies like a battlefield of trinkets, the scope of whose sojourns we can never see the end to. Playing at lunch supports an endless gullet: you fill yourself and never risk excretion or extraction. No one chokes around such a make-believe table because no one really eats, and everyone is sated by conjoined imaginings.

Chevalier Jackson's Tears: The Case of the Boy Who Cried

Sobbing is a(n) ~~function~~—emotional expression manifested by no animal other than man. It is involuntary ordinarily. The physiologic function of the larynx in sobbing is intermittently to close the glottis during inspiration, cutting short the inspiriting crying and phase . . . crying and laughing are emotional expressions also but are chiefly phona . . .

—CHEVALIER JACKSON,
incomplete handwritten notes, undated

"I didn't know the body had so many tears." I remembered those words from a woman with whom I shared a grief over the untimely death of another woman friend. Now a student in my poetry class had suddenly turned liquid while she sat across from me in the small anteroom that was my office at the State U, and I heard myself thinking those words again. The student wasn't crying because of anything I had said, but because of something she had said to herself. Something she heard herself say unleashed this watery torrent, and I was simply invited to witness it. I wasn't meant to staunch or cauterize these tears but to let her first shed them and then, as they rushed down her face, to watch her swallow them, thus

demonstrating a perverse misassumption tucked inside the stoic postula-
tions of that phrase, "to swallow one's tears." It seems a bare fact of being
human, for tears, once unleashed, to have nowhere else to go but, by dint
of gravity, drip down into the next available portal on the face.

William James would say the tears produced the feeling and not the other
way around, so what feeling is produced by the taste of one's own tears? An
oceanic primalness. A sense of bitter regretfulness. Not earthy like the taste
of your own sweat, the swallowing of tears might bring you into some dark
hollow of a place, the place of ducts rather than glands. The thing the student had told herself was that she wouldn't be able to go through with the
critique of her writing by her peers that was scheduled to occur that afternoon. Did it matter that she was the best writer in the class? I didn't tell her
this but pushed a box of tissues toward her, and, reminding her that this
was generally a fairly friendly group of people, asked her what was the worst
thing that could happen. "I'll start to cry," she said, "and uncontrollably cry,
and then will never be able to face them again." Thus I understood that the
student was using my office as a kind of backstage rehearsal space, performing before me the worst thing that could possibly unfold.

We sat in silence while she cried—my goodness, she could cry and
cry—we waited it out together while I said a few things to embolden or encourage her, and every now and then, one of us would say something that
had seemingly nothing at all to do with the display of her tears, something
distracting, funny, or mundane. She perked up to tell me, paused between
tears, that she had a special interest in the cognitive life of parrots and,
moreover, that she was both fascinated by and terrified of, in fact truly preoccupied with, the precarious proximity of the windpipe and the esophagus in humans. She consequently considered each act of swallowing that
didn't result in choking a major feat.

Call it a neurosis, but was it merely neurotic to let oneself be aware
of the wondrous and precariously weird dimensions of the human form?
Maybe she wasn't just a budding poet but a doctor in the making.

What's the worst thing that could happen? What was the worst situation
that the body could produce for the person who lived inside of it?

For this girl, it was that eating might make it impossible to breathe,
and vice versa: that breathing might curtail the need to swallow. That the
body's baffling relay of valves and flaps, or a misstep in the interplay of
the autonomic and the willed, might send a foreign body coursing down
the wrong pipe.

What's the worst thing that could happen? That the pain that is lodged inside of me might come out through my eyes for everyone to see. Or that my tears might produce more pain, a pain impossible to swallow.

What would Walt Disney do with *The Life of Chevalier Jackson?* There's enough pathos around animals in Jackson's book to recommend a tear-jerker centered on a boy and his dog, or a boy and his horse, but it would be difficult to translate the degrees of ravishment, rage, and violence in the autobiography into popular pablum or to disguise the literal bloodshed with allegory. The animals aren't anthropomorphized, they aren't stand-ins for human relations by other means or other names—though, as I will show later, they *do* bare the traces of an unspoken, displaced history of slavery in the United States.

   The Life of Chevalier Jackson gained a wide readership in 1938 because of the conventional features that could be found there—even if it was a strange, difficult, and disturbing book—and because the book brought together a number of elements that made it resemble other bestsellers of the time (see figure 19). Described in one review as a "medical romance suited to all medical students," it responded to a then-popular appetite

Fig. 19. Brentano's window display advertising the 1938 bestseller Life of Chevalier Jackson: An Autobiography. *Chevalier Jackson Papers, 1890–1964, MS C 292, Modern Manuscripts Collection, History of Medicine Division, National Library of Medicine, Bethesda, Maryland.*

for biographies of men of medicine and for nonfiction that took the form of popular science. The year before, Victor Heiser's *An American Doctor's Odyssey* had earned a place on the bestseller lists, and in 1938 Arthur E. Hertzler's *The Horse and Buggy Doctor* was published to wide acclaim. Jackson's book shared a popular stage with *Madame Curie* by Eve Curie and *The Evolution of Physics* by Albert Einstein and Leopold Infeld, while also enjoying the company of literary titles like *The Summing Up* by W. Somerset Maugham, *Out of Africa* by Isak Dinesen, *The Culture of Cities* by Lewis Mumford, and *I'm a Stranger Here Myself* by Ogden Nash. Doctor-novelist A.J. Cronin's *The Citadel* appeared near the top of the fiction list that year; it also featured life in coal-mining communities, but in Great Britain rather than the United States. Jackson's book could be seen to share an interest in medical ethics with *The Citadel*, which is largely concerned with the question of a doctor's willingness to treat patients who aren't prepared to pay for his services.

The novel that secured first place on the bestseller list for fiction, though, is the book that figures as the most striking analogue to Jackson's nonfiction. Marjorie Kinnan Rawlings's *The Yearling*, which would go on to win a Pulitzer (and had been edited by Maxwell Perkins, famous for his earlier work with Hemingway and Fitzgerald), told the story of a poor boy and his pet fawn. The deer is the offspring of an animal that the boy's father decides to shoot in order to use its heart to save himself from a snakebite. The harrowing denouement of the tale shows the boy having to kill his beloved pet in order to save his family—they have almost nothing to eat, and the animal is eating what little they have. *The Yearling* was made into a movie in 1946 starring Gregory Peck and Jane Wyman as the boy's struggling parents, and it would seem to anticipate the later 1957 Disney film *Old Yeller*, based on the young adult novel of that title in which, once again, a boy's route to manhood requires that he murder the pet that he loves, though this time the animal is a dog. The dog contracts rabies, and the boy's shooting of the animal is understood to be necessary if his family is to survive. An even starker version of this popular formula could be found in John Steinbeck's 1933 novel *The Red Pony*, in which a boy repeatedly tries and fails to save the animal placed in his care when he falls asleep each time the animal is sick. What's striking about Steinbeck's tale as a foundational narrative in a tradition to which Jackson's book belonged, at least in part, is that the horse in question requires a tracheotomy and the boy must tend the horse by cleaning out the contents of its breathing tube.

Dogs and horses take center stage in the emotional matrix of Jackson's autobiography, but their deaths don't serve the traditional narrative of rite of passage into proper masculinity. Other people carry out violence against animals in *The Life of Chevalier Jackson*, while Jackson fails to take his proper boy-place in such scenes: instead, he runs screaming from displays of the perverse forms that male heroism takes in his community, or cries himself into a frenzy or a stupor. The passages that picture cruelty to horses in Jackson's book—which Jackson counts as the "greatest of all causes of sorrow of [his] tearful boyhood" (*LCJ*, 9)—are practically impossible to read, so detailed, so carefully calibrated is Jackson's account of the severe mistreatment and exacting injury that he witnessed:

> Apart from gross cruelties inflicted in so many instances, practically all work horses were jerked, beaten, and battered into doing what they would have done willingly if taught what was required of them. . . . They were herded like cattle on the range with no knowledge of halter, rein, or bridle until three years of age. They were then lassoed, thrown, bridled and saddled with the cinch-girth that, with its mechanism like a compound pulley, compressed the chest almost to the point of suffocation. Before an admiring crowd a heavy horseman, thrilled with delusions of heroism, leaped into the saddle. The animal was ridden until he fell in a heap, limp and exhausted. He was then called "broken"—a not inappropriate term. Thereafter there was usually a sullen obedience to rein, whip and spur, notwithstanding an ulcerated back from the misfit saddle. (*LCJ*, 11)

The typical teamster, according to Jackson, was almost always "an ignorant, high-tempered, brutal, drinking wielder of the black-snake whip." All horses developed abscesses at the base of the skull between the ears as a result of their mistreatment, and many a day was marked by wagons and their horses entirely immobilized in mud, which would inspire a teamster to flog the animals with the blacksnake whip as a kind of exercise in masturbatory futility.

The horse might return as Jackson's gentle companion on the paths that his early work as a country doctor takes, and he might come to pride himself for commanding the animals as a team via love rather than cruelty, but the dog, mistreated by others but entirely loved by him, comes back into his life in a peculiarly vexing way. Before testing his mechanical methods for the removal of foreign bodies on living creatures, Jackson

practiced with a rubber tube and a cadaver. But before he dared to practice on the human body, he experimented with dogs. In *Peroral Endoscopy
and Laryngeal Surgery*, he states the case in literal, numeric terms when he
warns that "no one should think of attempting for the first time to remove
a foreign body from a human being until he has at least 100 times removed
a foreign body from a dog."

No dog died from the procedures that Jackson and his assistants carried out on them; no dogs were even injured, he insists. What Jackson
doesn't make explicit in his autobiography, though, is that in order for
the dog to help him with his work, the doctor needed actually to *implant* a
foreign body in the dog's esophagus or bronchus. He needed to force the
dog to swallow things. Jackson doesn't kill the thing he loves and thus secure a place on the bestselling grid of proper masculinity. No. He pictures
himself instead *rescuing* the dog that other people have abused; he sees
himself as making the dog into a compliant workmate. The dog is still, in
this sense, "sacrificed" without its having to die.

In one of many tributes to Jackson following his death, the instrumen-
tality of the dog is plainly stated:

> Dr. Jackson used to have an intern at the University of Pittsburgh Hospital
> insert objects into the throats and lungs of dogs and he would retrieve
> them for practice. He did not want to be told what the objects were. One
> day, the intern, Dr. I. Hope Alexander, now health director for the city
> of Pittsburgh, put an open safety pin into the lung of an animal. "Dr. Al-
> exander, putting an open safety pin into this dog's lung will prove to be
> the most brilliant act of your career," Dr. Jackson told him. "Neither this
> bronchoscope nor any instrument in existence can extract that open pin.
> So—we'll invent one."

Realizing he needs to, at worst, risk the life of that which he loves—the
dog—and, at best, compromise the animal in order to save the lives of
humans does seem to place Jackson squarely in the company of the boys in
The Yearling and *Old Yeller*. Still, Jackson did not wish for identification with
the mass of men or the mess of masculinity. Rather than shed blood, he
wished to count himself among the people who shed tears. He even comes
to distinguish himself this way: he is a boy who cries. And cries. From the
outset, he's a child with a body made of tears.

It is hardly evident from *The Life of Chevalier Jackson* that Jackson had two brothers, Stanford and Shirls; instead he paints a picture of profound solitude. "In my memory the tearfulness of my childhood and boyhood hangs like a pall over everything" (*LCJ*, 5), he writes. Fighting—treacherous, bloody, and atavistic; for sport, for pleasure, for money, or for no reason at all—is the order of the day in his hometown. "Other boys could look on, enjoy looking on, and seek opportunities to look on, at bloody cockfights, dog fights, man fights, and all similar contests. I always ran away crying and hid until it was over, in case such things came my way, unexpectedly; I never sought them" (*LCJ*, 6).

Jackson's fellows are tearless, whereas he is uncommonly gentle. He's the boy who recoils from the "crippling sports" of football and baseball with the effect of cultivating the "delicate manipulations" and "gentle touch" that will later be required by his work with the bronchoscope. Jackson is an unmanly boy and, by his own description, a female-identified boy, for he observes that, "in all the cruelties the sight of which made my childhood tearful, I never saw a woman or girl participate, either actively or as an onlooker" (*LCJ*, 18). He doesn't conclude from this that women are differently socialized—because, as he points out, the women, like the men, were equally unrefined, uneducated, and coarse—but that they, like him, are a breed apart, a species unsuited for cruelty and uninterested in perpetuating it for sport. By his estimation, "women and girls are better than men and boys" (*LCJ*, 18). In the final chapter of his book, "Introspection," he goes so far as to spell out his earliest conceptions—"that angels were women and all women more or less angelic. It seems to have been inconceivable that there could be such a thing as a man-angel. I always adored my father, whom I knew to be a good, honest, true, sympathetic, charitable man of good deeds, but the angelic conception was totally absent" (*LCJ*, 190).

Some reviews of the autobiography, from the *Dallas Morning News* to the *Washington Sunday Star*, picked up on Jackson's portrayal of an identity that took shape against the grain of masculinity and foregrounded that detail in somewhat unflattering ways. "Chevalier Jackson, Who Couldn't Be Tough," one headline read, while another lists among the book's subjects "Associations of Bachelor Femininity" (in spite of Jackson's long marriage). A fellow doctor used the word "fussy" to describe his adult demeanor, which is hard not to hear as a euphemism for gay. If the world of men that called to him both as spectator and participant only succeeded in making Chevalier Jackson cry, we could understand him, in more contemporary terms, as a survivor (or not) of a queer boyhood. What's interesting is that the autobiography as backward glance doesn't recount the tribulations of a crybaby from the point of view of the now triumphant adult, because, in many ways, Jackson does not ever become part of a larger social body. But he does use the occasion of his looking back to investigate more carefully the nature of his tears, as if to ask for all of us: What kind of tears do you cry? What makes you cry? When do you cry? And his answer, in this book and in his life's work, is as much a study of sympathetic forces and identificatory patterns, even ethics, as it is a physiology of fluids.

Three scenes in particular return Jackson to his liquid, limp self, all of which treat of death—of a baby and a horse, of a rabbit, and of a boy— but it isn't death itself that makes him cry. "The tearfulness and terror of my childhood," one scene begins, "seem to have been concerned with the cruelty and my helplessness to stop it, rather than with the gruesomeness of the sights" (*LCJ*, 15). At the age of nine or ten, Jackson is sent by his mother to buy some eggs from the wife of a teamster. The woman, Mrs. Murphy, sends him with her son, Micky, to search out more eggs in the haymow, when the boys happen upon a horrifying sight: the Murphy's baby lies on the floor of a stall near the hind feet of one of the horses, "evidently trampled to death." The utterly gruesome sight of the baby—its crushed and oozing brains—neither frightens young Jackson nor draws forth tears from him. He proceeds calmly to speak to the horse in order to drag the baby out from behind its hooves. Young Jackson carries the dead body toward his friend Micky's house, while Micky, overcome with guilt—he was supposed to be watching the smaller child—runs to get his mother. Jackson delivers the bundle of baby to its shrieking mother, then follows her command to find a doctor and a priest, while Micky is sent to wake his drunken father, asleep in a haymow not far from the spot where the baby was killed.

And here the emotional grain of the experience roughens for Jackson to the point of pain, for, upon his return, he finds his friend Micky standing at the opening to the stall and watching as his drunk father proceeds to whiplash the "trembling, quivering, crouching horse tied up in the stall" (*LCJ*, 15). Jackson, who was "tearless up to this time . . . burst out crying and ran till [he] got out of earshot of the lashes, the curses, and the struggles in the stall" (*LCJ*, 15). Jackson's recourse is to try to find his father, a trained veterinarian, who might be able to stop the "senseless cruelty."

One might pause here to remember Jackson's near contemporary, the German philosopher Friedrich Nietzsche, throwing himself onto the neck of a horse as it was being flogged, and the way the scene is made into the precipitating stroke of Nietzsche's descent into madness. One might recall any number of moments in the modernist pantheon too—crucial and cataclysmic episodes in the work of Dostoevsky or Kafka in which the sight of the beating of a horse by a human gives rise to a forever alienated male modernist self. In this same era, Freud wrote of adult fantasies so often recounted by his patients that he gave them their own titles, even their own genres: those fantasies in which "a child is being beaten." Freud uses the frequency of such scenarios in his patients' psychic life to remind us of two breaking (off) points in the lives of children: that moment when the child mind feels the smart of the betrayal of a parent ("He doesn't really love me. He hates me."), and the moment of stark recognition of an adult's superior physical strength.

Who can watch the struggle of the creature who is victim and not be flooded with grief and a commensurate will to act—not to be paralyzed but to be roused? If we found our friend standing back and merely watching such a scene, might we also imagine that he would be able to watch our own beating at the hands of adults? What's instructive here is the sense of what Jackson can or cannot look on: cruelty is already impossible for him to look at, and it doubly blinds him by bringing forth tears. The ghastly thrashing, the confinement of the horse in the stable, the impossibility of escape is rife with helplessness, but it is a defenselessness somewhat distinct from the vulnerability that caused the baby's death. The baby had neither the physical strength nor motor control to save itself, and the horse could not know it was killing a child. The death of a child by accident is sad, but it doesn't make Chevalier Jackson cry. Witnessing the unguarded, drunken father beat the horse is something altogether different and altogether overwhelming.

Continuing to explore "the character of the tearfulness of childhood" (*LCJ*, 18), Jackson recalls another tragedy with which he directly juxtaposes the earlier scene. Once again, he is sent on an errand, this time to gather strawberries, when he comes upon a beating scene. A teamster, driving a team of horses too hard, beats his son for not exerting enough strength and balance against the back brake of the cart as it is pulled quickly down the road. Jackson doesn't know how the scene concludes because he is driven away in tears by the sight of the father striking the son on the head with his "big dirty opened hands" (*LCJ*, 16). Later the same day, he sees the same wagon with the boy back-driver speeding down a hill, but the task of managing the wagon overwhelms the boy, who topples in front of the rear wagon wheel to his death. Boy Jackson calmly commands the horses to stop. Their halting hooves back rear against the load pushing fast against them and make a horrific jumbling sound. The sight of Tommy Walsh's body is as gruesome as the baby's was, and Jackson describes it just as coldly, in the language of a horror story, the eyes "squeezed out of their sockets" (*LCJ*, 18). But the dead human body (even if mangled and that of a child) doesn't elicit Jackson's tears.

Once again, he is sent off to fetch the town's doctor, and once again the father is drunk when he should be grieving. Evidently, the father went directly to the tavern while Jackson was fetching the doctor, and he arrives drunk with the dead body of his son at the cottage where his wife will receive the news:

> To my dying day, I shall never forget the piercing, agonizing shriek of the poor mother as she lifted the handkerchief I had laid over Tommy's ghastly, mangled face. Up to that time I had not shed a tear; there had been no fight, no struggle, no cruelty, no suffering. The boy had been killed before my eyes, but the death was obviously instantaneous and painless. But the anguish of that shrieking, sobbing, moaning mother, and her infliction, the helpless besotted father, were too much for me. I cried and sobbed all the way home; and even today, sixty-two years later, I gulp when I think of that wretched woman. (*LCJ*, 17)

Jackson describes a world in which children are expected to have the physical strength of adults or the emotional strength the adults only feign (because the adults, after all, are weak), a world in which implicitly helpless children must learn to survive at the mercy of even more helpless adults. He paints a picture of his child self as strong beyond his years, for here is a boy with the courage and fortitude and maturity to be able to act in the face of violent death, yet he also has the capacity to feel profoundly the pain of others to the point of being awash in it—he is a boy who is easily invaded.

All of this goes a long way toward establishing a groundwork of motivations for a later life devoted to rescuing children from accidents understood as the fault of their careless caretakers. And it explains his devotion to the creation of a different kind of mother in his relentlessly admonishing work, the call for a mother who doesn't turn away when her child is in harm's way. Resigned to the ineptitude and the hopelessness of fathers, Jackson seems unable to forgive the negligence of moms. But there is also a degree of protest in the pages of *The Life of Chevalier Jackson* against its author's own capacity for aggression, as though the major impetus behind writing the book was for Jackson to defend himself against a false accusation—and here Nietzsche as interlocutor returns. In a Nietzschean vein, the question "Who was that man?" translates into "Were you the man?"—were you the one responsible for the injury, the suffering, the inevitable pain? That's Nietzsche's account of the basis for modern self-consciousness, one with injury and punishment at its core, but it sounds as though it could be Jackson's too.

It is hard to imagine any person being able to put instruments down children's throats on a daily basis or perform tracheotomies on them without anesthesia—even in the name of care—who would not experience guilt in the process. Jackson had to be bold and, if not violent, then violating in his work. In a word, the ability to save lives in such heroic ways requires a degree of aggression, an aggression that he at all costs denies in his autobiography. In which case, his autobiography can be understood as an alibi for his later practice.

The conflict is apparent in the extraordinary outcome of one of Jackson's first cases involving a child. "One cold, dark, blackish-snowy morning in Pittsburgh," Jackson is assailed by a woman who tells him her husband is beating her child to death. When Jackson arrives on the scene, he realizes the girl is asphyxiating because of a "laryngeal obstruction" (*LCJ*, 98). He performs an emergency tracheotomy consisting of "two cuts in the front of the neck" (*LCJ*, 98), but before he can make the second cut, he is attacked by the girl's drunken father. After the father is taken away, Jackson finishes his work; after administering artificial respiration to the girl, he observes that she begins to breathe again: "her lips moved, and she began to cry. Tears rolled down her cheeks" (*LCJ*, 98). The girl's face, though, tells a mixed story of aggression in the black-and-blue marks that appear there, for when her face ceases to be blue due to lack of air, the bruises left by her father appear. And alongside those, one can only imagine the bruises left by rescue, of the surgeon's knife. The story the girl tells when she can speak is that she hid the family's last remaining dime in her mouth. She needed to buy bread with it so that her brother wouldn't starve, but she knew her father wanted it for liquor. Seeing her secrete the dime inside her mouth, the father attempted extraction by choking. Jackson arrives to rescue the girl from choking by cutting.

Thus Chevalier Jackson revisits the beating scenes of his own childhood and conquers his helplessness before them at the very site of hunger, speech, and breath: the maw. Jackson enters, and transforms tears of flight into a conjoined drowning. Together, he and his patients go down into an aqueous underworld. The patient kicks, quivers, struggles. He nearly suffocates by dint of Jackson's endoscopic method, however gentle. His eyes produce tears—tears, sword swallowers tell us, are always the effect of anything forced down the throat. But these are not crying or weeping or "physic tears," the biology of which is also a psychology of affect barely understood by we who shed them. Are these then "reflex tears," like those produced by an irritant in the eye, an onion, say? Or "basal tears," the lubricating solution that at all times prevents the eyes from drying out? No, the tears produced by forced ingestion must be a different kind of tears for which there is no name. The body turned inside out, a part of it seeping. The work Jackson does with his patients requires that they go under together—down, down, down—while staying awake; together they sub-merge, they suffocate, they drown, but with the courage to stay long enough, they find the foreign body lodged in them, released. They cry.

I gulp. He gulps. We gulp. To cry is to swallow. To swallow is to refuse to cry. Crying can make it hard to breathe, or swallow.

Fbdy (Multiple) #1173; Gavage: The Case of Joseph B.

Confronted by the fbdy collection's overwhelming scale, stirred and stunned by the volume it affords, visitors to the Mütter Museum find themselves asking a particular kind of question, a genre of inquiry on par with *Guinness Book* extremes: What was the strangest thing ever swallowed? Or the largest? How much money in all was collected from people's stomachs? What was the greatest number of things consumed by one person? Eyes widen and the mouth widens too to articulate the inarticulable, as though we're assembled en masse before a county fair's contest for whose stomach can receive the largest amount of pie. "Wow!" we hear ourselves saying, "Wow!"

Jackson, too, wasn't beyond identifying or delineating cases from the point of view of extremes, or what surgeon/writer Sherwin Nuland, in his book on medical myths, refers to as "the real *rarae aves*" (rare birds), "the one and onlies," novelty cases, peculiar phenomena, "wonders of wonders," that test the physician's confidence and skill in unpredictable ways, "oddities" mentioned in passing in medical school but that no doctor ever truly expects to encounter, treat, or solve. Nuland's example of the mystery case par excellence is none other than an unidentifiable stomach mass: a bezoar, or foreign body that forms as the result of an indigestible material held up in the stomach and unable to pass into the small intestine. Retrieving such masses from animal stomachs, humans have treated them as talismans. Inspiring equally fanciful responses, even if its origin bespeaks a person's severe distress, the bezoar most commonly found in humans consists of (ingested) human hair; in the medical realm, they call it the Rapunzel syndrome.

As we have already discovered, the ingested foreign body sends us to search out nothing so fervently as its origins. In the case Nuland recounts of a baby who had a ball of indigestible wax in his stomach, the origin of the "incomprehensible clump" "was not known" and "could not be imagined." The question remains, though, what we hope to find in our search for origins. What exactly do we want to solve, resolve, answer? Do we defer resolution and opt instead for a domino effect of infinite surprise—an orgasm of Wow? What if it's truth that draws us? Are amazement and a desire to know the truth mutually exclusive? And what constrains, determines, or necessitates our disclosure of the -*est*: the largest, strangest, most mysterious Thing?

It probably comes as no surprise that the extreme that most interests Jackson is one that privileges the operator's ingeniousness and skill. In other words, if Jackson is going to participate in a discourse of foreign body extremes, he will do so at the level of the most difficult case. Two cases jockey for this position from among the thousands, and though neither is interchangeable with the other, each is as interesting for what Jackson reveals about it as it is disturbing for what he leaves out—we might even go so far as to say for what he misreports about it.

The two cases, each coincidentally involving a nine-month-old child and a grouping of safety pins, are cross-referenced in *Diseases of the Air and Food Passages of Foreign-Body Origin* in shadowy reproductions of X-rays of the objects in situ alongside still shots of the objects dredged and excised, glimmering now in the light of day (*DAFP*, 157–58, 250–51). The first case, fbdy #1071—which is granted absolute pride of place by its additional and singular inclusion among photos depicting Jackson's life course in his *Life of Chevalier Jackson*—consists of

> four large, stiff, interlocked safety-pins impacted in the esophagus of a child, aged nine months. In addition to the interlocking and impaction from one month's sojourn the pins were bound together with an entangled mass of wool. The problem was rendered still more difficult by the enormous size of the pins and the small size of the passages in a nine-month-old baby. (*DAFP*, 250)

The four pins, splayed, fully open, and pointing upward, appear to dwarf the baby's ribs in the X-ray, and the image is nearly overwhelming as a representation of *that which does not belong*, as a record of an uncanny disconnect between a body's interior and a piece of the world trapped therein, between substance and context, stuff and location, the this and the there (see figure 20).

It took Jackson an inordinately long time to extract the pins in three separate attempts lasting thirty-six minutes, twenty-four minutes, and nineteen minutes. The feat is barely imaginable, and one can understand why he considered it his most difficult case. He first had to disentangle the pins without harming the child using an instrument the size of a straw. Then, relying on a retrograde method that I'm certain must have severely

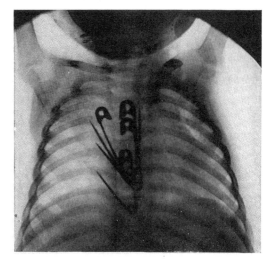

Fig. 20. An X-ray revealing the appallingly daunting case #1071, which Jackson described as his most difficult case.

strained his confidence, he was forced to place the two lowermost pins into the baby's stomach, later to recover them in the baby's stools. Then he closed and removed the two uppermost pins by his more regular peroral method—through the mouth. The case is neatly horrific, and he uses it again in his autobiography to teach by reproof, captioning photos of the X-ray and the four pins, which he reunited after the fact of their separation, covering over what he might have experienced as a failure tucked inside a success, with the lines:

> That the problem of the safe removal of this entangled mass of huge safety pins was solved does not alter the fact that when a nine-months old baby gets an opportunity to swallow such objects, some one was careless. It is a platitude to say that prevention is better than cure. (*LCJ*, penultimate illustration)

In a 1936 interview for Energine Newsreel, he had also put the case this way, noting that the fact that these "sharp, stabbing, potentially fatal pins were removed harmlessly and bloodlessly, through the mouth, does not alter the other fact that a nine-month-old baby could not walk to get the pins; someone must have left them within his reach. And worse yet, they left the pins open."

And here is where we must pause in a perusal of Jackson's most difficult case. Did Jackson forget entirely a significant detail of this case or just blithely ignore it as "no matter," because Emily van Loon supplies a missing detail that undoes carelessness as cause and replaces it with willfulness. "Probably his most difficult case," she reports in a tribute to him as president of the Woman's Medical College, "was in a nine-months-old baby whose older sister *had fed him* four open safety pins entwined with strands of wool" (italics mine). (As if case #1071 were not uncanny enough, serendipity also played a part in this child's treatment and cure. In one textbook caption, Chevalier Jackson explains that the baby had been admitted to the hospital for "operation for phimosis" or nonretractile foreskin, a condition which may or may not be pathological in infants, but that a nurse happened to find a safety pin in the baby's stool. This led to the decision to take X-rays, which then revealed the pins in his throat [*DAFP*, 124].

If human psychology cannot enter into Jackson's accounts of his most difficult case, it is because such admission would require him to revisit the scenes of his own childhood trauma. Maybe Jackson does not present all of the facts in the case, maybe he retreats again into carelessness as alibi because, while he can prevent certain forms of neglect by encouraging vigilance, he cannot, as his own life demonstrates, prevent violence. Jackson uses the verb "place" to describe his procedure with this nine-month-old baby, but no matter with what delicacy Jackson's angel fingers might move, I don't think that "place" accurately describes what he was forced to do with those bottom two pins: "push" might be more accurate. He was required to push the pins into the baby's stomach, to complete the act of (force)-feeding initiated by the child's sister.

Approaching the foreign body collection through the door of presumably tantalizing -*est*s and *most*s is more terrifying than fascinating in this way: doing so requires us to face not that which cannot be imagined but that which we do not want to imagine. Hidden acts of violence, peculiar in form and intent, lurk in Jackson's most difficult cases, and the question is whether we can account for the acts in which the foreign bodies originate or if, like Jackson, we find ourselves tempted to insert the things into a system in which the objects figure as evidence of mastery and control, in which the objects and our arrangement and rearrangement of them take on a magical aura, the vestiges of a mad science (see figure 21).

Fig. 21. Panels of fbdies containing case #1071 from the Chevalier Jackson Foreign Body Collection in the Mütter Museum. © Rosamond W. Purcell, 2009.

The case of the four open safety pins entangled in wool and ensnared in the esophagus of a nine-month-old boy is linked by dint of extremity to another uniquely astonishing, incomparably difficult, harrowing, life-threatening, and miraculous case, one rife with dimensions of seemingly incomprehensible violence that go unmentioned in Jackson's scrupulous documentation and discussion of it. While this case, too, features a nine-month-old boy and a collection of pins bound together, it distinguishes itself as a genre all its own: that of multiple fbdies all found inside the same body.

On a spring day in 1923, James B. brought his son Joseph B. to Jefferson Hospital in Philadelphia following a series of horrifying and baffling discoveries made by his wife and their family doctor. Little by little by little, bits and pieces of the object world began to spill from the baby's insides out. The discovery of odd objects—starting with buttons and unfolding into pins, cigarette butts, and burnt matches, starting with one object here, another there, and expanding into thirty-two objects (according to one account by Jackson), or thirty-seven objects (according to another account, also by Jackson), many objects, too many to altogether find or count—leaves us with a hollowed-out image of innocence confounded, because what must it have been like for Joseph's mother to receive these perverse hints and not know what to make of them? To rock the baby, witness the baby's discomfort, find and dismiss, find and pursue, to sleep and rise for several days without fully understanding what must have happened to her son, without her knowing that it did, that something indescribable, maybe even unimaginable, had happened to him, whose evidence she was receiving, if only she knew how to read it, if only he had words to tell it?

Most of the case histories that remain from Chevalier Jackson's foreign-body work are relatively short, one page, maybe two, but Joseph B.'s case spans several single-spaced pages and is accompanied by numerous X-rays, photographs, and displays (see figure 22). In a way, the case of Joseph B. is its own archive.

The baby starts by showing signs of a cough, and then vomits blood, which leads his mother to take him to the doctor. The possibility of a foreign body is ruled out when the mother informs the doctor that "the child was never permitted on the floor." The mother later finds a button in the baby's stool and imagines it to have fallen off his clothing. Several days later, the baby has a severe paroxysm of choking, leading the mother to attempt to clear his throat with her finger; she feels a "metallic object in the

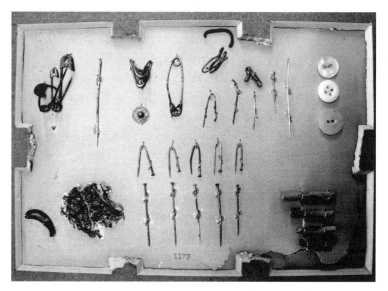

Fig. 22. A display of multiple foreign bodies removed from the body of an infant, case #1173, drawer 133, of the Chevalier Jackson Foreign Body Collection. Collection of the Mütter Museum, The College of Physicians of Philadelphia.

child's throat which she removed and found to be a bent pin." Soon thereafter, another bent pin, a needle, and three cigarette butts are vomited. A bowel movement reveals "two buttons, one bent hair pin, two safety pins (closed), two bent straight pins, and several burnt matches." One wonders if the mother simply described the objects to the nurse taking dictation in the case, or if she brought them with her to the clinic. Whether she counted them as a way of maintaining her sanity, or if a clinic staff member counted them in front of her like so much change, perfunctorily, with astonishment or without, with clinical aplomb. Did the tallying help to normalize what must have felt beyond the bounds of reason?

Upon X-ray of the baby, the following data emerged: "Six foreign bodies in the gastro-intestinal tract, and an open safety pin in the pharynx with an accumulation of wire on the hinge of the pin, which is open and the point is turned toward the mouth. Patient then advised to see Dr. Jackson." Subsequent descriptions of X-rays are more exacting:

There are three safety pins in the pharynx, one fairly large, one small one and another so bent that is it [sic] impossible to tell the size, but it is probably the same·size as the larger one above mentioned. This is about

1⅛ inches in length. . . . In the abdomen, there is a needle, a straight pin and a slightly bent pin without a head. . . . We are unable to say whether the pin is in the small intestines or the colon.

Jackson uses this case, designated as #1173, to exemplify a diagnostic mode that can be aphoristically summed up as "never rule out multiple foreign bodies." Had the staff in his clinic at Jefferson Hospital, preoccupied with the obvious ghastliness of the three pins wound together with a rubber band in the baby's upper torso, failed to consider and therefore failed to notice the pin in the intestines, this baby would have died.

Jackson's extraction of the bunch of pins, is, as usual, incomparably deft: using a child-size laryngoscope and special rotation forceps, he rotates the mass of pins so that they can conform to one of his cardinal rules—that "the points trail when traction is made upward." He removes them all, astonishingly, in under two minutes. The child is running a high fever at the time of the procedure and is later found to have been exposed to diphtheria bacilli, for which he is given an antitoxin; he undergoes upwards of twelve X-rays in the course of twelve days in order to monitor the remaining intestinal pin, and eventually, on June 18, 1923, undergoes laparotomic surgery under ether to remove the remaining, life-threatening fbdy located (the case study can now be certain) in the duodenum with the point perforating the intestinal wall. Having been admitted to the hospital on May 30, Joseph B. is discharged two months later, just under his first year of being in the world, on July 22, 1923, in "excellent condition."

Buried inside "the facts in the case" like a nearly throwaway line and never mentioned in any discussions of the case by Jackson, in spite of his multifold documentations of and returns to it for illustration, the following sentence appears in the case history under the heading Progress: "According to a statement made by both the father and the mother the child was cared for by a friend on May 28, and they believe that she deliberately fed these many articles to the child." Notwithstanding the fact that the date of May 28 has got to be wrong (since the mother was reported as having noticed symptoms of her baby's distress as early as May 26), the statement opens the case into a realm that we might not wish to enter. How can we reckon with the phenomenon of an adult forcing a child to ingest all manner of nonnutritive things?

What could the perpetrator have been thinking? "Thinking?" we might want to say. "She wasn't thinking." She was acting. She was hysterically

miming some portion of her inner life cut off from her, now newly dramatized in the forcing of her fist down the throat of a baby. The baby's
mouth and throat showed no signs of trauma. She didn't push, then, but
placed, and yet she forced. She fed the baby with a mind to form rather
than to content. When doctors act upon bodies in ways that are unimaginable from the point of view of laymen, we call it healing. What we usually
miss in our expectation of a more feeling-full relationship from our doctor
to us is that, though the doctor's subject is something we both share—the
body—he inhabits his body differently than we do our own bodies in order
to carry out his work. Doctor and patient thus share a body (insofar as each
of us is human) and live inside their bodies at a distance of radical departure. So, too, the force-feeder performs her task by way of an *idea* of the
body that she doesn't necessarily articulate but that is true for her and false
to the rest of us. The doctor, like us, is embodied, lives inside a body, lives
and dies, but he knows his own body as well as ours in uncommon ways, the
effect of which is to pretend it is not his body that he treats when he opens
us, that it is not his body that is being touched when he touches us. Not
his body. The person who filled a baby with things that his body could not
withstand worked from the opposite direction: if the doctor too fully dif-
ferentiates his body from that of his patient, the psychopathic feeder could
not distinguish that baby's body from her own. She acted upon a projection of herself—the baby's body as a phantasm of some piece of herself,
objectified *and* dis-embodied. She regressed to a primitive and unresolved
form of play—the baby's body as her plaything.

Maybe she was testing the baby's body or, then again, using the body
of the defenseless child in the way people had used hers: the female body
as depository, repository, or waste dump. Maybe her act was a literal stop-
gap. We equate gagging with choking, but here gagging was equivalent to a
form of forced swallowing possibly intended to stop the baby from making
detestable sounds: the sound of his need, want, discomfort, or hunger. To
feed the baby anything that was at hand was to gag the baby, to silence him.
Forcing me to eat, you prevent me from talking; you stop my voice or my cry.

Is there any realm so yoked to pleasure that also risks embarrassment,
an outer limit, or shame as much as eating? Where a certain liqueur dis-
tilled from rose petals is concerned, not until it is swallowed does a secondary flavor burst through: the essence of roses. Some people don't like to
eat flowers, they reserve them instead for their scent, but the taste bud and
aroma sensors are linked, so we might as well admit that to have a scent

waft over us is to drink it, to smell is to imbibe, just as to hear is to reverberate unceasingly. Everyone probably has some memory of water forced into a nostril—a taste that instead of *entering* the stomach *exits* through the mouth, of sea salt or soap bubbles, chlorination or river shoal. Or how about a tuft or blade of grass purposely sucked on or accidentally mixed in with a picnic repast and the sudden stinging bitterness of indigestible earth-stuff, the ground we walk upon. Cavities in adulthood link voracity with childish abandon—those years of eating pixie sticks in lieu of lunch, of licking the stickiness of marshmallows from palms and fingers, of tearing cotton candy into edible cloud forms, of sucking the sweet center of a water ice long after eating it, by licking the ring of color it has left around your mouth. For shame!

There are people who cover their mouths while eating and others who refuse to close them, quick chewers and slow, quiet and loud, happy and sad. Hunger is natural, but eating is learned. Or is it the other way around? Either I am taught how to want, or I am taught the proper way to get it. I can be taught ways of eating for the *share* of it—as if to say eating is a together act, so let me show you how to do it, the way that being taught how to crack the artichoke's code is part of the pleasure of eating it. Certainly the way that we eat, ingestion's form and formality or lack thereof, determines how we take food in and with what relish. Decorum, a *way*, can even make the inedible perfectly palatable—shoelaces spun with the proper attitude, twirled around a fork, just so, enable Charlie Chaplin to eat them, heartily, just as characters in Jan Svankmajer's film *Lunch* eat the flowers and the table, and each and every particle of their clothes from their suspenders down to their underwear when their waiter fails to serve them. So long as our bodies convincingly perform the dance of eating—dipping a starchy sock into a shoe's pretend well of gravy, looping a fork around those suspenders to approximate striped fettuccini, folding the underwear with a bread knife into the form of a compactly folded sandwich—we can ingest anything, these figures seem to say.

Adults and children, children and children, adults and adults: the scale and pace and power is different in each relation of force-feeding. Children test their own and each other's boundaries so much that inscribed in any one person's childhood are episodes we might liken to scenes from *Lord of the Flies*: the girl was mildly retarded and younger than the others who formed the group. It was a hot day—that's what made the earth so pliable—everyone was irritable, especially the parents, but the kids aspired to be "cool." They were weak and spindly but wanted to be able to climb, so they pulled themselves up to sit in a row on top of a four-foot-high wall. Perhaps it was the fact of a spoon out of place—because there lay a teaspoon in the dirt, on the sidewalk, who knows why?—that inspired them to convince the girl who was younger and slow that dirt was edible, it even tasted good, that she should eat some. I was part of this scene, and I remember running from it, crying. Let me try again. I was a member of the "they," and I stood on the sidelines watching. No. I was there, and I let the gaggle of these kids, "toughs" is what they were, rope me into confusing this girl even though I knew it was wrong. But if I dare myself to remember—truth or dare—that particular day, I'm afraid I was the ringleader of this team and I enjoyed it, that point at which the girl showed that she *believed us* by putting a spoon filled with dirt into her mouth.

An undated and unmarked newspaper clipping in the archives of the National Library of Medicine describes the case of Mary Genova, nineteen years of age. Mary "wanted to borrow a sled. In order to get the sled the neighbor's boy made her play marbles. When playing winter marbles he said you have to swallow them instead of shooting them. So Mary swallowed them, and here she is, in New York hospital." An X-ray appears below the article; it makes Mary's stomach appear to be filled with polka dots. Children forcing each other to *swallow* something in these two cases seem caught up in getting another person to *believe* something. These are games of lording it over someone, of manipulating trust, games of false conviction and betrayal.

That force-feeding happens between adults has led to its gaining a name: "gavage," they call it, but the French softening of the consonants does nothing to diminish the atrocity to which the word refers. Force-feeding seems to be a popular form of torture among humans—Serbs being made to eat paper and soap by Croats, Muslims being made to eat pork and drink alcohol by their captors at Guantánamo Bay. The hunger strike is a desperate form of defiance, mode of resistance, route to liberation, and it might work if it didn't inspire the violent insertion of a tube into a nose, leaving one to wonder how a person so defiled ever comes to eat again, or breathe. How she ever dares again to swallow. When the modernist writer Djuna Barnes submitted herself to this in the form of a journalistic stunt, an act of feminist solidarity with the suffragettes who had endured it, I believe she must have regretted it, that she really didn't know what she was getting into, how stripped she would feel of her body, how disoriented, how undone. If people force-feed each other in an attempt to subdue them, they no doubt oftentimes succeed.

And what of Joseph B.? Where did this episode of forced ingestion, adult to child, leave him? Did he eventually develop a cancer that cut short his life as a result of all those X-rays? Did he sometimes feel beside himself and not know why? Did he live long enough to have children of his own, and did he feed them lovingly, like a bird feeds its chicks small bits of bread? How long did it take for the scar of a laparotomy performed in 1923 to fade? And what about the "family friend"? Whose child was she, and inside what kind of rooms did she live out her life to its close?

An archive is a vestige and a vestibule, a place replete with remnants piled so high it sometimes blocks the view. Jackson exerted his designs upon this case as if to leave us with a tantalizing answer while erasing the question. He perpetually acts upon this case as if to right it, placing and re-placing its renegade pieces, on a tray or a plate, inside a frame, mixed together then unmixed again, so that we can, in a sense, consume them, take them in, and find them palatable. The items are striking, and the narrative attached to them is singular in the way that it enters into realms of atrocity, violence, in contemporary terms, of abuse and rape. But stowed as they are, positioned and recounted inside Jackson's cabinet, they refuse, in a sense, to be grasped even when they are literally pinned down. They recede and advance, recede and advance, asymptotically: never quite constituting the reality of the bodies from which they hail, nor quite crossing the Rubicon of dreams. Stowed in the cabinet, the fbdies that comprise case #1173, like all items in these drawers, are strangely equalized. They form a mass inside the cabinet-as-stomach, and even if we try to regard or re-regard each particular with wonder and let our imaginations work on it, we're still drawn into a process of ingestion and digestion, a churning of our stomach-minds that transforms the collection into chyme ("chyme" being the word for what food becomes once the digestive system begins its work). Should the case of Joseph B. for a special category be reserved? Call it the fbdy case that *cannot be taken in.*

Jackson's photograph in *Diseases of the Air and Food Passages of Foreign-Body Origin* of the thirty-two objects retrieved is remarkable for the way the objects are painstakingly ordered therein (*DAFP*, 158). He not only identifies each object by name—distinguishing a "glove fastener" from a mere snap—but he numbers and alphabetizes each one, starting with A and ending with N, and in this way *exhibits* the things. "Ladies and Gentleman,

I present you with Exhibit A," he seems to say, and now the fbdies take on the character of evidence, but not as telltale items remaining at a crime scene or personal effects to be presented before a judge and jury in a court of law. In this form, this incarnation, the fbdies function as testimony and testament to nothing other than Jackson's and his fellow operators' skill. Jackson subtly separates out the items he extracted by positioning them in the upper left-hand corner, like a medieval letter in an illuminated manuscript. The things merely "passed" by the passive (if it can truly be called that) work of the patient's body know themselves only in relation to the extracted safety pins as herald.

As we arrive before each incarnation of these things again (and again), if we come now to encounter them in person, in actuality, in drawer #133 of the Mütter's cabinet, and especially if one knows their backstory, they take on a haunting volubility that cannot be undone by their arrangement (see figure 22). Witnessed, the things that the baby passed through his bowel seem to have traces of manipulation, as indices of some other human having acted upon them: she who forced the child to ingest them, to take them in. One safety pin, for example, seems disturbingly to have been bent entirely in half. This makes it hard to place but easy to swallow. This makes it seem as though she tried to make the object edible, swallowable, because certainly it is no longer usable in the way we know a safety pin to be. It has become something else, bent between two fingers, strong fingers, because it would seem to require a tool to do this—or did she crush the pin between her teeth before she fed it to the baby? What we can't see in Jackson's photograph of the objects but only "in the flesh" is how beautiful the buttons are, and how small: together they run the gamut from translucency to opacity, all in shades of white. Jackson has arranged them to ascend in size from smallest to largest, and then, in order to harmonize the whole, he's arranged the burnt matches also in terms of scale, but now from large to small. The snap-piece, what Jackson calls a glove fastener, is alarmingly odd for its difference among these things; more like a sad nipple than a thing, it seems to comment on the rest. And then the whole ensemble resembles one of those activity boards made up of levers and shapes that babies are meant to push and pull and handle. Ah, but there is also an item that leaps out like a crazy squiggle—it's a bunch of something, it's static, it's not happily arranged, it's a trace of perverse expressivity— Jackson's or the babysitter's? It might just be the rubber band displaced after all these years, disintegrating.

A clump, a pile of regurgitated cigarettes. Along with these, Jackson admits, "some unidentified objects." Placing, re-placing: the pins appear alone again, because we can also find these emblems of Jackson's two most difficult cases—case #1071 and case #1173—extracted from their home within the drawers and thrown in with the mix of scores of safety pins, their kin, what I have called Jackson's alphabet of pins, pins turned into cuneiform, piercing, punctuating, staying the page. Here, in this setting, the "most difficult" are now submerged—you have to search to find them, you have to know to know them—as if to say that *every case is difficult,* and most of these pins are open, even though Jackson closed them in order to remove them, he reopens them to show us what was what (see figure 23).

What will we use the case of Joseph B. to understand? How will we

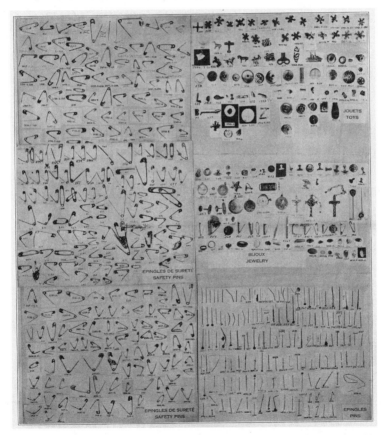

Fig. 23. An alphabet of safety pins in which cases #1071 and #1173 appear. Chevalier Jackson Papers, 1890–1964, MS C 292, Modern Manuscripts Collection, History of Medicine Division, National Library of Medicine, Bethesda, Maryland.

make meaning from it? What can we claim now to know because of it? If we turn to it in an attitude of amazement, does that mean we can't also be interested in determining the truth of the matter, a handling and begetting of the underlying facts in the case?

What do you give to the man who has (kept) everything? What kind of object can a patient give Chevalier Jackson as a token of thanks? The rooms behind the doors that front the Judy Garland *Wizard of Oz* glass-slipper display in the Smithsonian Institute's National Museum of American History harbor a paperweight, an ungainly thing, made out of 2,400 coiled wires, inscribed to Chevalier Jackson: "In grateful appreciation of faithful services rendered to Miss Ethel Hogan, 12/5/22, New York Telephone Company." In Australia, on the grounds of the Melbourne Boys' High School in Forrest Hill, South Yarra, a tree was planted in 1936 as official thanks to Chevalier Jackson by the Australian State Department after Jackson removed a nail from the lung of three-year-old Kelvin Rodgers.

The case of Joseph B. distinguishes itself in this: deftly sent, bestowed with gratitude, attached to the pages of the case study appears a gift. Someone has seen fit to send Chevalier Jackson photographs of the boy at various stages of his life to show how well he grew. Many years pass between each snapshot, each a sporadic sign of the continuance of life, each a marker of some moment of pause or of reflection on their bearers' part, of cataclysm or crisis, some confluence of forces of an afternoon, or maybe it impresses them in the middle of a night, a moment powerful enough to lead the family to remember again and assign a meaning to the day that Chevalier Jackson saved their baby's life. Here's Joseph perhaps at eighteen months: he's standing with the help of a nearby table upon which his left arm rests while the other hand squeezes the sides of his baby clothes, a one-piece outfit that balloons outward like knickers atop a very fancy pair of striped elastic socks and two-tone button-up shoes. He's not exactly smiling but interpreting with his gaze what a figure outside the frame might be expecting of him. He's reading a face we cannot see. "Hold on to the table": he seems to hear this command, but one foot steps forward because he must want to toddle toward the voice that speaks to him rather than rely on something so hard as a table to hold him in the alone-space that is the photo. His family calls him Josie. This we learn from the inscription on the photo, and they send another one of the child in which he looks to be about six. Is there a word for the pose the boy takes in this photo, fetching as freckles (though he has none)? (See figure 24.) One leg is bowed while

Fig. 24. Joseph B., the nine-month-old victim of Case #1173, as a boy. Chevalier Jackson Papers, 1890–1964, MS C 292, Modern Manuscripts Collection, History of Medicine Division, National Library of Medicine, Bethesda, Maryland.

the other crosses over it in an attitude of adult nonchalance or breezy confidence. One arm rests upon a hip, akimbo, while the hand of the other arm settles once again upon a convenient piece of furniture. His black patent leather shoes are spic-and-span for the occasion of a portrait in a photographer's studio arranged with urns and vases filled with flowers. It's a sumptuously fashioned scene that seems to expect the wedding party of which he is a part any minute to arrive. He's wearing shorts—too casual, perhaps, for a cherubic-seeming ring boy, but just right for a party that might happen upon a green. Someone has combed and then slicked down Joseph's hair, someone has parted it for handsomeness with loving care. By age fourteen, Joseph appears to be nearing manhood; it's November 15, 1936, according to the photograph's penciled note, and he's agreed to pose outdoors, this time wearing the argyle socks that were the fashion but apparently ill-at-ease and stiffly awkward: he's arrived at adolescence and is much less darling for it.

In X-ray, to the untrained eye, every body, including that of a baby or child, appears to be adult. The fact of the human skeleton either ages us or is timelessly opaque. The X-ray of Joseph B. (see figure 25) is a far cry from the photograph of the full-bodied boy. In X-ray, he is parsed into pins extruding out from bones. Their points and protrusions are horrifying; in bold relief, they seem to scream, and the baby's opened mouth—he, too, must have been crying—is ghoulish without the features of the baby's face.

Among Chevalier Jackson's own personal effects, one might have found a lockbox, a container for keeping not radiographs but photographs of the people attached to the fbdy Things. Or maybe the pictures could have hung in the clinic's waiting room, over-brimming the bulletin board the way any modern veterinarian's office beams with photographs of treated cats and dogs even if only their owners can distinguish them by name. Paper-clipped to the case, such pictures function as part of the case's proof-giving data. Held between the fingers of a biographer, they seem to exist in order to excite an intimacy with strangers poised on a bridge of unforgiving time. Root beer soda, buttered bread with honey, hard candy,

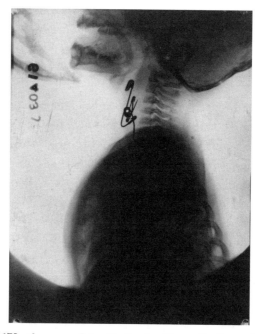

Fig. 25. Fbdy 1173, the case of Joseph B., in X-ray. Radiographer, Dr. Willis F. Manges (1876–1936). Collection of the Mütter Museum, The College of Physicians of Philadelphia.

lime. I imagine the boy imbibed such things, and heartily, well beyond his trauma.

Jackson attached to the case but not the person, and that's OK. If we reattach the boy in places, it can be to remark how at age six he stands *unsubdued*. If we attach not simply to a detail of these photos but to the spirit of them—these signs *as* life—we have to admit that being force-fed was not the only thing that ever happened to Joseph B., even if it was a truly horrible, possibly formative thing. These photos' auras—I don't know what else to call them for the way they attach to a part of consciousness more nearly akin to dreams—hover inside our cabinetry with a graceful insistence that, sigh and sigh and sigh, catastrophe was averted. Remaining steadfast to the case study as such, they take on the designation of Joseph-as-robust-specimen. Detached, reattached, remaining, they remind us of the heartbeat in a line: "Thorax: examined with difficulty because of patient crying."

Fbdy #2440: A Perfect Attendance Pin

> *I shivered at the slightest pretext. I knew, for instance, that if the physician made a mistake it would be the end of him and of all those who came after him. What could one expect, after all, from a Negro physician? As long as everything went well, he was praised to the skies, but look out, no nonsense, under any conditions! The black physician can never be sure how close he is to disgrace. . . . I felt knife blades open within me.*
>
> —FRANZ FANON, "The Fact of Blackness"

The Thing that is "A Perfect Attendance Pin" attaches to story in ways that scores of fish bones never will (see figure 3). The pin lures and enchants and makes us want to manufacture a scene, and it is those two little words that inspire us to do this: "perfect attendance." The presence of an inscription compels us to restore the sentence the pin has been struck from, to reconstruct a syntax, grand or banal, for the day that issued the pin into its recipient's world and the day the pin fell out of place too meaningfully, rearranging that world irreparably. With the Perfect Attendance pin, we want to reattach the charm to its bracelet, and we want to laugh or cry at the irony of the accident—the sad twist of fate whereby that which was supposed to bestow honor brought calamity instead.

To hold the material trace of someone's medical ordeal between your fingers is a sacrament, but the excitement I feel when I happen upon the actual case report for fbdy #2440 in the National Library of Medicine is anything but reverent at first. I'm seduced by the novelty of this object as fbdy and its oddly humorous aspect, until I begin to read this case's sad details: that the pin belonged to four-year-old Fred J.; that he, unlike the vast majority of Jackson's patients, did not survive the removal of the pin; that he was African American, unlike the vast majority of Jackson's patients, who were white. To have the pin but to have lost the boy is horrifying. I become attached to the fact of Fred J.'s address, "24 Newcomb St. Phila., Pa.," and try to locate it on Google Earth, but from the disappointing distance of a satellite, I mostly find dead ends and parking lots, no trees. I think about the tragedy as part of Fred J.'s family history. I wonder how or if it is remembered by his parents' descendants, and who now lives in that house where his mother returned to mourn: a house whose rooms were tinted with calamitous death, the loss of a child. A preventable disaster?

Fred wasn't feeling well when he swallowed the pin—he came to the hospital with pneumonia—and I picture him putting it in his mouth as a form of self-soothing. According to the report, his mother stated

> that about 6:00 PM last night child had a pin-button in his mouth. He talked and then exclaimed "he had swallowed the pin." She patted him on the back and he choked and gagged and "his chest heaved" but the foreign body was not recovered. Then mother rushed him to the hospital where he was referred to Dr. Jackson's Clinic. No attempts at removal. Patient is having difficulty in getting his breath and complains of pain in his stomach.

I learn that Fred J.'s mother was named Agnes, and that she and his two sisters and one brother were "l. and w." (shorthand for "living and well"). That she brought her son to Samaritan Hospital, not far from their home, a facility established in 1892 by Dr. Russell H. Conwell (founder and first president of Temple University) on the principles of Christian charity and with the intention of treating the city's sick poor. In 1930, Chevalier Jackson established a bronchoscopic clinic there. Fred J. entered the hospital on January 14, 1930, and died the next day at 1:55 P.M. Chevalier Jackson was his endoscopist, assisted by his son, Chevalier L., Emily van Loon, and R.P. Smith. I can't tell from the case history why they had to put the child through the ordeal of the extraction if the pin in his stomach wasn't a threat to his life, an extraction that took twelve minutes and thirty-nine seconds, sans anesthesia.

In addition to "broncho-pneumonia," Fred J.'s final diagnosis includes "mediastinal emphysema" (the usually painful condition of air trapped in the space between the lungs) and "acute mediastinitis" (inflammation and possible infection of the middle section of the chest cavity). In *Diseases of the Air and Food Passages of Foreign-Body Origin*, Jackson explains that "Mediastinal emphysema may follow a perforation of either the cervical or thoracic esophagus. It is usually associated with subcutaneous emphysema and may prove fatal whether infection follows the leaking air or not." Was the leaked air in Fred J.'s chest the result of the pin's perforating an already damaged esophagus, or had the instrument introduced a tear into Fred's airway or foodway? Had increased pressure within the lungs or excessive coughing associated with the pneumonia ruptured an air sac inside the boy's lung? The case history simply lists the conditions without venturing a precipitating cause. According to the report, a doctor named Harold F. Robertson, who attended Fred on January 14, wished to give the child molasses in small doses, thinking it would "do no harm . . . hoping to coat the opening over and stimulate a reparative process." "The "opening" to which Robertson refers must be the otherwise unspecified tear, the source of which we cannot know since the details of the gastroscopy—"report attached"—is missing from this file.

Once having identified the boy to whom the pin belonged, it would seem unfair—though I'm not sure to whom—to yoke the peculiarly compelling case of the Perfect Attendance pin to a history of racism in the United States, but that's the door it's wedged beneath, that it holds in place, unopened. Jackson tried so hard to detach himself from the social body that the larger world begins to take on the power of a phantasm, but this particular object makes him part of it again, as if to re-embody the doctor precisely at those points at which he'd prefer to disappear.

Chevalier Jackson lived so long, so much longer than Fred J., that his life's work spanned more than one major historical shift and change: he was born into Reconstruction and died on the eve of the civil rights movement. His first birthday coincided with the legalization of segregation marked by the Supreme Court in *Plessy v. Ferguson*, and in the very last years of his nearly century-long life, he saw that landmark race decision overturned. Racism manifests in different ways in Jackson's life's course and serves as a point of return in the letters he left behind. This racism with a capital "R," which risks abstraction, is never simply anecdotal or ascriptive, but is available when he needs it—a cultural repertoire that he draws upon in times of stress. More profoundly, race is the foundation for a burgeoning selfhood in *The Life of Chevalier Jackson*, and later on, the sail he raises on those occasions, like an available expediency, when he is buffeted by life's unpredictable winds.

What part does race play in scenarios of delicacy and trust at the site of the mouth? What happens if we bring race onto the stage of the history of endoscopy? Coinciding with the early rocketing of Chevalier Jackson's career was the 1901 publication of a novel by Charles Chesnutt, the African American writer and practicing lawyer who could pass for white but chose not to. *The Marrow of Tradition*'s politics were so confrontational and real that the book ended Chesnutt's career as a writer. Based on the 1898 Wilmington, North Carolina, riots carried out by whites against blacks whose voices and voting power the upper and lower crust hoped to suppress, the book hinged on an episode in which the infant son of a white North Carolinian patriarch got something caught in his throat.

Depending on who is observing the boy, he can be understood as a sign of a bright (white?) future, even of *life* itself, or of an ominousness that must be guarded against and that manifests in the form of a birthmark, a mole that appears on his neck just beneath his left ear. His father, a Major Carteret who works daily against the changes announced by the conclusion of the Civil War, experiences his newborn's "first cry as a refreshing breeze from the distant ocean" and a predictor of glorious days ahead, whereas the baby's black nursemaid—Old Mammy Jane—regards the baby's presence as foreboding. She thinks the mole might be the sign of something immanent but unspoken, and Chesnutt relies on a strangulated language to bring it into view—in short, the baby's birthmark and (maybe too his birthright) leads Mammy Jane to consider that lynching might be in his future, but she doesn't know how it could be if he's white. "Had the baby been black, or yellow, or poor-white," the narrator muses,

> Jane would unhesitatingly have named, as his ultimate fate, a not uncommon form of taking off, usually resultant upon the infraction of certain laws, or, in these swift modern days, upon too violent a departure from established social customs. It was manifestly impossible that a child of such high quality as the grandson of her old mistress should die by judicial strangulation; but nevertheless the warning was a serious thing, and not to be lightly disregarded.

The position of the mole, Mammy Jane later notices, is in fact "just at the point where the hangman's knot would strike" even if the boy's class and race would make him immune to such violence. It's as though the boy comes into the world with the violence of his historical moment written on him, a violence that the likes of his family have carried out and will continue to carry out, but the effect of which is to make him seem the most vulnerable of all.

Chesnutt takes great pains to spoof the baby's robustness as a sign of racial purity. In one episode, little Theodore is passed around the table and duly admired: "Clara thought his hair was fine. Ellis inquired about his teeth. Tom put his finger in the baby's fist to test his grip." In Mammy Jane's words, "dis chile is a rale quality chile, he is,—I never seed a baby wid sech fine hair fer his age, ner sech blue eyes, ner sech a grip, ner sech a heft."

At some point in this admiration fest, the baby starts to choke, and Mammy Jane, being the most observant of all of his caretakers, notices that he is gasping for breath. The mother can't imagine what could be causing the child to breathe so heavily, with a strange whistling noise, but Mammy Jane diagnoses a fbdy instantly, determining in no time at all that he has accidentally swallowed part of an old yellowed rattle that had been strung around his neck. The dilemma now, as in all foreign-body cases of the day, is how to remove it and whom to call upon to perform the work, but instead of telling the tale as so many newspapers would have recounted it—of babies traversing great distances to Chevalier Jackson's clinics where they were, in no time, saved—Chesnutt asks us to imagine not exactly a medical but a social "complication." In an age when white mobs routinely "stretched the necks" of blacks, how could blacks trust their babies' tender necks and throats to white hands, however "caring," and what would it take, under what circumstances and on what terms would it become acceptable for a black man, first, to be allowed to earn a medical degree and, second, to treat white bodies?

The local doctor, a white Southerner named Price who is also the "family physician and father confessor," examines the baby and concludes his diagnosis with language that could be derived from many a Jackson case study. "It's a *curious* accident" (and don't we know it; italics mine). "So far as I can discover, the piece of ivory has been drawn into the trachea, or windpipe, and has lodged in the mouth of the right bronchus. I'll try to get it out without an operation, but I can't guarantee the result." Unable to dislodge the fbdy, Price concludes that "it will be necessary to cut into [the baby's] throat from the outside"; normally, he would undertake the operation unassisted, but because he knows how much the Major "values" this baby, he explains that he would like to call upon a specialist to help him, a specialist from, of all places, Philadelphia.

The Marrow of Tradition weaves the life and work of Chevalier Jackson between its lines. Jackson's clinic was in Pittsburgh, not Philadelphia, at the time of the novel's publication, but it is easy to imagine Chesnutt reading some sensational story attached to Jackson's pioneering work and drawing from it in establishing his novel's premise. But with a twist. Because he uses what he might have read of Jackson's feats with people's airways and foodways to attenuate the meeting of race and body politics—in short, to foreground the politics of medical practice, even to wonder about the strange superimposition, the uncanniness of the development of a medical specialty focused on the throat coinciding with a period in which one group of Americans was routinely choking another group to death.

As the plot unfolds, we might imagine Charles Chesnutt having created a sort of racially split version of Chevalier Jackson, because he introduces both Dr. Burns, the white specialist who will make the trip from Pennsylvania to the South, and Burns's former student Dr. Miller, a black doctor who, like Jackson, not only studied in the North but in hospitals in Paris and Vienna. Miller has made the decision to return to the segregated South, where he is establishing a teaching hospital for the black community in his hometown. He and Burns happen to meet on the same train, and Chesnutt uses the occasion of the two doctors meeting, one white, one black, ruthlessly to expose the double and triple standards of Jim Crow: the conductor, assuming that Miller is Burns's servant, reminds Burns that the laws require Miller to sit in a separate train car. When Burns suggests that he will fight fire with fire simply by moving with Miller, who is not his servant but his friend and colleague, to the "colored car," he is informed that he is not allowed on that part of the train either; in this way, the conductor explains, both parties are served. Burns and Miller will make the rest of the trip in separate cars, but their plan, based partly on Burns's having read an article by Miller detailing a rare and remarkable case he's treated, is to meet at Major Carteret's house where they, one white and one black doctor, will together perform surgery on the white child.

Even with the baby's life in the balance, once Burns has arrived, he and Price and Carteret spend time arguing over whether Miller should be allowed into Carteret's house, and, if so, whether he should use the front door rather than the back door. This is a place where unwritten laws—"certain inflexible rules of conduct by which [Carteret] regulates his life," certain sacred principles "lying at the very root of our social order, involving the purity and prestige of our race"—dictate that black doctors are not allowed to treat white patients. Carteret wins the argument on the basis of his also having "personal" reasons for not wanting to let the black Dr. Miller into his house, and the operation, about to proceed without Miller, is interrupted by the foreign body having shifted on its own. It is released through the child's mouth thanks to a few sure claps between the baby's shoulders from Burns (a fictional treatment method, to be sure).

Little Theodore's body, nevertheless, remains not only central to the narrative, it frames the book: that something might get stuck in the male heir's throat rendering him unable to breathe, speak, or swallow is the novel's defining anxiety, beginning and end. The book reaches its climax with Theodore falling ill in the middle of the riot of white against black, leaving Carteret no recourse but to turn, after all, to Dr. Miller to save his child's life. The child has developed "membranous croup," he "struggles to cough up the obstruction to his breathing," he gasps, but the town is in chaos and there are no other doctors to be found, certainly none who can perform the necessarily "delicate" operation (once again, the kind of operation that Jackson was expert at, a tracheotomy), that would free the child's windpipe and enable him to breathe. One of the victims of the massacre is Miller's only son, who has been fatally shot by a stray bullet in the violence that Carteret was a key player in fomenting, thus presenting Miller with an ethical dilemma that seems impossible to solve.

The reckless precariousness not of the black male body but of the *white* male body gets top billing here. The maintenance of the integrity of the white male body is imperative, according to *The Marrow of Tradition*, and no black doctor is going to be allowed access to or penetration of his white American counterpart; subsequently, if not exactly vice versa, black patients will have reason to mistrust white doctors for decades to come.

It would be interesting to imagine what position Jackson would take if he were the white Dr. Burns—or, alternatively, if Jackson as we know him attempted to fill the shoes of the black Dr. Miller. Or what if Jackson were the white teacher of the black student? What if Jackson, instead of having children rushed to him for treatment, took his practice south?

In his lifetime, Jackson did go south, where he picked up postcards, maybe in train stations, where, as an unhappy traveler, he languished, maybe on the run without much thought to content, but more likely carefully he chose a postcard from a kiosk, and more lovingly than obligingly affixed a stamp. The ink from his fountain pen took to the cardboard like blood to a blotter on which he fashioned short notes bound for home, and the people waiting there and the place he missed: the security of his study, where he wrote undisturbed; the quiet of his dining room, where his wife served him daily. On August 2, 1930, he chose a tinted photo of a "Negro Baptism, Near Norfolk, Virginia" (see figure 26) to send to his live-in sister-in-law, Jo. Yellow-painted boats teem, over-brimming; they're filled with bobbing red hats, white lace, brown jackets, and bowlers. Sailless masts crisscross the sky like divining rods or searchlights; projecting

Fig. 26. The Chevalier Jackson Postcard Collection, Conwellana Templana Collection, Temple University Libraries, Philadelphia, Pennsylvania.

a fanfare of guide wires, the boats tilt without toppling toward telegraph poles that careen like scarecrows. A boy's face reflects itself in the water, while the men who surround him bend their necks humbly toward the pool. Jackson is inspired: he heads his note with a funny caption: "Amos Nandy get religion." The letters bleed into one another, and the script is shaky as though written on a train; unembarrassed by the public-ness of his joke, he nonchalantly records his bearings: "still on way south but start home tonight Love Chevie."

In the 1930s, black Americans appear on postcards as though they are a site on a tourist's itinerary, an ethnographer's find for white visitors, the featured attraction for the white person traveling south, a bit of local color. Perhaps knowing his father's tastes, Chevalier L. chooses another "negro scene" to send his father while on a trip to Cincinnati but with the inscription "homeward bound." It's 1939, and the photo is of a work scene on a pier with the title "Loading Cotton on the Riverfront" and an accompanying explanation—"Loading cotton: Husky, singing negroes handle these great bales of cotton as most people would handle bed pillows. On the great Mississippi river, packets and barges are piled high with the billowy white cotton, tightly encased in burlap wrappings."

Jackson did travel south; even earlier in his life, this southward movement forms a substratum. When he makes the move for a second, more permanent time, it's from his clinics in Pittsburgh to Philadelphia. Though it's considerably early in the century, he's no longer a boy; he's a man gaining accolades for his humanitarianism and medical advances when he writes his mother:

September 30, 1917: The large estates of the wealthy suburbanites remind me so much of England—and the weather has been very English. I know you would like a ride through the suburbs; but you would not want to be bothered with the raft of servants these big places need. Help has been mostly Irish, but now there are many negroes from the south. Many of them very repulsive looking.

The letter continues as though nothing untoward or out of keeping has been said:

If you want to talk to me anytime, Stanford can get me on the Longnecker phone and I will send money to Stanford for the charges.

> I hear a church at one window and Estery's organ and piano Building
> on the other, so I get plenty of music here at the office. Wish you could hear
> some of it.

The racist inlay seems to be a way of remaining familial and parochial in spite of his move to work in Philadelphia, a way of not straying far from back-home ways. While Jackson writes of the "repulsiveness of negroes," has someone brought a black child in to receive his care? Or is this the private glue that makes his familial feeling stick, a privacy we have no right investigating, incommensurate with the public man?

In his autobiography, Chevalier Jackson takes great pains to assert the rare equality that characterized his practice. In one episode, he explains how he gives equal credit to "the colored woman who wheeled patients in and out of the operating room" as he does to himself; he even thanks the woman, named Hattie, for helping to calm his child patients by whispering encouragements in their ear (*LCJ*, 160). In another instance, he ventures a form of medical ethics when he writes, "With physicians a patient is a patient; race, religion, color are considered only in so far as they may concern the scientific problems" (*LCJ*, 184). Of course "the scientific problems" are never neutral, but that contradiction aside, we still are left with all manner of paradox. Jackson wanted to convince us that in his world, the "colored nurse" was not only admitted but given equal credit for an operation when we know that, as late as the 1930s, in the larger world of which Jackson was a part, black doctors, including those trained at the Woman's College that he at one time presided over, were routinely turned away by the hospitals where they sought employment. What Jackson wants to claim about his medical ethics doesn't hold up alongside his personal correspondence, nor does the personal note accord with public knowledge. Can a doctor, can anyone, separate out the racism of his everyday life from the way he apprehends his patients inside the four walls of his medical practice? Is it possible to be racist in one part of one's life and in another, not? There's unconditional love, and conditional racism. There's no such thing as a little racism or a lot. What sort of gleaming surface or foreign body facade could reflect an answer to the fundamentally irresolvable question of the 1930 case study: why did four-year-old Fred J. have to die?

> Yes, in retrospect it's curious to note
> How a series of events seemingly remote

Dovetailed together with uncanny precision
To help me arrive at a great decision.
I acquired an array of unrelated knowledge
Aside from facts I learned from college.
As a plumber's cub in my father's hotel
I learned fundamentals that served me well,
And later saw a curious parallel
Between plumbing pipes and valves and tubes
And the pathologic mechanism of bronchial tubes.

—*Pittsburgh Historian*,
undated pamphlet in the National Library of Medicine

At the Idlewood Cottage Hotel, dinner was served between one and three o'clock and supper from six to seven. Boiled corned beef and legs of mutton in caper sauce were the featured hot dishes, while the cold part of the menu included sugar-cured ham, roast beef, and tongue. Cape May tomatoes, Winslow's corn, hominy, new beets, and cabbage could be had, topped with relishes that ran a short gamut from horseradish to tomato catsup. Almonds, figs, cream nuts, and filberts comprised a modest dessert for the summer-dwelling businessmen, doctors, lawyers, judges, professors and their families who chose to stay at the Jacksons' establishment over and against a more fashionable and far-flung watering hole. From ages nine to eighteen, Jackson worked alongside his family to maintain this "family hostelry without a bar" (*LCJ*, 44) that was his father's attempt to recover from a bankruptcy following a trusted employee's embezzlement of funds.

On Friday evenings, chicken and waffles were served, and "hops" were held inside a large pavilion built for the purpose just a little beyond the hotel's curved entryway. A three-piece orchestra of cello, violin, and cornet might furnish the music for dancers who waltzed to tunes with timely titles like "Telegram" and "Hydropathen" or listened to quadrilles whose pastoral undulations mimicked the hills and valleys where the cottages nestled. On Sunday evenings, a Dr. Tindle would gather people in the parlor of the large edifice that was the main building to sing Moody and Sankey gospel hymns. The women among the families who were regulars at Idlewood spent most mornings in idle gossip—indeed, Idlewood was an idyll for the newly idling classes—and one woman recounted how one day, amid fancy work and fast talking, the most talkative among them opened wide her mouth and swallowed a fly, much to the amusement of the others. One writer was known to visit the hotel, and she could be seen at a distance penning her pages in solitude beneath a willow tree.

Cows roamed beyond a high hedge while visitors set skiffs carved out of shingles onto the quiet waters of a shallow fountain pool whose waters gurgled more than they rose in the dim light of hushed conversations and the loud pranks of kids. Mulberries could be fresh-picked, and an apple orchard attracted children to pluck its fruit even before it ripened or convince Jackson's older brothers to let them ride atop the fodder brought back in carts for the cows. On one adjacent slope, fearing no nostalgia for the city they'd return to on weekdays, the men tapped croquet balls lightly, or with a thwack stopped the sound of a red or yellow roller lost in the pith of unmown grass. They pitched quoits or whittled wood and hours away, convinced that the country could be a cure for the urbanity their families thrived on, preferring for a spell the smell of boiling tar used to seal the cans inside a tiny tent alongside the vegetable garden to the dark and heavy smog that seemed to seal the city into itself. The children knew the horses by name—Dick, or Bill, or Barney—big sorrels and a powerful gray that hauled the busloads of tenants, mostly businessmen, daily to and from the Idlewood stop en route to Pittsburgh on the Panhandle Railroad just a mile away.

Ads for the hotel in the *Pittsburgh Dispatch* explained how "the proximity of Idlewood to the city, and the fact that, at moderate cost, business men and their families can enjoy all the pleasure of rustic surroundings there while keeping their business hours with the same facility as if living in the city, makes it a permanent favorite." The hotel, "situated upon an eminence that commands the loveliest of inland views," worked well for the people who spent their summers there, but the venture never yielded the profits that Jackson's father had hoped. At Idlewood, Chevalier Jackson mostly worked. And worked. And worked, "sixteen or seventeen hours out of the twenty-four" (*LCJ*, 45). The stable, the dairy, and the vegetable garden required constant tending, and the various social functions—ranging from concerts to amateur theatricals—needed to be hosted. Eventually, spring water was pumped into the establishment, and Jackson's father rigged a complexly designed but also dangerous gas-generating plant to illuminate the place, a setup that was in constant need of repair but that Jackson learned to fix by apprenticing as a plumber's cub. Still, the benefits of Idlewood, from Jackson's point of view, were multifold. For one thing, he got to study painting with two different visitors there, the artist wife of Judge Kennedy and A. Bryan Wall (1861–1935), a well-known local landscape painter and friend of Thomas Eakins. Imagine a small five-by-seven oil color as the product of those days: in it, fluent lavender clouds throw purple shadows on a house diminished by trees and by the central solitary figure, the painting's focal point, wending his way down a road. The small painting's stiff board has been ripped down the middle and then taped back together with broad bands on its back, but a fissure remains, the way time and work engrave deep lines into human skin, or the way, in an etching, an artist insists on a horizon line for the sake of perspective. That frustration and yearning—the sign of the small painting's tear and repair—was precisely the profit of Idlewood for Jackson, what he called its "impetus": the model provided by the educated upper classes with whom he got to mingle, seeking an antidote to the "dread" that he might never leave the coal-mining district and its brawling masses.

In the wings of this rags-to-riches fantasia, buttressing the story of Jackson's country home for class mobility, a group of stagehands held the scene together. Members of Pittsburgh's nineteenth-century black community served Chevalier Jackson as a mirror that deflected rather than reflected an image; they represented what, in Jackson's mind, he must not become. Young Jackson wanders down alleyways in the area that as early as 1850 was known as "little Hayti," the Wylie Street district of Pittsburgh, where runaway slaves had settled. He's sent there on "emergency errands" to gather four to six waiters, whom he has to convince to walk six miles back with him to the hotel if they want work. Most of these men take jobs that neither whites nor immigrants want: they are janitors and porters, coachmen and teamsters, who might work ten-hour days and earn just $2. Barbering was the only "elite" position available since the white male population relied on black men to cut their hair. If any of these barbers happened to cut the hair of a fellow black man, however, he'd lose his right to serve white bodies. In this very neighborhood, the famous black nationalist Martin Delaney co-edited the nation's first black newspaper, the *North Star*, with Frederick Douglass. Delaney had tried to train as a doctor, and white Pittsburgh physician/abolitionists helped to give him his start, but after being accepted into Harvard's medical school, he was later dismissed when white students protested his presence there.

Jackson is maybe a teenager when he is sent to round up—in what almost sounds like slave-picking—"recruits" to wait tables at Idlewood. As an adult looking back, Jackson paints his black employees as squanderers of their hard-earned dollars, people with a hopeless relationship to capital. As soon as they earn a little money, they piss it away in "poolrooms" and "saloons" and "dens of iniquity," and it's hard, if they've already got some coins jingling in a pocket, to get members of what Jackson calls the "happy-go-lucky, floating negro population" to work. The dilemma, in Jackson's words, has to do with black desires for independence, and one almost hears a proslavery rationale in his narration. "So long as any money remained" in the pockets of his would-be recruits, "an impenetrable armor of independence resisted all inducements" (*LCJ*, 47). What's the proprietor of a rustic white watering hole to do?

"Woo them with food" seems to be the answer Jackson supplies for himself, and he describes how not every man who agrees to follow him actually makes the steep climb to Idlewood but that each is encouraged by his offer to feed him the leftover "plate scrapings" that the "colored cook" will have waiting, simmering on the stove's back burner.

Once there, the black help would exceed their duties by supplying the white tenants with entertainment. "After dinner they would get very jolly, dance jigs, sing plantation songs, do impromptu minstrel acts" (*LCJ*, 46), which was all well and good until more black friends showed up with whiskey. Hilarity would soon give way to brawls and a "walk-out of all hands" (*LCJ*, 46), leaving Jackson no recourse but to resume his Wylie Street recruitments.

Jackson strains to find a lesson in all of this, some tidbit useful to the future making of the self-made man. Recalling a fight between two black men flashing razors, "blood . . . squirting" from the combatants, "tears streaming" from his eyes, he muses: "I little thought then that these razor cutthroat cases were to furnish me in later life with unique opportunities for the development of a system of laryngeal surgery" (*LCJ*, 47). It's left to us to decide if Jackson meant that he, as a budding physician, learned from black Americans (from barbers with razors, in fact) how to cut, or if he is trying to tell us, with blithe disregard, that their wounds were the basis for his later achievements.

There's so much that we cannot know but must needs picture. Occasionally, Jackson will take his recruits to the train station rather than walk to Idlewood. He doesn't describe their inevitable, mandated separation inside the cars, but perhaps we can imagine it: Jackson in one car, his recruits in another; how it felt to him to sit up front alone, how it felt to them to sit together.

. . .

"You have seen how a man was made a slave; you shall now see how a slave was made a man." What could this famous line from Frederick Douglass's autobiography have to do with *The Life of Chevalier Jackson*? Jackson was a white man, and his book was written in 1938, not in the 1840s, but his autobiography bears traces of the slave narratives that were being published at the time of his birth. Strange as it might seem, Douglass's oft-quoted line could describe the founding premise of *The Life of Chevalier Jackson*: it's a classic example of a white writer using America's slave past as an afterimage in forging the origins of his white self. Fantasies of abject blackness birth him.

Hear how the opening sentences of Chevalier Jackson's autobiography are marked by the terms of a pre– and post–Civil War nightmare-turned-dream:

> From the cradle to threescore and ten, I have been a slave to an innate and insatiable urge to make things, to achieve; though never for the mere glory; the achievement itself was the objective and the source of temporary satisfaction. The satisfaction was ephemeral because each achievement was quickly followed by another slave-driving urge to finish another task. (*LCJ*, 4–5)

At the moment of my birth and for all my life thereafter, I've been a slave, the physician's life-writing begins. Not a slave like those who taint the history of white America's past, however, not a slave to *labor*, but a slave to advancement; not the subordinate of another, but to myself as master; slave to a passion, not savage, but refined.

Chevalier Jackson's life and *The Life of Chevalier Jackson*, like any life, are, as I have stressed before, "scenic," rife with mementos that seem scored onto celluloid, that recur or fade with time, suddenly flash or hum, into which he inserts himself, out of which he makes himself—episodes that orient a "life story," sometimes as acute as life sentences. Numerous scenes in *The Life of Chevalier Jackson* compete for emphasis, but none quite outstrips what we could call a master scene, an origin scene, a this-is-what-has-made-me tableau, a point of direction and of no return and of perpetual return, that is the happening of young Jackson upon a "huge, burly half-drunk negro" lashing "four beautiful, well-built young horses . . . hitched to a hopelessly sunken, heavily loaded wagon" (*LCJ*, 13). Because Jackson has no "prestige" at this point in his life, because at this stage of the game he lacks the "prestige" of a physician (yes, he says it twice), he can't hope to coax the "savage brute" (*LCJ*, 13) carefully to unload the wagon, release the empty wagon from the mud in which it has sunk, and then reload it. This is something that only his father is capable of, and he's not there.

Instead, Jackson is forced to watch as the "negro bellowing like a bull and roaring curses . . . [lashes] his bleeding team *seriatim* . . . beating the leader over the head with the butt" (*LCJ*, 13). Jackson's recounting of the memory is fierce and exacting, picturing for his readership the force of the blow, the helpless flinching, how "at each savage onslaught the hit horse would plunge into his collar" (*LCJ*, 13). Blinded by his tears as though it is he who is being beaten, Jackson beseeches the black teamster to stop, and expects to find a sympathetic community among the crowd that has gathered. "We will help unload," he shouts, but his pleas are greeted with threats of violence from the teamster, who cracks the blacksnake whip in the boy's direction. As if this were not enough to mark the scene as one of unforgettable horror, something entirely unexpected and more unspeakable occurs.

The crowd begins to gather fence rails—to build a platform around the horses, Jackson hopes—but instead of releasing the horses of their load, they use their new proximity to beat the horses into further submission in concert with the teamster, and with "hickory coal-pick handles" (the words themselves are ghastly-sounding) as their aid (*LCJ*, 14). A robotic frenzy now sweeps the crowd as each man places himself directly next to a horse, so that each may beat the horses "synchronously" while the teamster continues his "seriatim" clarion call (*LCJ*, 14). If we reinsert this scene into the history from which it issues as a kind of fantasy, the crowd appears to behave like any number of late-nineteenth-century lynch mobs: ecstatic, motivated, working in unison, fascinatedly, to brutalize black men. In Jackson's story, though, it's a horse that is being beaten rather than a man, and the black man is one of the animals' persecutors—in fact, he's responsible for stirring up the mob.

Did this really happen? Could Jackson truly have witnessed a black man performing violence in front of a white crowd who comes to join him in the 1870s coal-mining districts of western Pennsylvania? Perhaps. But the relative probability of the event does not preclude its functioning as a powerful *fantasy* in the story Jackson will tell himself about who he is and whom he would become; nor does it mean that we cannot learn a great deal from the language that Jackson calls upon in remembering it and reattach it to the complex racist history of which our doctor is a part.

Jackson positions this tableau as a founding trauma that, psychoanalytically speaking, would carry the weight of a "primal scene." For weeks the episode comes "back upon [him] so suddenly and overwhelmingly that, repeatedly, [he] burst out crying" (*LCJ*, 14). But the effects do not end there. The story follows him for the rest of his life, still returning, acutely, even at the moment of his writing it: "Hundreds of times in later life the memory of it has rushed back with a vividness that has marred many a moment. Even as I write today, notwithstanding the fact that the horses are dead, the teamster is dead, all the men of the crowd have probably passed away, that horrid memory lingers" (*LCJ*, 14).

For Jackson, the "terrible picture of it is burnt in my memory, like the red-hot branding iron that seared the Western horse" (*LCJ*, 12). By this account, the scene makes him into a slave, for slaves were also branded. But no, his sympathies, his identifications, are with the horse, not with the man. Like little baby Theodore in Chesnutt's *The Marrow of Tradition*, he really cannot be marked by his race in the way his black colleagues or his black patients are. He can't be stigmatized even if he feels as though he has been; he can only be marked for glory and prestige. The horse-beating scene isn't, then, something that only happened to Jackson; it was something that took up residence inside him, told him where his body began and ended, and left the impression of a distinction he had to hold fast to—the fact of being white rather than black—if he were ever to become a doctor. Left to die in a coal pit as a child, Jackson reappeared, in his neighbor Biddy Welsh's words, "blacker 'n a nayger in a tar bawl," and likely to "skeer yer mither tah death" (*LCJ*, 36), and his colleagues warned him that treating his assistants as his equals would lead his students to lick "all the 'lasses off his bread and then call him nigger" (*LCJ*, 155).

Characters in *The Marrow of Tradition* are the collective victims of the mass trauma that was the end of the Civil War. The novel is populated by people who are operating under severe distress, which Chesnutt represents in the form of perpetual "shocks" to his characters' nervous systems: at least one character actually dies of shock when she is robbed by a white man in blackface. The novel is keen to document the "effects of slavery upon the human mind," white and black, and Chesnutt understands better than anyone that if the order of things is going to change fundamentally, psychic transformation must occur as well. Jackson's pivotal formative scene, on the other hand, serves a more personal and individu-ating purpose. Jackson isn't trying to study race-based trauma or illumi-nate anything about our nation's past; instead, he's drawing from that past as though from a reservoir of templates in his effort to picture nothing so much as himself. He relies upon a culturally available whipping scene, in other words, to distinguish himself—literally to imagine his own distin-guishing features, the brand that marks him and his difference.

There's nothing, however, original about Jackson's gesture: students of psychoanalysis and race have long noted the extent to which the mod-ern self relies upon "finding one's place within the *mise en scène* of racial trauma" (Calvo) and how Freud's early-twentieth-century patients used Harriet Beecher Stowe's *Uncle Tom's Cabin* as the basis for the beating fan-tasies that they shared with him. Race-based slavery became a peculiarly available and convenient screen for white people's dramatizations of their own complexes and conflicts. Into this mix, Jackson adds another ingre-dient drawn from the 1890s—the animal rights activism that reached its first fervor with the founding of the SPCA. At a moment of intense disap-proval of the granting of rights to black citizens and the inception of new-found exclusionary, segregationist practices, a great many Americans saw fit to take up the cause of animal rights instead. The perverse replacement or substitution of man with animal is underscored by literary historian Jennifer Mason, who explains how early activists actually replaced the fig-ure of an enchained slave that had served as the masthead of abolitionist William Lloyd Garrison's *Liberator* with a beaten horse. Charles Chesnutt, she points out, expressly wished for *The Marrow of Tradition* to become the "legitimate successor of *Uncle Tom's Cabin*." Instead, Anna Sewell's *Black Beauty: The Autobiography of a Horse* (1877) came to fill that role, when, as Mason explains, MSPCA president George Angell discovered the book in 1890 and "promptly printed 600,000 copies," heralding the book on its title page as "The *Uncle Tom's Cabin* of the Horse."

Chevalier Jackson seems to have wished throughout his life to extricate, insulate, and isolate himself from the social body even as his life's work entailed treating individual bodies, but, as Jackson's self-mining demon-strates, he was very much a man of his time. *The Life of Chevalier Jackson*'s primal scene mimics a popular sentiment of the 1890s—that the "negro's" "savagery" was a rationale for lynching. It introjects and reverses a form of violence commonly found in slave narratives, for the kind of, degree of, and regularized, even syncopated, brutality that the black man visits upon the horse was enacted by white men against slaves. We could be reading a slave narrative. But we're not. Presumably we're reading the life story of a remarkable physician who changed the face of medical history. Just as the slave master lingers long after he is dead in Harriet Jacobs's *Incidents in the Life of a Slave Girl,* just as he remains as terrorizing eyes and threatening phrases planted inside Jacobs's ears, so, though all the violators at the scene are dead, they somehow continue to live in Jackson. That intractable living memory, intolerable as a foreign body caught in the throat, uncomfortable as a rigid instrument slipped in, forces him back not to the scene of his own victimization, but to a scene of forced voyeurism.

Chevalier Jackson, we might have to note, runs from what he finds captivating and recaptivates us with his description. Or maybe he draws us only to repulse or repel us. It's a tug of war, a tourniquet applied, a vying for attention, a jockeying for position, a shade that follows him, forcing him back to look again, to watch once more, perpetually to refind his place at a site of violation. Something is disintegrating, that's for certain, and Jackson's writing is an attempt to reintegrate it. He's not after truth. No, he's struggling with metaphor, because truth, as Chesnutt's narrator reminds us, "sometimes leaves a bad taste in the mouth," while the Fred J.'s of the world are caught in the crossfire.

"Strange Things Were on the Run from Mary's Deepest Depths": Hardware, Swords, Scopes

"Animals can be tamed," Winnicott wrote ominously, "but not mouths."
—ADAM PHILLIPS, *On Kissing, Tickling, and Being Bored*

The Chevalier Jackson foreign-body collection is certainly singular, but it's not solitary. In Rosamond Purcell's words, "the doctor as collector of medically engendered detritus persists throughout time." Thus it should come as no surprise to read a 1930 *New York Times* article that pairs Jackson with a French colleague who also kept "a large and varied collection of strange objects removed from patient's lungs, among them being false teeth, pieces of money, and one overcoat button which was swallowed by a baby."

West, East, North, South—a quick trip down the Roadside America Web site reveals more museums of curiosa than meet the eye, several of them featuring fbdy displays. The Allen County Museum in Lima, Ohio, is home to a miniature (working) model of Mount Vernon that takes up an entire room; the largest collection of albino animal specimens in the world; and a macabre, whirring wonderland of taxidermied creatures proceeding along a conveyor belt in an imitation of Noah's Ark. Formerly coin-operated, the moving diorama was fashioned by an Ohioan undertaker who turned to selling shoes and who entertained children with the display in his shoe store. Such charming novelties, ingenious forms of kitsch, share a space with a local Dr. Yingling's collection of pins, dentures, and buttons swallowed and retrieved, each one centered and sewn onto a paper card, identified by patient's name, age, and date, then thumb-tacked in long rows upon a board.

If the endoscopist retrieves and then collects, he also makes something out of his findings. Rosamond Purcell identifies a strange collection of "(carefully ordered) needles" dating to the mid-nineteenth century, removed from the body of an insane woman addicted to morphine. The needles are assembled "tidily," and Purcell remarks the "peculiar sensibility of whoever arranged the morbid collection with such care": "It is as though the needles, once a source of frantic and fruitless anticipation, might now be used methodically by a person mending clothes, as if the gruesomeness of their history could at least be somewhat tempered by presentation."

Extreme acts of swallowing seem to engender equally peculiar extreme "crafts"—of mounting, exhibiting, or transforming the items and their etiology into works of, for lack of a better term, "art." Each fbdy collection serves its own conscious and unconscious, ascribed and denied, practical and imaginative purpose, but it's hard not to notice an affinity between fbdy displays that originate in acts of mental instability or hysteria, especially when the patients-subjects-swallowers are women and the physicians-operators-collectors-artists are men.

Sometime between the years 1927 and 1929, an unnamed woman (we might consider her a sort of never-to-be-hailed Unknown Soldier on the battlefields of the history of psychiatry) undertook a swallowing project of mammoth proportions that eventually precipitated her death. Other patients in the ghastly-sounding State Lunatic Asylum No. 2 in St. Joseph, Missouri, witnessed her swallowing Things, and she was rushed into surgery, but without the benefit of Chevalier Jackson or any of his disciples, she died on the operating table. The hospital's surgeon discovered enough hardware in her stomach and bowels to constitute a collection in itself: 453 nails, 9 bolts, 115 hairpins, 42 screws, assorted buttons, pebbles, and

942 various pieces of metal, including earrings, silverware handles, and salt and pepper shaker tops. Is it quality or quantity that matters? To me, the choice of salt and pepper shaker tops seems more significant than the number of bolts consumed. I wonder if a special pathological category should be reserved for the person who counts the Things and records them in a ledger, bent on getting the number right. Imagine the number of times whoever counted the nails, exasperated, had to start over, until, checking and double-checking, he was able to breathe a sigh of relief and say, "Now we know." But what do we know?

It's strange to find a short article on these things in *Self*, a magazine focused on fitness, health, and nutrition for women, but even more startling to find it featured on "extreme craft" blogspots. Here it's not the act of swallowing that is the focus but what Dr. Ralph Edwards, a pathologist at the hospital in the 1920s, did afterward with the swallowed things: he sewed them onto a large piece of cloth, then ordered and arranged them to approximate a pattern. What is now called the "stomach contents display" is on view in the Glore Psychiatric Museum.

Sometime in 1968, George Glore, a lifetime employee of the Missouri Department of Mental Health, began to assemble a collection of mental health ephemera that he exhibited in an abandoned ward of the state hospital to celebrate Mental Health Awareness Week. The museum that grew out of this collection offers a one-of-a-kind tour of centuries-old treatment devices for the insane, who appear as mannequins in the assorted little-shop-of-horrors exhibits. The stomach contents display, though, distinguishes itself to this day as the museum's most talked-about item, no doubt for some of the same reasons that the Chevalier Jackson collection is among the Mütter's most popular exhibits—they both assert a *Ripley's Believe It or Not* appeal. Just as powerful as, if not more so than, the fact of the things and the unnamed woman's acts, however, is the truly weird suggestion of Edwards's arrangement of the objects swallowed: neither a meticulous cartography, documentary, or cabinet of wonders, the stomach contents' afterimage resembles nothing so much as a pulsating mandala (see figure 27).

Buttons cluster in the center of the design like an archetypal navel; pins and needles swirl in carefully composed circles as if to suggest the hub of the universe itself. More than ordering disorder, the foibles-turned-mandala translates the Things swallowed into a form of the sublime, however cheap and raggedy, for it's surely not transcendent and is hardly

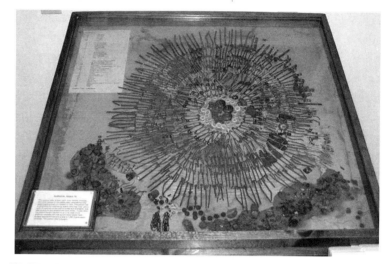

Fig. 27. "The Stomach Contents Display." The St. Joseph Museums, Inc./Glore Psychiatric Museum, St. Joseph, Missouri.

beautiful, though it does seem on par with the terrible and awful. Foreign bodies swallowed fasten on our imaginations, but the pathologist's mandala seems to say, "It's too difficult to make meaning out of this." However the patient hoped for her disorder to act upon herself or her interlocutor, whatever it was she was making or making *of* herself by such acts, it is subsumed by the force and weirdness of the pathologist's design.

It's not a competition, nor is it a you-say-po-TAY-toh, I-say-po-TAH-toh sort of difference, this affinity and distance between the act of swallowing and the act of assembling. Nor do I think Edwards fancied himself a Jungian in his off-hours or hoped to treat other patients in the asylum with the soothing effects of a meditative prayer wheel. At best, he was trying to tame something wild; at worst, he let the remarkable nature of her act—the titillating aspect of its extremity—override whatever the patient was trying to say. He was inspired but not informed. He extracted the showy, the *monstrum*, from inside the monstrous; he translated the abominable act into a transcendent symbol rather than an exorbitant sign. As if to say let's take this moment of hysterical departure to a point before you were born and after you have died and hang it here, and marvel at it.

Chevalier Jackson's collection has the power to occlude others, just as, in some sense, identifying collections the world over risks normalizing his. For every robust and fanciful foreign body collection, there are no doubt dozens more quiet and banal versions languishing behind closed doors. In the Mütter Museum itself, one outspoken foreign body collection is on permanent display (Jackson's), while another lies hidden in a recess of the archive (see figure 28). Two mica-like, nearly translucent, razor-thin slivers approximating the porous sheath that is human skin stand upright inside beakerlike containers. Charred black flecks coat the containers' rims—traces, the museum's administrative coordinator explains to me, of a sealant made of pitch that has since flaked off. The specimen dates back to 1840s Philadelphia. It consists of rows of pins and needles—but the pins seem sharper than the ones we use nowadays, and the eyes of the needles are so fine as to require a magnifying glass for threading them. The pins are also headless—recommending thimbles on more than thumbs, lest you risk pricks and cuts and bloodstains. They're filamental as fishbones and wispy as a lock of hair. They've been separated out, the pins from

Fig. 28. Pins and needles extracted from the body of a "young hysterical female" by Thomas Dent Mütter sometime in the late 1840s, mounted on isinglass. Collection of the Mütter Museum, The College of Physicians of Philadelphia.

the needles, and mounted, which is to say, mildly etched and glued into isinglass in neat rows of six. Today they've lost some of their adhesiveness and are deteriorating; unloosed, a few lie detached from their mounting at the bottom of the jar. The ones still adhering to their surface seem like splinters caught under a nail; their placement in evenly paced rows upon a backing makes the specimens resemble a still-playable musical instrument, kind of like a Jew's harp, requiring both a finger and a mouth.

Oh, but here's the most astonishing detail: they were extracted by Thomas Dent Mütter himself, and the slips of pinned and needled isinglass could have been his calling cards—they're just the right size. Like the Glore extravaganza, this more modestly delicate display also references a case of *purposeful* ingestion, the only data on the case being its specimen number drawn on a label yellowed with glue, 13410, and a sentence in one of the museum's catalogs: "Needles and pins removed by Dr. Mütter from different portions of the body of a young hysterical female, 1849."

What compelled Mütter to keep or dump, mount or discard? Unlike so many of his specimens, this one is not anatomical per se, but a trace of a will. What exactly could this neatly separated display teach? Mütter was among the earliest practitioners of plastic surgery and of operations to treat scalds and burns. This case might testify to a delicate incursion into the skin—"Look, I extracted them whole!" What else do we know about Mütter? In a posthumous reminiscence by the famous Dr. Samuel D. Gross, we learn that he was married to a woman considerably younger than he; that he died young, at forty-eight, and that "no children blessed their union." That he was "the pink of neatness." That he had a strong and clear voice and cut a distinctly physical figure on the streets of Philadelphia, where people couldn't help but notice "his tall grey horse, his low carriage, and his servant in livery." Chair of surgery at Jefferson Medical College for a time, he was nevertheless not, from Gross's point of view, to be counted among the finer surgeons who were his peers. Though he "wielded his knife" with grace and self-possession, he was "deficient in boldness," according to Gross. Moreover, he had "no fondness for authorship," and "did not possess much ability as a writer." Gross tells us that neither was Mütter much of a reader: "His library was small," writes Gross, "and he did not read much beyond what was necessary to enable him to keep abreast of the knowledge required for his lectures." I sense that Mütter was a kind of showman: he was "fond of anecdotes and had always a good supply on hand for ready use," Gross adds. In other words, he was a *collector*, and one wonders if he would have been remembered by medical history if not for his museum. Perhaps he went at medical knowledge through the door of things rather than ideas.

Like the woman in the Glore case, next to nothing is known about Mütter's 1840s "hysterical female." What remains of her act is this specimen in a jar. If the Missourian woman's collection is weighty, if it astounds us for its heft and shape and magnitude, the Philadelphia woman's pins and needles bespeak uncanny transport. Today they might appear no more than corroding stripes on a translucent card, but this kind of ingestion hints at waywardness, of a body's giving itself over to multiple forms of departure and arrival.

Beneath a photograph of the specimen by Rosamond Purcell for the book *Mütter Museum of the College of Physicians of Philadelphia*, we read: "Pins and needles that have been ingested orally may work themselves out through the walls of the gastrointestinal tract and become lodged elsewhere in the body." In his own treatise on fbdies in the airways, not the foodways, Samuel Gross caught that peculiarly menacing effect of the ways, once inside the body, certain kinds of foreign bodies can move:

> Finally, the foreign body occasionally, though very rarely, escapes through the walls of the chest, by retracing, as it were, its former steps, or retraversing the route by which it entered. In some instances, again, also very uncommon, it forms a new passage, just as tubercular matter sometimes does. Lastly, the extraneous substance may leave the lung, and pass into the cavity of the pleura, where it may either become encysted, or, as more generally happens, excite fatal inflammation.

Once inside the body, it's anybody's guess what path a pin or needle will follow; so light, they seem to swim. The horror of these particular things ingested isn't only that they're sharp, but that, carried through the body's interiors without benefit of peristalsis, they are errant and directionless—we don't know where or how they'll reemerge.

How can I make a pin once ingested or a spoon handle *mean*? How can we reattach the thing not to cloth or isinglass but to history, to story, to the body, to the mind? There must be clues that we're missing that tell what couldn't be told. I might swallow a spoon handle because I'm using it to make myself throw up rather than to shovel something in. I might be redressing spoons as implements to scoop the body with. J. Marion Sims, the so-called Father of American Gynecology, invented the first speculum by bending back a kitchen spoon. Maybe I'm turning the spoon against itself as enemy rather than against the man, though it's he who is now required to fish it out of me.

As for "pins and needles," therein lies a tale. Of nervousness, excitement, and anticipation—it's the path that nerve-ways take or fail to when shut off. They're the implements of women's work, the tools for mending and of livelihood, of social staying, of gender placement: if I pierce myself, will something open that is otherwise shut? Can I imagine myself as a cloth in need of stitching, in need of being fastened, or held in place, pieced together again? Tell me a story while I work, of a girl sent on an errand to her grandmother's house who meets a wolf who asks which path she'll take—the one of "pins or needles"? Give me an ending in which she neither ends up in the belly of the beast, nor is rescued by a huntsman, but frees herself to take the deepest path into the darkest unmapped wood, the way of pins, the way of needles. Early versions of "Little Red Riding Hood" proposed these paths to the girl—a choice between the pleasure principle and the reality principle, according to Bruno Bettelheim. "Don't amuse yourself along the way," some versions of the story have the mother tell the girl, certainly don't eat the pins and needles, but our hysteric does.

Every doctor makes something out of what the patient gives him: a diagnosis, an interpretation, a treatment method. A mandala, a specimen, a collection. When the swallowing of fbdies is intentional, the case is rife with things we dare not understand. Our own unconscious processes, for example, as well as the patient's, re-inspiriting the body, its pleasures and its perils. The body as a place of egress and entrance, as receiver and begetter, as consumer and producer, as me and not-me, as that which goes into me and that which goes out of me—my words and yours.

> *But besides this quality of the stomach, there is another more strange, when some can eat and digest coals, sand, lime, pitch, ashes, and such like trash. This is called by Physitians a disease, under the name of Pica, Citta, Malacia; but I think it proceeds not only from a distemper in the stomach, and malignant acide humors impacted in the membranes thereof; but also, and that chiefly, from some occult quality.*
>
> —ALEXANDER ROSS,
> *Arcana Microcosmi* (1652), book 2, chapter 8

Foreign bodies stretch the viscera in ways doctors supposed was not possible, but they stretch our imaginations too, and the limits of our credulity; subsequently, they make interesting demands on our language.

Multiple foreign bodies. Numerous collections. A panoply of orifices. Competing accounts. The language that Chevalier Jackson lent to his endoscopic practice was sober in comparison to so many ecstatically charged books on the subject before and since his remaking of the field. I can take the strange-but-true *National Enquirer* approach to foreign-body ingestion, I can write with more or less of a lilt, unironically or fascinatedly. Of course, Jackson's tonal control hardly ever lets a stray fantasy or impulse enter into his prose. His purchase on the impossible borderlands of foreign-body lodgment is always a hermeneutic one: an occasion for a disquisition on a mechanical problem and the particular instrumentarium it calls into being; the implements and methods required to cross a seemingly impassable bridge; the tools and technique and wherewithal that need to be invented so as not to get lost in a pitch-dark wood.

Once in, how do *I* get out? Once in, how does *it* get out? These are the questions upon which Jackson's prose tirelessly touches down, and they provide enough investigation for a lifetime, but they cannot temper the generative nature of the foreign-body phenomenon, the uncontrollable and the inexhaustible, the perpetual fund to which the caught foreign body gives rise.

At the time of Samuel D. Gross's own *Practical Treatise on Foreign Bodies in the Air Passages* in 1854, only a handful of books and papers from France, Germany, and the United States existed on the subject, according to Gross. The very first thing that Gross notes isn't the particular nature of each case's specific challenge but the amplitude beyond measure, the "exceedingly diversified character" of fbdy things caught, the endless endlessness, the everything and all-full-ness that the human body can incidentally ingest. The mid-nineteenth century represented a different material landscape than the one we inhabit now, but history books cannot really compete with the picture made by the sounds of the names of things swallowed by people in 1854. Breathe in the ferule of the rib of an umbrella containing a piece of whalebone, breathe out persimmon seed; breathe in some sewing silk, breathe out a tamarind seed. Breathe in a sprig of cedar, cowrie shell, a plum-drupe. Breathe out a fiddle-peg, some locks of tow, or millepods. In me are caught some beech-nut burrs, ears of grass, and rye and barley. Some pipe-stems, worsted yarn, and button-foils. There are artificial teeth with their blocks and pivots, a puff-dart, a piece of feather "nearly two inches in length and still furnished with some of its plumage"; the berry of the bladder-senna; a pellet of paper, such as is used for enveloping "sugar kisses" "about the size of a dime and with very sharp angles."

The names are enchanting. but they spell out forms of death that are sadly similar and an array of crude and gruesome attempts at cures. A person might be treated with emetics, "sternutatories" (sneeze-producers), the inhalation of iodine, or, with the intuitively sound but unfortunately ridiculous inversion of the body. Surgery was so often fatal, but the alternative was "leeches and blisters . . . applied several times to the right side of the chest" (this, for a person who had inhaled a nail); the regulation of the bowels with castor oil or calomel and rhubarb; the control of the cough with "occasional doses of hyoscyamus," derived from a genus of plants named henbane or hog bean and belonging to the nightshade family. Known for its hallucinatory, sedating, and hypnotic effects, henbane contains the colorless, crystalline, and highly poisonous alkaloid hyoscyamine.

Several decades after Gross's treatise, a French surgeon named Alfred Poulet compiled his own two-volume *Treatise on Foreign Bodies in Surgical Practice*, though he admits that two volumes is hardly enough to contain "all the curiosities of this kind, which are little known and scattered throughout the annals of science." The thing about foreign-body work is that it is *beyond us*, not only in its vastness and measure, in its multifariousness and its refusal to adhere to any norm. It is beyond our understanding, and therefore has the potential to severely strain a doctor's confidence. "Take a student who has passed through all the medical grades, and is on the eve of entering civil or military service: place him in the presence of even the simplest cases of foreign bodies—a small stone or a pea in the ear, a metallic splinter in the cornea, or a catheter broken in the urethra— and the anxiety and embarrassment which he manifests will show how insufficient is his surgical knowledge on this point." This is how Poulet announces the impetus behind his book, but the resulting two volumes don't so much impart surgical knowledge as they pursue off-limit realms of the Gargantuan and Lilliputian. We could be reading Rabelais or Swift, or the bizarre mythology of an as-yet-undiscovered culture.

In the alimentary canal, it is possible to find the foot of a chair, or a long hair pulled out by a mother. It's the stuff of nightmare, or of whimsy—see the eyeglasses swallowed by a maniac trying to do himself in. Here are two iron forks swallowed by a girl during typhus that made their exit by means of "suppuration through the abdomen," and the story of a group of Royal Guards who, after an orgy in which they had drunk a great deal, "broke their glasses and swallowed the pieces, thereby causing death." The digestive canals of the insane are especially secretive, for their intestinal tracts often become "a rendezvous for the strangest articles," often considerable in number, and often only discovered upon autopsy because few believed the patient when he or she confessed to swallowing things. The poet Gilbert introduced the key to his room into his fauces (the back of his mouth) and thereby died. No one believed he had swallowed the key. The same could be said of persons who had swallowed a thousand shoe nails, and a game of dominoes.

Of course there are people who haunt public squares with no other intention than exhibiting their "skill in swallowing pebbles, nails and glass," Poulet notes. Run out of ideas for how to make a living? In the case of Henrion, called Cassandra, born in Metz in 1761, "not satisfied with the various trades he followed in his youth, he began to force himself, at the age of 22 years to swallow pebbles." Henrion pretended he was an "American savage" by first heating the pebbles and then plunging them into cold water.

Sometimes people swallow things out of devotion or fidelity to a cause, as in the case of strategists and spies who make their way through enemy lines and then poop their war secrets at the foot of Napoleon.

A waiter in a café opens a bottle of champagne with his teeth and swallows the cork. A practical joker throws a chestnut into the opened mouth of an onstage singer where it lodges and asphyxiates.

An eel or a mouse enters the mouth of a sleeping person. No, this doesn't really happen, but people say it does, or fear that it will. What really happens is worse, as in the person who uses one fbdy to extract another fbdy and ends up swallowing both, or the person who has the misfortune of swallowing something before Jackson opens up shop and must submit himself to instruments shaped like hooks and levers, whips and even chains. Or the person whose opened cadaver reveals fourteen knife blades in his stomach. What compelled him to compete with sword swallowers? What compelled Poulet to note that, while some of the knives were rusted, one still showed clearly the name of the cutler?

Order and control aren't really what Poulet is about, though his book is a gathering and a collecting and a sorting. The book becomes dimensionless in its consideration of fbdies introduced into *any and all* of the body's orifices. Fbdies introduced through traumatism, introduced intentionally through malice or accidentally in depraved sexual manipulations; fbdies voluntarily concealed in the rectum or entered into orifices for curative purposes by both ignorant persons and medical men. Is it buffoonery or a physiological condition that leaves a person unable to eat peas without blowing one through his nose? Here's a tender tale of a child who held a ladybug "in the half-closed hand, and held his fist against his ear in order to hear the buzzing of the insect," then felt the bug actually enter "the auditory canal while endeavoring to escape." A whole host of rationales accompanies the instances of fbdies in the openings of the genitals. Sometimes Poulet links such to identities—the pervert, the addict, the deviant; other times he yokes his examples to "idleness, solitude, and stupidity," because he really can't explain people's "sickly curiosity" and "strange manipulations," their tendencies toward violent self-pleasuring, to climaxing at all costs and perpetually. So a monk loses a key in his bladder, or a woman who, having tried to kill herself, apparently successfully, is found with an open compass in her vagina.

"The reader will not have forgotten the monstrous histories, the scene of which was laid in the rectum" one paragraph begins, and we might feel as though we're inside of (but now that innocent prepositional phrase feels tainted) a Gothic novel of scatological proportions. Even (or is it mostly?) civilized folk have been known to punish each other by inserting things into the rectum of those accused—of adultery, for example, in the Greek practice of *rhaphanidosis*, whereby "a peeled radish covered with hot ashes" was entered into the rectum, a practice that morphed in the Victorian era and into contemporary S/M usage as "figging," the forcible insertion of peeled ginger into the anus. While such examples might test our squeamishness or make us ill to contemplate them, Poulet's detailed narration of a case of live snails up the arse wins the prize for the most entirely gross. "When the index finger was introduced into the rectum to .08 [centimeters] above the margin of the anus, it came in contact with a series of hard, smooth bodies, of the size of a large hazel-nut, swimming and clashing against one another in a liquid mass" reads the report from 1875. "After the patient was anaesthetized, the three first fingers of the right hand were introduced into the rectum, and forty-five small snails were extracted in succession, together with hardened faeces." While the patient reported eating the snails, the doctor concludes that they were entered into the anus. On a dare. Following the taking of some wine.

Poulet's book is a bit like the famous folk poem that begins with a

woman swallowing a fly, "I don't know why": that crucial line gives way
to the woman swallowing a spider, a bird, a cat, a dog, a goat, a cow, and
a horse, from which she dies, "of course." The invocation of the great
chain of being, a predatorial hierarchy, a dilation of examples, each one
outstripping the one before it in size or maw—in Poulet's menagerie, in
grossness—shows the poet and the doctor, annoyed or enfeebled by this
difficult "why," responding by flexing. Frustrated by the detachment that
might be required by the question, or even just the alienating horror of
the fbdy lodged, the writer opts for indulgence, because there's definitely
something voyeuristic and (dis)gustatory about Poulet's book, something
brimming with guilty pleasure. The physiology of swallowing and the psychology of swallowing are fascinating, but the urge to collect and report
extreme instances can make for pornographic compendia, the point of
which seem to be to hang out on the outskirts of decorum, to get really
depraved, all the while still, significantly, authoritatively, wrapped in your
lab coat.

If I collect stray instances of swallowing—rather than matchbooks,
cow-shaped creamers, or albino animals—does that make me like Poulet?
Recently, without the benefit of Jackson, the world's largest man was instead called in to reach into the throat of a struggling dolphin and release
the plastic lodged there. Articles on the subject were so delighted by the
image of the man with the overly large arm functioning as superhero that
they overlooked the environmental tragedy of dolphins swallowing plastic.

Some indigestible stuff they can't put a price on. A whale belch can be
heard for miles around, and out plops ambergris. At first the stuff stinks
until the ocean leaches it, and then it's mined by perfume sellers for its
incomparably sweet aroma.

The euro has been found to be more swallowable than other coins:
there's a factoid we might find humorous so long as we're no victim of the
new economy. Snakes swallow their young to protect them from danger,
then spit them out when the danger is passed. In yoga, the throat chakra
is imagined as an endlessly opening lotus flower made up of sixteen inter-
secting petals, blue-green and silvery as moonlight. When the energy that
founds the universe is kindled at the base of the spine, it's said to bound
upward like a snake. I'm not sure why, but I picture the snake coming out
of my mouth.

Recently, a man in the Urals, complaining of a pain in his chest, was discovered to have a tiny fir tree growing in his lung. Complete with needles
but devoid of sun. Had the man, snoring during a midday nap, inhaled a

seed as it fell from a tree? The fear this tale—tall or short—taps into is of that which grows inside of us, is always growing inside of us. Is it death? But the beauty of it and the chill of it is its entwining—when the fir tree comes to be inextricable with its host, like a Hawthorne character's birthmark. The power of the alien thing taking root within us.

It has been said that poets are people who love the names of things. In the realm of medicine, to name something is to begin to know it, but also, in various crucial ways, to be done with it. The Greek suffix "-phagy" in particular takes us into relatively unspeakable realms. Take "placentoph- agy," the practice of eating the placenta following childbirth, where the afterbirth is understood to be a double of the fetus, a highly nutritive life support that had performed all of the major organ functions for the fetus before birth, a substance that is to be treated with awe and with rever- ence, thus leading to some people's ritual consumption of it. Or "polyph- agi," the word for a glutton or a person who overeats for sport, or who is compelled by others who need to watch a person eat to excess for their own amusement. "Polyphagi" are perfect contenders for fbdy-discourses- as-pornographic-compendia, accounts in which the writer seems to take as much relish in reporting on the phenomena as the glutton's audience was amused and disgusted by it.

Pagophagia: excessive eating of freezer frost. *Acuphagia*: swallowing sharp objects. *Amylophagia*: ingesting laundry starch. *Cautopyreiophagia*: doing the same with burnt matches. *Coprophagia*, feces; *foliophagia*, leaves, grass, acorns, pinecones; *geomelophagia*, raw potatoes; *geophagia*, dirt, sand, clay; *lignophagia*, wood, bark, twigs; *lithophagia*, rocks, gravel, peb- bles; *trichophagia*, hair. All of these neologisms were invented to exemplify a more global diagnostic term for a form of disordered eating called pica.

Pica refers etymologically to a genus of magpies, birds known for their insatiable or indiscriminate appetite. From the sixteenth century onward, it has been used to refer to "disordinate longing," "deprav'd" or "per- verted" appetite, "untoward hankerings of nature," "morbid craving," and "desire for innutritious substances." Because there is no definitive etiology for pica, the term is relatively useless, but, as we can see, it has generated a boundless set of companionate lingo. It can afflict pregnant women, autis- tic individuals, people with developmental disabilities, psychotic patients, prison inmates, and people suffering from nutritional deficiencies, which are hardly groups in common. Best of all, as Lillian N. Stiegler points out in "Understanding Pica Behavior," "many individuals with normal intellect report that they engage in pica simply because they take pleasure in the texture, smell and/or taste of the items they ingest."

Pica appears to be a bona fide DSM-IV category, and yet commentators on the (presumed) disease note with surprise that pica receives scant attention from psychologists in the literature. Dr. David F. Gitlin observes that "most reports on intentional swallowing do not appear in the psychiatric literature; rather, they are found in the surgical and gastroenterological literature, and they focus on complication rates and surgical techniques for removing the object. They contain little to no commentary about patient intentions, psychological meaning or psychopathology." Perhaps this is why treatment methods for dealing with people presenting with the disorder are as barbaric-seeming as many of the horror show techniques featured in the Glore Psychiatric Museum. According to Lillian Stiegler, the hell realm that a pica patient might be made to enter includes having hot sauce squirted into his mouth or ammonia forced up his nose; being outfitted with a fencing mask, mesh bags, or a hood to cut off access to his mouth; or being made to wear a specially constructed helmet made from "sheet metal and plexiglass and pop-riveted to a jacket that laces up the back." "Over-correction" methods—an interesting euphemism for forms of punishment—are also used, such as requiring the patient to immediately brush his teeth with strong antiseptic mouthwash for five to ten minutes following a pica attempt; such methods demean the sufferer, and "work" only temporarily.

Just as no one specialty is adequate to treating the complex matrices that form the human swallow, so behaviors or conditions that fall under the category of intentional swallowing of nonnutritive substances in humans are too diverse to be adequately named. Of course we name things so that we can treat them, but oftentimes we name things so that we can dispense with them, or at least stop thinking about them.

One thing that can be said for pica is that it is as generative, as proliferative of categories as its origins are diverse. No matter how carefully researchers try to systematize it and, in systematizing it, treat it, pica remains utterly baffling and impossible to regulate. Sufferers of pica are sort of like what Ian Hacking (1999) calls the "motley of impaired individuals that at different times, and in different ways, have been handily lumped together as schizophrenics." These people are not "of a kind," Hacking argues, and it only takes some reading in the primary documents that constitute the history of the term "schizophrenia" to see that people like E.E. Southard, who lobbied for its replacing "dementia praecox" as a diagnostic category, saw themselves as creating taxonomies of humans.

Since the advent of pica as an identifier of a type of mental illness, other, more contemporary eating disorders are being named, like night eating syndrome (NES), the consumption of nonnutritive, high-caloric items all through the night; nocturnal sleep-related eating disorder (NS-RED), people who eat while sleepwalking, typically high-fat and high-sugar foods; and orthorexia nervosa, which is so new it has not yet earned an anagram: people so obsessed with eating healthily that they no longer enjoy food and consequently begin to isolate themselves.

When Dr. Samuel Gross applied the word "outré"—as in "There is hardly any substance, however singular or outré, that may not enter the air-tubes, and give rise to severe, if not fatal mischief"—he took a word that we usually associate with human custom, social decorum, and the boundaries of behavior and applied it to the object world, as if to suggest that when objects enter the human body, they become animated, almost as if they had a will of their own. It's a fanciful idea indicative of the excitement—in medical terms, the efference—produced by fbdy narratives, whether the items are ingested or inhaled, and most especially when the incorporation of a foreign body is intentional. Reading through an article on pica today regarding the proximity of pica to autism and the various "treatments" employed (many of which seem inhumane), it becomes clear that, for some people, the presumably odd or unbelievable or incredible is part of a daily, profoundly difficult "norm" (especially if they are parents of developmentally disabled pica sufferers). Stiegler quotes one exasperated father, who, writing in an online chat group, asks: "Is there no end to the variety of odd objects autistic children will eat? There are days when I believe my son would be quite happy with a daily menu of baby lotion, rabbit food—and perhaps a little toilet paper for roughage!" Finding accounts of fbdy ingestion in some strange way thrilling might depend on where you stand.

Swallowing that which is nutritive seems to require degrees of imitation and intelligence in humans. And yet, as a poetry student of mine once put it, riffing on John Ashbery's line "All things are secretly bored," perhaps "All things are secretly edible." Perhaps none of us, if we really thought about it, could supply a simple, true, or definitive answer to the question Stiegler tells us people suffering from pica are asked after they've been put through enough rounds of aversion therapy: the intensely bewildering "What is food?"

The kind of girl I was, I could swallow ink. Paper, too. A hangnail, laces, possibly a fin, a dove, a jack-in-the-box, cement, and, with a little urgent purpose, someone's dry wrap, a buoy.

—DAWN RAFFEL,
"We Were Our Age," *In the Year of Long Division*

In notes, handwritten or typed, tacked onto case studies or incorporated therein, in articles and in textbooks that Chevalier Jackson authored in the long course of his career, he never used the term "pica" to refer to acts of intentionally swallowed foreign body Things. He used the word "hysteria."

"Hysteria" is no less ambiguous or problematic than "pica" and "schizophrenia" are as descriptors of human behavior or states of mind, but the term both enables us to access psychoanalytic (rather than psychiatric) discussions of the phenomenon and lends a historical dimension to otherwise free-floating curiosities. Is it possible to attempt an explanation of hysterical behavior—the swallowing of hardware in large quantities, for example? Can we seek to understand what might be going on there, without resolving the uncanny cast of hysterical embodiment and its potential to unnerve us? "Hysteria" as a semantic envelope might make it possible for us to hold voluntary forms of untoward consumption before us so we can study them without quite pinning them down.

In 1909, Jackson published an article in *Laryngoscope* called: "Voluntary Aspiration of a Foreign Body into the Bronchi, Removal by Bronchoscopy." The case involved a forty-one-year-old woman who was referred to him by a doctor in New York City. Jackson carried out the removal of two tacks from a posterior branch of the right inferior lobe bronchus at the Eye and Ear Hospital in Pittsburgh. In one amazing paragraph, Jackson explains that, after the tacks had been removed, the patient swallowed and aspirated more tacks, and therefore had to undergo bronchoscopy once again, this time at the French Hospital in New York City, to which Jackson traveled:

Four months after the removal of the tacks, as reported in the foregoing, the patient came to Dr. Cole's office at the suggestion of Dr. Geo. W. Bogart, stating that she had the same old symptoms, and she thought there must be more tacks there. She further said that the tacks Dr. Jackson took out were corroded, yet the last just coughed up was bright and new. A radiograph showed one tack on each side of the thorax . . . not so near the periphery as the previous tacks. The question then arose how could the patient get the tacks into the bronchi voluntarily, as it was clear that she was a hysteric, if not demented. Dr. John W. Boyce, in consultation on this point, said that by throwing a number of tacks into the pharynx and taking a deep inspiration, she might get one or two down, but in so doing she would swallow many more than she could aspirate, so that, if not too late, a radiograph would show tacks in the alimentary canal in progress of passing through.

Jackson concludes that the "sympathy" the patient received combined with her case's "sensational features . . . evidently appealed to [her] neurotic temperament . . . and developed the hysteria which now is most troublesomely manifest in ways unnecessary to enumerate here." Jackson's attitude toward human psychology is what it always is here—impatient, incurious, and dismissive. The human psyche is an annoyance he'd rather dispense with when it interrupts his work on the body, but is it possible that the hysteric in this case doesn't want necessarily to be treated by him but to baffle him? In presenting a case of presumably voluntary aspiration, she outwits the doctor and even projects a certain mastery of physiology without the trouble of book learning.

Hysteria includes acts of purposeful swallowing of things and is also the category for which is reserved, in psychoanalytic parlance, the utterly menacing "phantom foreign body"—a sort of false foreign body or felt foreign body that is and is not real. We have to love Jackson's seemingly oblivious misuse of the phrase to designate phantoms produced by errors, which are therefore correctible—when the X-ray machine is dirty, for example, or when patients have faulty memories of the Thing, which an X-ray machine then corrects. In his 1934 work *Annals of Roentgenology: A Series of Monographic Atlases*, phantom fbdies of this kind are in these ways easily explained and easily eliminated. The examples are plain and simple:

> Phantom foreign bodies may be the result of dirt or extraneous objects in the cassette or elsewhere about the equipment. The cassette and all other pieces of apparatus should be kept scrupulously clean. We have seen a number of errors result from failure to insist upon this rule. In one instance error was due to accidental partial exposure of the film before it went into the cassette. Usually phantom foreign body is eliminated by its failure to appear in all of the films made.

Never take it for granted that the foreign body of which the patient gives a history is necessarily the one that is lodged in the patient. For example, a supposed bone in food was a pin that fell from the cook's clothing. Conversely a supposed pin was a radioparent bone. We have had a number of such cases. All examinations should be complete for radioparent as well as radiopaque foreign bodies regardless of the history. In one instance a supposed oyster shell turned out to be a cap off a catsup bottle.

In Jackson's world, phantom foreign bodies can only be signs of failure to remember or to carefully observe. Reliability is his bottom line; he needs to know exactly what he is dealing with to exact a cure. The psychoanalyst, however, needs to be open to ambiguity and an inexpressible center, to the possibility of "phantoms" that are reliably there, on one level, and entirely illegible on another.

Practically concurrent with Jackson's discussion of phantom fbdies in the early twentieth century, psychoanalyst Sándor Ferenczi, an original thinker who was also a reluctant detractor of Sigmund Freud, was writing about two kinds of hysterically induced phantom fbdies: *aerophagy* (the hysterical swallowing of air to simulate a pregnant belly) and *globus hystericus* (the production of a lump in the throat often accompanied by severe dysphagia). When we are children, we might believe that pregnancy is a result of something going into the mouth, that kissing is where babies come from. So the aerophagic hysteric reverts to this earlier assumption and, for any number of reasons, makes herself pregnant. When we consider that the contraction of the upper esophageal sphincter during inspiration probably serves to prevent inhalation of air into the esophagus, the purposeful ingestion of air must be quite a feat: in hysteria, the involuntary nature of the swallow mechanism is overcome, rerouted, perverted, and undone.

Globus hystericus, a quite common occurrence among Ferenczi's early-twentieth-century patients, introduces even more complicated implications. The conundrum that Ferenczi observes is that the lump in the throat is a phantasm produced by the hysteric *at the same time that* "a kind of foreign body, a lump, really is brought about." In the early pages of his essay "The Phenomena of Hysterical Materialization" (1919), Ferenczi interprets such symptoms almost always genitally. So, in the case of *globus hystericus*, "on analysis, the lump certainly appears as a quite peculiar and not harmless foreign body, but one with an erotic significance. In not a few cases this 'lump' moves rhythmically up and down and this movement corresponds to unconscious representations of genital processes." Ferenczi's theorizing doesn't end there, however; he doesn't rest easy with the "mysterious leap from mental to bodily" processes featured in hysteria but admits to vast lacunae in our knowledge of these matters and remains determined to find a language for the hysteric's ability not just to manifest a feeling (I feel like I have a lump in my throat) or fantasize a bodily state, but actually to bring the physiological state about. In a separate fragment titled "Materialization in Globus Hystericus" (1923), he offers further proof of this strange mental process "by which an idea actually becomes true in the flesh" by citing a story told by another psychoanalyst in which a doctor feels the tumor or lump about which the patient complains, his fingers inside the patient's throat, only to discover no "malformation" upon further surgical inspection.

Ferenczi's cases are beyond intriguing: in them, people make of themselves a foreign body, they introduce foreign bodies into themselves from inside themselves. This is especially apparent in patients' manipulations of their digestive tracts. Exerting great control over their intestines, "our neurotics, especially the hysterics," Ferenczi remarks, make "it possible to retain a faecal mass or gas-bubble at some place or other, and compress, so to say shape it." One of Ferenczi's male patients offered the analyst the opportunity to "study the hysterogenic role of the rectum and anus for months on end" until together they concluded that, "with the help of the contractile rectal walls," the patient "was compelled to mould for himself a male organ—the member of a consciously hated opponent—from the plastic material of the ever-present rectal contents that could not remove itself from the rectum till the conflict was solved." Ferenczi understands these internalizations as substitutes for withholding of information, or retention of desires, and he refers to the creation of fbdies inside oneself as "auto-plastic tricks" that are the precursors of art (the difference between the hysteric and the artist being that the former manipulates her own body, whereas the latter manipulates material from the external world).

Ferenczi doesn't settle for one interpretation of *globus hystericus* or autoplasticity. Are we witnessing the bodily expression of something psychological? Is what's going on the result of internal stimulus taking precedence over stimuli from the outside world? And how is it that "in hysterical symptoms . . . organs of vital significance subordinate themselves entirely to the pleasure principle, regardless of their own particular function in utility"? Ferenczi is convinced that something instructively unusual is occurring in *globus hystericus*, neither a hallucination nor an illusion but, in his coinage, a "materialization." The word carries connotations of spiritualism, ghosts, and the occult; in fact, the word "magic" enters into Ferenczi's exploration of the problem.

Contemporary feminist social scientist Elizabeth Wilson mines Ferenczi's speculations toward a radical understanding not of spirit but of biology and the body—not the body understood as that which opposes the spirit and is flatly concrete, but the biological as a realm of dynamic thinking all its own. In a startling essay, "Gut Feminism," Wilson reopens the lacunae that had necessitated Ferenczi's writing in the first place by proposing that we suspend our investment in hysteria as a form of psychosomatic projection. Hysteria's body isn't a passive recipient of psychological conflict, she argues, but a reversion to an earlier body. In such instances as *globus hystericus*—those Ferenczian materializations—or bulimia, in which the person appears to have gained unusual control over the gag and retch reflexes to such an extent that she can will food back out of the stomach, Wilson wants us to consider that a profound and particular kind of regression is taking place. A primitive form of thinking vested in the organs themselves takes over where the psyche fails. I cannot begin to do justice to the subtleties of Wilson's proposal, via Ferenczi, of a "biological unconscious," but can only reiterate what distinguishes the mouth, the throat, and the human swallow as the place in the body where the most is going on. In Wilson's words, the "back of the throat is a local switch point between different organic capacities (ingestion, breathing, vocalizing, hearing, smelling)" and "the fauces is a site where the communication between organs may readily become manifest." Our organs communicate with one another, but in the transformations engendered by psychopathology, one organ can also take on the function of another. In Wilson's example of the bulimic, "ingestion has become a technique for expulsion rather than digestion."

Phantom fbdies, autoplasticity, aerophagy, *globus hystericus*: these are not conditions that can be bronchoscopically treated or even glimpsed, though it might be significant that the introduction of hardware into the gullet and the onset of these biopsychological states were contemporaneous.

The Notion Department contains merchandise assembled according to its uses and made of the most varied materials. To most people it looks like a

mixture of small articles which have no relation to each other. It sometimes
seems to be the place for all the things that cannot be classified under any
other name. . . . Arrangement of one's stock is not very different from the
arrangement of one's ideas. Every time we put a thing where it belongs we
see more clearly its use and its relation to other things around it.

—M. ATTIE SOUDA, *Notions* (1922)

Sometime in the early 1930s, according to an article for a then widely circulating newsweekly, the *Literary Digest*, a display of fbdies had been assembled at Brooklyn's Kings County Hospital as "mute testimony to the resilience of the human stomach." The astonishing collection, described under the heading "museum" in the article, is no longer extant; all that remains is its media trace in "Iron Rations: Fakirs Swallow Swords, but Amateurs Take Cake Lunching on Hardware," a jaunty piece of journalism that presents the patient, Miss Mabel Wolf, as an amateur when compared to a knife-swallowing Indian magician, but one whose staggering feat far outstrips his. Each sentence is accompanied by a wink and a nudge as if to admit the extremity of her act while keeping all that is disturbing about it at bay. Mabel Wolf had swallowed a staggering 1,203 pieces of assorted hardware. "When she felt depressed," the journalist jokes, "she cheered herself up by indulging in a little nut-and-bolt snack." Wolf, who worked in a notions department in a New York store, arrived at the hospital in March 1934 and deposited (delivered? gave over or gave up? relinquished? manifested?) the following collection of fbdy Things:

588 fine upholstery-tacks	3 picture-frame hooks
144 carpet-tacks	2 large, bent safety-pins
2 chair-tacks	1 small safety pin
1 round-headed thumb tack	1 head of a nail
3 ordinary thumb tacks	3 brass nails
46 small screws	83 pins
6 medium screws	1 matted mass of hair
80 large screws	containing screws and pins
1 hook-shaped coat-hanger	59 assorted beads
30 small bolts	4 pieces of wire
47 larger bolts	89 pieces of glass
3 nuts	1 teacup handle

A close second to Wolf's mosaic glass and metal assortment was the collection retrieved from the insides of Mrs. Paul Pappas of Nyack, New York, who, "in February 1935 had 234 pieces of assorted hardware removed," including a "meat-skewer, teaspoons, pins, links of automobile chains and fragments of bed-springs" as well as "rounded and curved bits of glass in assorted sizes."

"Aim-inhibited eating." "Eating in the absence of nourishment." The "mouth's extraordinary virtuosity." These are phrases that appear in British psychoanalyst Adam Phillips's essay on a banal, peculiar, deeply pleasurable human habit—kissing—but they could just as easily serve as grounds for understanding such scarily self-penetrating acts as swallowing hardware. Miss Wolf and Mrs. Pappas aren't *eating*, per se. Theirs is a form of swallowing without chewing (there should be a word for it) since it's not "mastication," and it's not about nourishment, though it may indeed be about appetite. It points up the vitality of the mouth-hungry versus stomach-hungry distinction, and yet the stomach still plays a role—in this case, perhaps becoming a cabinet or drawer, an endlessly expansive tool chest, a place for stowing or hoarding and for keeping a collection, the self transformed into a warehouse complete with inventory.

Hysteria's stomach is like those one finds in myths and fairytales where human beings are swallowed whole, in which the stomach is not a place of digestion but of capture. In "Little Red Riding Hood," the stomach is a place from which you wait to be rescued; in Jonah and the Whale, it's a darkly separated interior where you hang out for an age, contemplating the nature of God. In these fantasies, the stomach functions more like a womb; or maybe the tales express a wish to enter another and not be changed in the process—to be held rather than digested, to be churned out rather than to be born. When a tack or nail or bolt goes in, the body (the self) becomes a place where things end rather than begin. And yet a world does emerge, even if you don't want it to, even if the upholstery-tack snack was only ever about getting the impossible *to go down*. If you swallow enough items, you can create a world, or someone else will do so for you, re-creating it according to his own taxonomy. Man and the creation of the human is necessitated by a woman's inability to resist putting something into her mouth. This is where the world begins—according to at least one famous account, it issues from the ingestion of a forbidden object.

The hysterical swallow relieves but does not satisfy. It seems to require a fixation, and it delivers much like a fix. It's a form of self-soothing, and a form of self-harm. When does it begin? Because there must be a first time, a moment when the first nonnutritive item goes in, but you might say, no, it's just a repetition of what one has always done, there's nothing new here. But, then again, yes, there is a difference here, the breaking of one habit by the establishment of a new one. Or maybe it's a mix: it's the continuation of something old, and the establishment of something new. The first time a bolt goes down is the culmination of a process that has been ongoing. After which nothing is the same.

We speak of an inner psychic reality, and I wonder where in the body we locate that entity if not in the head, and if it is commensurate with the place we reserve for the idea of the soul. For swallowers of hardware, the stomach seems to be the seat, center, inner sanctum, and nexus of significance, as though the mind has shrunk to the size of a pouch at the center of the self, and a one and only question of expansion and accommodation and contain-ability.

Tempting tolerance or elasticity, when people expect too much from us, we can experience our inability to meet their demands as a lack of capacity. "I've had it up to here!" we exclaim, hand held just beneath the chin as if to keep down a rising gorge. "I'm fed up!" we say, in place of "I'm angry" or "I'm frustrated," where anger and frustration are understood as having too much of something, of having something alien inside oneself. "I haven't yet taken it in" tells me that to face, accept, acknowledge, or realize demands incorporation. To make sense of something is to find a place for it *in me*, but the hysterical swallower challenges this model by redrawing the lines between what is supposed to be kept out and what is acceptable to let in, rendering what *should* remain outside and what *must* enter in ambiguous—or, for that matter, what should be confessed and what must be kept secret. Whether one "confesses" to what one has swallowed or not, whether swallowing brass nails, picture frame hooks, and teacup handles is something one does in the privacy of one's notion counter or something one does for everyone to see, whether this is something we do together or alone would seem significant, especially since the act appears so very isolating. What's worse? The hiding of a message inside oneself or the assumption of self-sufficiency, an attempt to be everything to oneself, when, in swallowing hundreds of pieces of hardware, a person meets her needs in ways that no one and nothing else can—or so she thinks.

The women in these cases from the 1920s and 1930s who swallowed hardware were not developmentally disabled, pregnant, or schizophrenic, as far as we know. I've opted for the term "hysteria" rather than "pica" in naming their malaise because it was the term that Jackson used to describe similar cases, but I wonder if these otherwise inexplicable and unimaginably motivated acts can be understood as instances of what Ian Hacking (1998) calls "transient mental illness"—and ones, in this case, for which there is no name—if swallowing hardware in quantities great or small exemplifies "an illness that appears at a time, in a place, and later fades away."

From a contemporary psychoanalytic point of view, the women in these cases were suffering from a surfeit of incorporations; taking into account the era in which they lived, their acts are an index of modern life. They could be Charlie Chaplin, whose lunch hour is being forfeited in *Modern Times* by a time-saving device. With the Billings Feeding Machine, the worker is strapped in place while a set of mechanical arms brings soup to his mouth and wipes it too, but the machine goes haywire and accidentally forces two bolts down his throat.

To swallow hardware is to swallow the entrails of machinery.

What was hardware anyway, in the machine age that preceded our own computer age of wares soft and hard? It was the stuff that held the machinery together, the minutiae that made possible the bridges and fences, the silos and chutes, rivets and tractors and lampposts. Who hasn't experienced the allure of the hardware store with its parts and cubbies, its taxonomies—"Would that be a hex bolt or a carriage bolt I'd be needing?"—its assurance that everything in the store fits into everything else: the hardware store as a life-size Erector Set. Inside any hardware store is a skyscraper waiting to be born. It's the "stuff" that keeps the humblest domicile together, and the everything required to build a new one. Inside any hardware store, important distinctions inhere: between tools, which are forever (like the simple fact of a hammer), and gadgets, which are of the moment (like talking bottle openers or pocket drill-bit holders).

I wonder if, when Mabel Wolf swallowed items from her notions counter, she heard the pound and speed of traffic through her window, or the click, punch, ring of her cash register, or the liquid screeching of steel on steel of a passing train, the *ping* of her counter's brass bell, or the rumble and hum of a nearby escalator, built on the same principle as the assembly line. In department stores, consumers are moved as swiftly as possible, the better to traverse the distance of so many things available for purchase; in the factories, the things are moved past the person-worker stilled into freeze frame as he adds his part to the thing again and again and again and again.

If you think hardware stores are reserved for male roaming and grazing and fiddling, consider how much more territorial are lumberyards, which are practically cultish, or car mechanics' offices with their obligatory *Play-boy* calendars. Department stores brought women into the public sphere to shop—to consume but not entirely to own—and as saleswomen to match in figure, face, and stance the type of store in which they operated. To meld. When a woman swallows hardware from a notions counter in the machine age, she announces the store's ordering system as delusional, she makes the immanent but not apparent grand plan of little things in boxes a jumble once again, a primordial mass inside her stomach. Literary historian Elaine Freedgood (in a work-in-progress on the nature of "thing-ness" in the Victorian age) wonders if an increasing identification between people and things expresses a desire to be more machinelike, and if to be more machinelike is to be self-regulating; to be insured, like a commodity; to be better connected to the world.

Were these female consumers (so to speak) trying to make themselves into that which was valued more highly than themselves—the machine—or were they attempting, in halting or bypassing or denying digestive processes, to slow the production line on which they played a subordinate part?

To my great sadness and surprise—I suppose because I had invested the Chevalier Jackson fbdy collection with the romance of the cabinet of curiosity—the original drawers in which the items were stowed were not wooden but metallic. They resembled industrial ware or army surplus furniture, a stand of interlocking toolboxes colored "vomit green" (as the Mütter Museum's administrative coordinator appropriately described them while showing me photographs). They didn't resemble a nineteenth-century doctor's medical chest, replete with pharmaceuticals in neat and colorful bottles, with recessed crannies and hidden slots for portable vials. They stood for the era in which the collection was founded—squarely situated in the industrial age. The newer, wooden set of drawers displaced the metal armature when the museum underwent renovation in the 1980s and reflects an attempt to better match the collection with the overarching aesthetic of the museum.

Jackson's work, as he understood it, was in many ways made possible by the machine age. In a 1935 article on "Benign Laryngeal Lesions," Jackson attributes the modern diseases of the throat he encounters in his practice to "the noise incidental to our modern life." The machine age is bound to cause voicelessness, it seems: "To talk in a subway train is utter ruin to the larynx," Jackson warns; "railroad trains, omnibuses or automobiles are almost as bad. Certainly to converse in the average city street involves abuse of the larynx." Over and against and in addition to these problems, women (and men) came to his practice beset by hardware. In a 1928 article for *Grit*, a photo of a pile of washers, nails, nuts, bolts, and screws forms a lurid mass atop the caption " 'Junk' Sidney Barne Had in His Stomach 27 Years." We don't learn if Sidney Barne's ingested hardware was a work hazard or if he can join the ranks of the women who swallowed hardware on purpose. A headshot of him staring up at a ceiling simply informs us, "And Here is Mr. Barne Himself."

Cases of purposeful swallowing in Jacksonian archives maintain an aura of sadness and distress. As in the case of Mrs. Nannie T.W. of Richmond, Virginia, who, at the age of forty-nine in 1927, attempted suicide by swallowing hairpins. The case study cites the woman's husband's death as the cause of her despondency and depression, and notes earlier attempts either to starve herself or to harm herself: "ate some glass with no harmful after-effects," "X-ray was taken and revealed a penny in the stomach . . . which patient states she swallowed one week ago." Examination is difficult due to the "highly nervous state of the patient," and though a "Dr. Royster closely questioned pt.," she "refused to answer."

Alongside Mrs. W., we could place nineteen-year-old Anna M. of Utica, New York, who, more dramatically and symbolically, swallowed a crucifix with several beads attached to a rosary chain, which lodged in her cervical esophagus. Endoscopy exacts a removal of the Thing but fails to help her otherwise, describing her as "apparently mentally unstable," hailing from a history of familial insanity, presenting with teeth that are stained and bloody, and needing to be subdued with morphine owing to her becoming "violently insane" following the removal of the foreign body: "She attempted to injure the nurse and scratched her severely." Like Mrs. W., Anna M. "will make no attempt to answer questions or to speak." The coincidence of purposeful swallowing with the loss of voice, in the figurative and not just the literal sense, in the willful and not the accidental sense, is a reminder of hysteria's (mis)use of the body to say what can otherwise not be said.

Let us take stock: what we need to understand about hysterical swallowers is that they are not *eating* hardware, they are *swallowing* hardware—they have separated out one function from another. I need to be able to swallow in order to eat, but not all swallowing is in the service of eating. There are numerous ways to understand what is happening here, none of which is equivalent with the other: a bodily function that is usually integrated is cut off; something reserved for one function is pressed into the service of another and becomes exaggerated or takes on hyperbolic significance. Even to begin to render the hardware gobbler intelligible, we need to be able to acknowledge forms of ingestion that don't have digestion in mind, forms of inhalation that don't have breathing in mind, forms of intake that don't have incorporation in mind, or those instances where mouthing becomes more important to the organism than eating. Take, for example, smoking—we enjoy inhaling something other than oxygen for its pleasurable effects—chewing gum, or sucking tobacco. We swallow a great many things in the course of a day, week, or month without eating those things and with more or less thought involved in the process—consider saliva, phlegm, or cum. We have trouble understanding why someone would ingest hardware, but we name dishes on diner menus "The Kitchen Sink." (Stranger yet, we live in an era of vomit- and booger-flavored jelly beans— call it *Harry Potter* product placement.)

To perfect one's ability to swallow without eating is to make oneself independent of the world outside of one: it's as though the hardware needs the person, or at least the body—the gullet that can withstand it or the stomach that can contain it—more than the body needs the hardware, in the way that a person needs food in order to live. A hysterical swallower doesn't need hardware in order to live, but she needs it in order to desire. In which case, her existence depends upon it.

A student of mine once wrote a fascinating essay on the array of mustaches a man could sport, the many ways in which a mustache could change a man's face and even signal a repertoire of manly types. Not until I heard the student read the essay in public did I notice that when she referred to facial hair on a man, she spoke of his "mouth" ("mustache" and "mouth" must be etymologically related), but when she referred to facial hair on women, she used the word "lips" (the phrases "hairy lip" and "lip mop" were especially prominent). Mouths and lips are definitely not the same, and it occurred to me that the student was onto something, some taken-for-granted insight about the gendering of orifices, some illumination of the matter of what bodies we're allowed by virtue of the bifurcated genders we're ascribed.

To insist on differences between men and women usually does no favors to either sex. Still, I wondered if it were possible that, culturally speaking, men had mouths and women had lips. Where lips emit and perform, mouths desire, grasp, and get. Mouths swallow, whereas lips blow, as in "Put your lips together and . . ." To mouth words might mean to say them without meaning them, but mouths are more about the fulfillment of desire than are lips. Lips pay lip service. Lips kiss, curl upward, or frown. Women's genitals are thought of as lips—terminologically, the labia and the labile are liplike. Which doesn't mean they are malleable or facile, though these words seem to be kin. Women's lips are injected with silicone—the better to pleasure you with. To say "she has a mouth on her" is to imply an illicit relationship to language, as if a woman can only have a mouth when she's saying something mean or dirty—in which case the mouth is very unladylike and does not become her.

A truly masculine man's lips are not supposed to purse (nor are they supposed to pout), but when men get clubby, behind closed doors, they can be femmie with each other in ways they'd never permit in public. This is how I imagine a glee club of ear, nose, and throat specialists preoccupied with asserting the manliness of their profession—their authorial protocol—at the same time that they cozied up to one another to sing pep-rally songs like a group of giggling girls. At their annual meetings, members of the Triological Society, aka the American Laryngological, Rhinological, and Otological Society, apparently crooned like barbershop quartets songs that they'd written in honor of Chevalier Jackson.

Imagine the white-tie, black-tail gathering at which John Finch Barnhill proclaimed his "Introduction of the Living Ex-Presidents of the American Laryngological, Rhinological and Otological Society." He presented Jackson with the following bit of doggerel, recited at a dinner in the honor of ex-presidents at the Hotel Raleigh, Washington, D.C., on May 4, 1928:

Chev. Jackson's is a name on which
It's easy to make verse,
Because the name has spread around
The entire universe.
In America or Europe,
In Australia or Cathay

All foreign bodies are removed
The à la Jackson way.
Now Jack can slip a bronchoscope
Into a bronchiole
As deftly as an artisan
Pounds sand into a hole;
And can take out bits of hardware—
Till the numbers mount and mount—
As easy as a bride elect
Can spend a bank account.

It's interesting that out of all the work that Jackson was known for—from tracheotomy to new diagnostic procedures, from lye legislation to the perfecting of the instrumentarium—the verse in his honor chooses to highlight a case like that of the unknown woman in the Glore display, a hysterical imbiber of vast amounts of hardware. Did Jackson even ever treat such a case as Mabel Wolf's or Mrs. Pappas's? It's not clear that he did, but such examples seem to yield the greatest entertainment value for a group of doctors bent on securing medicine as a male domain. This isn't high art, to be sure; it's more like the fodder Freud so well exploited in *Jokes and Their Relation to the Unconscious*, because the poem certainly performs, in condensed fashion, a whole host of regressive fears and anxieties and even ventures its own interpretation of hysterical swallowing. By evoking the bride-elect's spending capabilities, the verse likens the hysterical swallower to a hyperconsumer who will waste what her husband earns, squander what he banks, and accumulate hardware with the same fervor with which she spends coins.

Lyrics from the 1911 *Triological Songbook*, from the society's seventeenth annual meeting, held in Atlantic City, are even more elaborate in their misogyny. Someone hits middle C on a piano and the bright-faced singing physicians begin:

Poor Mary was a sufferer,
    Poor Mary was insane.
Poor Mary filled her lungs with things
    Which ne'er came up again.
Poor Mary had a hankering
    For hardware on the brain,
Poor Mary's taste was queer. . . .

Chorus (after each verse):
Smoothly, smoothly slips the tube in,
    Brightly, brightly burns the light,
Quickly, quickly pass the forceps,
    When all is working right . . .

Chevalier was called in haste
    Poor Mary to relieve.
Soon he came with all his kit,
    Great wonders to achieve.
The first assistant took her place,
    A stop watch on her sleeve,
The time to ascertain.

Down went the speculum,
    Down went the swab;
Down went the bronchoscope,
    For Jack was on the job;
Down went the forceps,
    Mary's lungs to rob,
Then down and down again . . .

Cheva-Cheva-Chevalier
Cheva-Cheva-Chevalier,
Cheva-Cheva-Chevalier,
Your fame is marching on.

   Once again the hysteric serves as centerpiece to an evening's entertainment just after cocktails and before dinner and cigars, during the party portion of a day spent delivering papers and discussing advances in the field. The woman hardware swallower is chosen over the scores of quirky, curious, strange, or stirringly oddball cases the songsters could have drawn from. The stopwatch really does bring home Taylorism and the factory context of such acts, the relation between Jackson's methods and then-popular efficiency studies, measuring of workdays, and standardizing of time/output quotients. But the remainder of the song adds the creepy dimension of a male doctor inserting something into a woman for sport.
   How could Jackson have responded to these boys' club cheers—he who was bullied for his outsider status for the better part of his childhood? He

who in so many ways cut a figure of unmasculine manliness? Could he possibly have liked this form of adulation, or did he feel he was being made to
participate in the kind of savage cheering—"Cheva-Cheva-Chevalier"—
that he warned was ruining many a football fan's voice in those days? I first
encountered this song in the John Quincy Adams Library of Otolaryngology in Alexandria, Virginia, but a second, longer version came to light
in the Smithsonian's collection of Jacksoniana, which I only discovered
because of Jackson's handwritten instructions to turn the page over, as
though he had anticipated a future reader and fellow appreciator of these
lines, which are to be sung to the tune of "John Brown's Body":

Down went a button first,
   Then down went a pin;
Down went a peanut,
   Deftly breathèd in;
Down went a toothpick,
   Which somewhere else had been;
And then down went a cent.

   . . .

So quickly slid the bronchoscope
   Deep into Mary's lung
At most but half a second passed
   Before the deed was done.
And then in but a second more
   Strange things were on the run
From Mary's deepest depths.

Up came the button first,
   Then up came the bone;
Up came the pin again,
   Up came a stone.
But, when he fished the toothpick out,
   Poor Mary gave a moan,
Her dearest treasure gone.

About the further course of things
   But little need be said;

For Mary had a free movement
   And freely vomitèd
Soon Mary had a hardware shop
   Around her in the bed,
Nothing was left but gas.

Final Chorus:
Cheva-Cheva Chevalier
Cheva-Cheva-Chevalier
Cheva-Cheva-Chevalier
Your fame is marching on.

I'm struck by how this song explodes into a celebration of bodily effluvia (vomit and gas); how it pictures the woman as a kind of automaton or burping doll who coughs up all manner of stuff if handled and shook enough, if properly acted upon for a marveling audience's delight. "Strange things were on the run / From Mary's deepest depths"—that's a suggestive line, but it might be more indicative of the psychic mayhem, the id-like upheaval, the competing thoughts and feelings that had run amok in the minds of the medical men who wrote and performed the song, than reflective in any significant way of what women who lunched on hardware were trying and failing to cope with.

Imagine a woman naked but for her foreign bodies (see figure 29). At

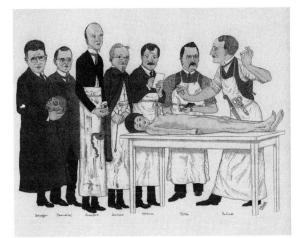

Fig. 29. A detail from the 1923 C. Miksch caricature of Jefferson Medical College faculty with Chevalier Jackson fourth from left. Courtesy of Thomas Jefferson University, Archives and Special Collections.

the head of the table on which the naked woman lies, distinguished only by her rings, pert nipples, and a fetching spit curl that mimics the curvature of a stomach, stands Chevalier Jackson. The head of the table would be the proper place for him, since he must stand behind her head in order to enter in. He wears a cape in lieu of a jacket, a paean to his effeteness (or to his love of France) and suited to his goatee. His right hand pulls on the fourth finger of his left hand the way a baby might suck on a thumb: the pose bespeaks some mild embarrassment over the long arrowhead of the bronchoscope that hangs in front of him and to one side. Here Jackson is part of an all-male lineup, a pantheon of faculty of Jefferson Medical College sketched by a Dr. C. Miksch in 1923 in imitation of Adrien Barrère's "Nude Lady," a caricature of a similarly posed Medical Faculty of Paris dating from 1906–7. Each man appears in caricature, his face collapsed beneath crinkled brows and sternly pursed lips. Not only are these men not naked; they are actually overdressed, each one provided with an accoutrement representing his medical specialty, the organ or body part as emblem of the branch of medicine to which he is devoted. Most wear a kind of blood-bespattered winding sheet atop their suits rather than a lab coat, the joke perhaps being that they may as well be butchers rather than doctors. The figure at the head of the table, DaCosta, wears a full apron into which is tucked an enormous pair of scissors and a butcher knife. He leans over the woman with the forefinger and thumb of both of his hands pinched together in the manner of a chef about to prepare the female patient for cooking rather than for operating. Or maybe just for seasoning prior to chopping. The strange presence of the woman's jewelry on her otherwise stripped-down body makes her nakedness all the more apparent, obvious, and humorous.

At least two women endoscopists worked alongside Jackson in the course of his career: Ellen Patterson, his closest female colleague in Pittsburgh, and Emily van Loon, his closest female colleague in Philadelphia. It's hard to imagine all that they had to negotiate in order even to inhabit the role of doctor or to carry out their work. This patently sexist centerfold—or, more to the point, panorama—is hardly an urtext in the history of medical misogyny, but it serves as an apt bookend or frame for the sorts of songs and ditties found in the annals of the Triological Society. It points up the extent to which practitioners of the healing arts came to confuse science with sexual mastery, intent on keeping others, and outsiders, in their respectively abject places.

Something happens in the history of having a body and examining bodies that makes possible even as an *idea* the insertion of a rigid metal tube into the esophagus and later into the bronchial tubes. Something, too, happens in the history of having a body and examining bodies that makes possible as an *idea* the swallowing of huge amounts of hardware. Jackson daily put hardware into people's gullets and called it an advance in medical science; wielding his rigid scopes, he was a pioneer on a bold new frontier. Women put hardware into gullets as well; it was considered a perversion entirely apart from Jackson's practice, a psychopathology. We could say that what distinguishes Jackson's act from that of hysterics was that he was sublimating—he obsessively inserted hardware, yes, but he did it in the name of a higher, greater good. Is the difference really that clear-cut, though? Are hysterics simply perverting something wholly reasonable, transforming it into an abomination, or is there more going on that we cannot easily account for?

Which came first? The swallowing of hardware by depressed women, or the insertion of hardware into the human gullet as a new form of healing art? I believe that the advent of esophagoscopy and bronchoscopy made possible the swallowing of hardware, and that their coincidence is a result of a new way of thinking about the body: of apprehending the body as a machine. If the model of body-as-machine is traceable to the seventeenth century and Descartes, the body's machinic incarnation was newly attenuated in the late nineteenth century; by then, as Carolyn Thomas de la Pena notes, "it was common for books on popular health to refer to hearts as 'motors' or 'pumps' and food as 'fuel.'" Acknowledging, as we must, that various forms of instruments were introduced into the body's orifices as early as Greco-Roman times doesn't let us off the hook of discerning historical difference: the question that drives the need that forms the desire that incites the interest *to enter in* does not remain the same across millennia, or across cultures, and the endoscope as we know it is a product of modernity.

Ralph Major's wonderful essay on the history of the stomach tube documents ancient objects that range from feathers to long leather glove fingers stuffed with wool to, in the sixteenth century, hollow, perforated tubes made of lead, silver, or copper, but these were mainly evacuative and not examining devices. A Roman used a feather to relieve himself from overeating; a kind of artificial finger was used to purge, cleanse, or to expel a poison. Other types of early instruments were used to push a fbdy or caught food into the stomach, or, crudely, to catch hold of fishbones stuck in the throat, but most of Major's examples are devices that served the purposes of cleansing or emptying the stomach of its contents. In a sense, these instruments were aiding a natural process or stimulating a reflex (to help a person to vomit), whereas the insertion of Jackson's rigid tubes required that the body's reflexes be subverted or subdued.

We are in the realm of thresholds and of distinctions, because there is a difference, isn't there, between one's body being entered by a manufactured tool and one's body being entered by the body of another—by tongue, penis, or hand, or by another person's words, a voice inserted into an ear and down a throat. Is it personal predilection or acculturation that renders us docile in the face of invasive medical procedures—which is to say, most medical procedures in the Western world? What makes dentistry so unpleasant to most people is that it involves the insertion of instruments into the most delicate and vital and precarious of bodily orifices. Would we rest easier at the dentist if he were able to do his work using only his hands? I think I'd prefer flesh on flesh to metal probes inside my mouth, but maybe I'd most happily opt for neither. The speculum, that famously unseen instrument, is every woman's nightmare. The "speculum" is in fact misnamed because it is not a mirror (as its etymology implies) but is, in a sense, like a bronchoscope, an instrument that makes possible a direct rather than a reflected view and that requires a secondary light source. Doctors were initially more willing to put instruments into the orifices down below than those above, and some of the first esophagoscopes were based on scopes for examining the urethra and bladder. Again, what would you prefer? For your gynecologist to open you with her hands or with her instrument? Or maybe not to open you at all?

Products of the industrial age, Jackson's tools have examination, visual exploration, manipulation, and mastery in mind. They are first and foremost scopes—and ones that fulfill an interest in peering into the *living* body. The long view of endoscopy as a practice shows it to be a product of the Enlightenment, and the history of endoscopic instruments to be inextricable from the history of light. Endoscopy as an idea is literally driven by a desire to bring light into darkness—to see one's way in the dark—and to test the limits of the human perceptual apparatus to, if properly applied, see further, clearer, more fully and entirely into realms otherwise reserved for a higher power.

Phillip Bozzini, who between 1803 and 1808 developed what is considered the first true endoscope, virtually defined the instrument as a vehicle of light in the very name that he gave to it—he called what he had designed the *Lichtleiter*, or "light conductor." Medical historian James Edmonson's indispensable article "History of the Instruments for Gastrointestinal Endoscopy" describes the trial and error that accompanied various lighting systems in endoscopy's history: candles reflected in mirrors, oil lamps and alcohol-turpentine mixtures, the burning of magnesium wires and loops of platinum charged with an electrical current that proved so hot that a cooling system was also required. Each of these methods deterred potential endoscopists and discouraged endoscopic development until 1879, when Edison's incandescent electric light offered an unsurpassed possibility for peering inside. The substitution of platinum wire with a tiny incandescent bulb in 1886 rendered an instrument designed by Johann von Mikulicz "the first truly usable esophagoscope," according to Edmonson. In Jackson's scopes, the distal lamp (or light carrier, as it was also called) consisted of a handmade battery-charged lamps the size of a grain of wheat mounted at the end of an exceedingly thin rod that was slipped inside the scope. Sleekly penetrating and perfectly luminous, it's no wonder that Jackson named one of his scopes "the velvet eye" (*B&E*, 27; see figure 30).

When Jackson accesses the body via one of his famous bronchoscopes, he is moved not only by the visual display the device affords but by the part the instrument allows him to play in a grand machinic process.

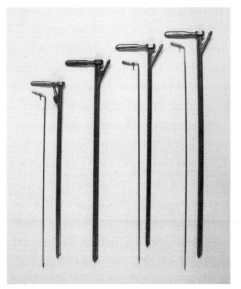

Fig. 30. An array of scopes from Jackson's vast instrumentarium with accompanying distal lights. Collection of the Mütter Museum, The College of Physicians of Philadelphia.

The particular problem that Jackson faces is a body imagined as a machine that is not equipped to process the foreign object that has fallen into it. Jackson, in turn, makes the body—via deft positioning of head, neck, and throat, the acts of assistants upon the body, and an inventive set of instruments that he introduces into the body—into another kind of machine, one from which the foreign object can be extracted nonsurgically.

Although Jackson removed foreign bodies through the mouth without surgery and engineered forms of entering the body without cutting into it, his procedures are not really "operations" in the strict sense of the word, yet he called the room in which the ingested items were removed the operating room, and the doctor who performed the removal was not the surgeon but the "operator." What exactly is the doctor operating if not operating *on* something? Is he operating the instruments or the body-as-machine into which they have been inserted, or both?

Here's an illustrative tale: to demonstrate the need for legislation to protect children against the ingestion of lye, Jackson photographed himself next to a particular type of machine—a wooden-cogged mortise wheel and iron pinion known as a "man-eater." What was the logic here? Jackson explained that "arms, heads, or anything that got caught in the inmeshing side of the gears [of this machine] *went through*," thus eventuating the requirement that this "dangerous machinery" be guarded by screens and covers. Jackson used the machine to emphasize, by contrast, the lack of legislation to protect children from the dangers of lye. The connection is made by inverse analogy: the mortise wheel, an inorganic thing, has the ability to "eat" a person; and a person has the ability to "eat" an inorganic thing. In both cases, something has gotten into the machine (mortise wheel or body) that wasn't meant for it, necessitating prophylactic measures, protective screens that, in the case of real machines, might work, but in the case of human bodies, much to Jackson's frustration, almost always failed.

Here's Chevalier Jackson as foreman, hoping to monitor ingestion like clockwork. There he is intervening at the scene of a body's irregular inspiration hoping to restore the smooth functioning of interrupted cogs.

By inserting rigid tubes into people's gullets in order to examine their insides, he was reinventing the body as a kind of machine, but its protective reflexes had to be disabled in order for his tools to enter in. He was a master of getting people and their bodies to cooperate without being cut. The very image his patients had to have of their bodies in order to allow Chevalier Jackson his work is the same image that a woman capable of swallowing hardware had to have of hers: a body that could expand and withstand (in medical terms, a body that could "tolerate") all manner of parts. Were hysterical hardware swallowers simply rehearsing what medicine in the machine age was heralding and propounding as inevitable? Readying themselves for the next machinic insertion, and the next.

Therefore I do not much wonder that the Ostridge can eat and digest iron. . . . Leo Africanus saith, that they swallow whatsoever they finde, even iron. . . . As for Pliny, he saith plainly, that it concocteth whatsoever it eateth. Now the Doctor acknowledgeth it eats iron: Ergo, according to Pliny, it concocts Iron.

—ALEXANDER ROSS,
Arcana Microcosmi (1652), book 2, chapter 8

For more than 2,000 years the sword swallower had solved the problem of the stretching of the mouth-pharynx angle. This teaches us modesty! . . . Notwithstanding the fact that they have rendered good services to the development of esophagoscopy, there is hardly any literature on sword swallowers. Now . . . there is certainly a reason to give credit to them because this interesting guild will probably soon be extinct. . . . We have come a long way from Kussmaul to Jackson.

—EELCO HUIZINGA,
"On Esophagoscopy and Swordswallowing"

The taboo which has been violated is, perhaps, one of the oldest known to human beings—that the interior recesses of the body are not merely private to others, but peculiarly private—that is expressly forbidden—to the owner or inhabiter of the body.

—JONATHAN SAWDAY, *The Body Emblazoned*

That some people have taken to swallowing Velcro at first seems hard to believe until you think about the deeply satisfying press-and-rip aspect of that substance, the way it mimics eating with its tiny teeth, or enmeshing, or textured attaching and holding in place. Perhaps those who swallow Velcro are convinced the act might lend them some of its clearly magical properties. Velcro probably feels good on the way down in that indescribable way, like a backscratcher meeting the itch of an otherwise unreachable spot. Researchers of pica don't appear to be kidding when they designate people who like to ingest blood "Draculas," rather than invent a more official-sounding *-phagia* for them. Velcro and blood seem far afield, yet both are specific enough to make us realize how acts of swallowing leave new forms of identity in their wake: is a Velcron like a Klingon or someone less strange, as neighborly as the man next door? And when was the last time *you* admitted to or checked your own vampiric tendencies?

One type of human swallow can be likened to a disappearing act, as in the case of a vaudevillian who ate glass, matchbooks and lit matches, flowers (stems and all), and an entire newspaper without a hint of where it all went. (Did he really swallow that stuff or just pretend to?) Another type entails repeatedly swallowing a pellet tied to a string. Over a number of years and with recourse to increasingly larger pellets, a person can enjoy a throat pouch suitable for smuggling things, and thus the possible exploitation of the body as a truly secretive place.

Swallowing *acts*. Swallowing *tricks*. Swallowing as a form of defiance. Swallowing as a test case for the limits of sense and nonsense, as in the example of "H.F., male, aged twenty-three years," who, according to the 1922 *New York Medical Journal and Medical Record*, was "showing a little boy the trick of inserting a penny into his nose and withdrawing it from the mouth. He thrust it too far back and it became impacted in the upper esophagus." E.L., a seven-year-old contemporary of H.F., exerted an impish, stubborn use of the mouth when, "in the course of an argument as to who should carry the money," herself or her sister, as they walked to the store, she "swallowed a twenty-five cent piece. She was seen five days after the quarter went down."

Should I believe myself or believe the instrument that examines me and, which, in entering me, reads me? Does it tell me *my* truth? Does it see me fully and conclusively? Apparently "hysterical," "S.S., female aged thirty-nine years presented with the inability to swallow anything and the conviction of a tumor" that "she localized below the clavicle." Esophagoscopy presumably cured her by passing the tube under local anesthesia into her throat. At the aperture that is the mouth, we therefore see enacted a battle over belief. Teetering on a threshold of the real, she is convinced by the instrument that something is open rather than closed, available to light rather than dark, passable rather than impassable, fluent rather than blocked. But does it clear everything up? Is the application of medicine's instrumentarium entirely demystifying?

There are spectacular swallows and celebrity swallows, and spectacular swallows that make people overnight celebrities, but what kind of star is born of an unusual ability to swallow? Chevalier Jackson saw Bing Crosby once or twice as a patient, treating the overworked singer's throat. You can discover this in Crosby's biography but not in any of Jackson's work. Notoriety of this sort did not interest Jackson in the least. Other celebrities' swallowing accidents postdated the life of Chevalier Jackson. Places are reserved in the popular imagination for Elizabeth Taylor's chicken bone, Jimi Hendrix's vomit, and Mama Cass's (apocryphal) ham sandwich. In Cass's case, the coroner, confusing Cass with a kind of circus Fat Lady, concluded that she died of self-engorgement when in fact the ham sandwich she was supposed to have inhaled sat by her bed, untouched. Cass died of heart failure, possibly brought on not from overeating but by the numerous crash diets she was compelled to pursue.

There's Ronald Reagan's peanut kernel, George W. Bush's pretzel stick, Carrie Fisher's brussels sprout, and Cher's vitamin pill—these all appear together in a 2006 *Talk of the Town* story in the *New Yorker* about the independent film *Choking Man*. The article centers on a bizarre coincidence: Mandy Patinkin, star of the film, finds himself choking on a piece of Caesar salad and is saved by the Heimlich maneuver, fast on the heels of doing a good deal of research on various "asphyxiation scenarios" in preparing for his role.

Then there's an entertainer whom no one today remembers but who was known in his time as the Human Ostrich. A 1922 article by George G. Hopkins in the *Brooklyn Medical Journal* describes a man who worked as a "freak" at one of the "cheap shows" in New York. He was in the habit of swallowing things that members of the audience would pass up to the stage. Regularly, in an evening's performance, he would swallow "80 pins . . . and a lot of hair pins and long wire nails, most of which passed through him without doing any harm." What brings him to the offices of Dr. Hopkins is the (more or less) accidental ingestion of a four-foot-long window chain. Usually, he performed with the chain attached to a string: first swallowing the chain, and then pulling it back out of his mouth by the string to which it was attached, as though flossing the center of his being. On this night, he lost his grasp of the string.

Dr. Hopkins is incredulous before the Human Ostrich until he fishes around in his feces, from which he recovers "two horseshoe nails, one wire nail, and 19 ordinary pins." "Hoping to get some more of his intestinal hardware," the doctor feeds him some bread and crackers followed by cathartics. His patient, in tremendous pain, begged for Hopkins to operate on him, and he did, and he discovered, upon opening his stomach, the following inventory: "129 pins, 6 hair-pins, two horseshoe nails, 12 half-inch wire nails, 2 door-keys, 3 chains, and a large ring."

Hopkins's article is accompanied by a long and narrow collage assembled after the surgery that resembles a hieroglyphic tablet or a kind of Dead Sea Scroll of the stomach in need of an interpreter. The Human Ostrich, chastened by his medical ordeal, decides that "he will not swallow any more truck" but will instead "spend his time selling pictures of the cut" the surgeon's "knife inflicted on his stomach." "The object lesson concerning the limitations of the human digestive tract" (in the doctor's words) was, however, lost on the Ostrich—as was, I'm sure, the pun in the phrase "object lesson"—because the nineteen-year-old youth returns to the hospital in a few months' time with more stuff inside him. Was it really the case that swallowing objects had become compulsive for him, though, or was it that the audience couldn't stand *not* to see him swallow things, having gotten used to his particularly graphic performance? He went to the hospital after a group of men recognized him in a bar and forced him to swallow "2 wire nails four inches long, an ordinary nail, and a piece of bone two inches long."

He refuses a second operation and claims his pains have subsided, leaving us to imagine him walking in the direction of certain death, beyond the doctor's office door, into unsafe streets and even less safe entertainment halls. The swallowing man is a caricature of celebrity: too recognizable, he is open to punishment for his daringly self-penetrating acts, destined to repeat what his audience can't bear to watch and yet can't keep themselves from wanting (because isn't it ambivalence that drives such titillation?), needing him to perform for them at all costs like diabolical babies insistent that the adults throw the ball, tickle them under the chin, or play patty-cake once more, delirious with the pleasure of their new word: "Again!"

The Human Ostrich seemed to perfect his act onstage, discovering what he was capable of with each new performance, but a special place needs to be reserved for the sword swallower who stands before us only after years of practice in private. No one "spots" for the sword swallower: he's not an acrobat, though he has been grouped alongside the *saltimbanco*—literally, from the Italian, a person who jumps or somersaults onto a bench. The sort of performer who stops traffic to claim your attention, who interrupts the proper use of a bench by making it into a stage, who subsequently lures you in and, like a charlatan, cons you in some way. Most sword swallowers also obviously use a piece of the object world in unanticipated ways, but they aren't illusionists: they want you to believe, yes, but what they want you to believe is horrifyingly real.

In what furtive corner of a day—with the shades drawn or raised—does the sword swallower ply his trade? I picture the novitiate in the bathroom, basement, or garage, or perhaps the type of seedy chamber built of concrete blocks where boys perfect an unknown martial art. An open field will do if sufficiently far from people set before their easels, people running with kites, or throwing Frisbees on a green. Plein air might be perfect for this act that raises ceilings and looks to the sky, but I can only imagine a tiny room of banishment inside a domestic scene as the sword swallower's proving ground. I picture a utility closet where no one expects to find him—he's hardly missed—but out from which, in time, he emerges triumphant. Daily and for years he strikes the pose: the attitude of any number of ecstatics and ascetics and saints: the head thrown back beyond repose, and then the sword thrust in . . . but only after the head's thrown back, almost as a punishment for ecstasy rather than its source.

It's hard to say whether sword swallowing is on the decline or on the rise: a renowned performer named Dan Meyer (aka Halfdan, an old Viking name for "Half Danish") is one of the few practitioners left in the world, but he can't keep up with the demand for shows in every part of the world. Meyer came to sword swallowing expressly as an alternative to magic; not only are the swords he swallows quite real, but, he jokes, the act requires "pinpoint accuracy and razor-sharp concentration." The range of arenas that showcase his work is wide: from a spot on "Food Magic," an episode of *Unwrapped* on the Food Network, to gigs before scientists at Cambridge University, Harvard, MIT, Oxford, and Imperial College; from appearances in Ripley's Odditorium to shows for the Wellcome Trust, London's prestigious library for the history of medicine; from demonstrations for videos like *99 Most Bizarre Self-Inflicted Injuries* to inspirational, motivational, and even religious venues.

It's fascinating to see Meyer adapt his work to suit the occasion. Performing a sword-swallowing act before a Christian audience, he prefaces his show with a compelling set of analogies between Jesus and himself: just as Jesus was thought to be a magician by those who didn't believe, so are sword swallowers. But Jesus said, "Blessed are those who have seen and believed; even more blessed are those who have not seen and yet believed." Like Jesus, Meyer will risk his life to make an impact on your life (which isn't to say he expects to die on stage, but that he might). Sword swallowing, he explains, is a perfect example of the amazing work of God, he who fashioned such an incredible thing as a human body capable of swallowing swords. Like a sword swallower, all Christians could afford to be more real, Meyer explains: this, not magic, is how to bring people into the fold. Pushing the string of metaphors further, he closes by describing the word of God as the sword of the spirit, and recommending that we try to swallow the word of God each day.

"Laugh, then think" is the motto of the Ig Nobel Prize committee, a group that celebrates science's eccentric side and has honored Meyer. Organized by the Annals of Improbable Research, Ig Nobel Prize events have featured the inventors of the plastic yard flamingo and of karaoke. They've honored physicists studying how sheets become wrinkled, chemists working on extracting vanilla from cow dung, linguists studying the problem of the word "the" for anyone trying to create an index, nutritionists "looking into the seemingly boundless appetites of human beings by feeding them with a self-refilling, bottomless bowl of soup," and the inventors of a "centrifugal-force birthing machine" that, according to the *Guardian*, "spins pregnant women at high speed." The Ig Nobel Peace Prize for 2007 went to an Ohioan group that had instigated "research on a chemical weapon to make enemy soldiers sexually irresistible to each other," while the prize for aviation went to an Argentinean group for the "discovery that Viagra aids jetlag recovery in rats." Meyer and the British radiologist Brian Witcombe won the prize for medicine in 2007 for an article they co-wrote for the *British Medical Journal*, "Sword Swallowing and Its Side Effects."

"In non-medical terms," Dan quips in an appearance on the Food Network, "I cram two feet of solid steel down to tickle the bottom of my tummy." In medical terms, what he does is much less whimsical and staggeringly complex. On a Web site he runs for the Sword Swallower's Association International, Meyer describes how

> physically, in medical terms, the blade goes into the mouth, the epiglottis must be flipped open, the alignment and placement must be just right, so that the blade goes into the glottal chamber behind the prominentia laryngea, the voice box, past the pharynx, through the cricopharyngeus or upper esophageal sphincter (UES), down the esophagus, between the lungs, nudge aside the heart, past the liver, relax the lower esophageal sphincter (LES) so the blade goes into the stomach at or near the duodenum—each step must be done correctly and very precisely—one slightly wrong move and you could puncture any of those organs and kill yourself.

In ever more exacting terms, the sword swallower alters the shape and direction and relationality of mouth to throat to esophagus to stomach, as a book excerpted on Dan's Web site titled *Bizarre Medical Abnormalities* explains: "In the first place the head is thrown back so that the mouth is in the direction of the esophagus, the curves of which disappear or become less as the sword proceeds; the angle that the esophagus makes with the stomach is obliterated and finally the stomach is distended in the vertical diameter and its internal curve disappears, thus permitting the blade to traverse the greater diameter of the stomach . . ."

Amazingly, two reflexes are brought under the sword swallower's control: the gag reflex (which prevents passage of unwanted, forced, or inedible substances down the throat), and the retch reflex (which prevents passage of the same into the stomach). Bright-eyed, blond-haired, ever-energized Meyer adds that the peristaltic reflex—the twenty-two pairs of muscles that move the bolus of food down the esophagus—must also be brought under his control. These reflexes are, in Meyer and Whitcomb's words, "desensitized," while the pharynx, esophagus, and horizontal fibers of the cricopharyngeus, "which are not usually under voluntary control," need to be relaxed. Without this "relaxing"—though "relax" cannot really capture the transformation of the body by a sword swallower—the throat can close up, a person can become asphyxiated, or a sword could even get stuck in its human sheath.

Dan talks about the control of reflexes as the place where the psyche enters in, in a mind-over-matter sort of way, but I don't know if the mind and the body can be so neatly severed in making sense of what the sword swallower's body becomes, what he masters and what he serves, and all else that is going on at the scene of the sword swallower's body—which is really a culmination of a series of previous acts—that the mere spectator doesn't really see.

Chevalier Jackson was often keen to point out that the esophagus is the most intolerant of human viscera. Poulet (that nineteenth-century compendia maker whom we visited earlier) would have disagreed, as he emphasized how the purposeful swallowing of fbdies "shows how great the tolerance of the digestive canal may become through habit." Jackson claimed a failure to understand that, in order to develop a habit which is pleasurable, a person might have to put the body through unpleasurable paces, to overcome an initial distaste in order to acquire a new taste. "Everyone knows that to learn the tobacco habit requires overcoming distaste and nausea. Why do it?" he asks (*LCJ*, 171). It's as though Jackson cannot understand masochism but only sadism, or he cannot fathom the human enmeshment of pleasure and unpleasure. But this entry through a painfully difficult, seemingly impossible set of doors in order to arrive at a place more exquisitely painful is what sword swallowing is all about. The audience to one of Dan Meyer's performances witnesses a shocking act that lasts but a few seconds. The act is powerful, but so long as we don't think beyond the moment of its startle, a disconnect maintains between the spectacle and the potentially more powerful, strange, and compelling route the sword swallower had to take to get there. What the sword swallower keeps to himself, what he does not publicly perform but which might be more meaningful than the culminating thrust is the self-disciplining, acclimating, retraining, and reconditioning of the body that he pursues via "practice" twelve times a day for at least three years before being able to swallow a sword.

We see the lunge and plunge, but we don't see the disciplining of the body, the radical reorganizing achieved, the familiarization with intrusion, the overriding of tendencies of the autonomic nervous system, the establishment of an independence of parts—in short, an overturning of what most of us think of as a nonmanipulable real (in which case, the sword swallower *does* perform a kind of magic). He brings under control what is not supposed to be controllable. He's a submissive (he throws his head back), and he's a master (he thrusts his sword), all at the same time. He is self-taught, but how can we describe his resulting expertise? He's an expert in himself as his greatest obstacle.

"The gag reflex is desensitized," Meyer and Witcombe explain, "sometimes by repeatedly putting fingers down the throat, but other objects are used including spoons, paintbrushes, knitting needles, and plastic tubes before the swallower commonly progresses to a bent wire coat hanger." It's possible, then, that hysterics who swallowed large quantities of hardware in different shapes and sizes were also bent on controlling their gag reflex and relaxing their lower esophageal sphincter. That in both cases, an experiment is perhaps being carried out that is not only physiological but ontological: if part of the body no longer reacts, recoils, or protects, what becomes physiologically possible, the hysteric and the sword swallower seem to ask, and what, subsequently, does the body-as-the-person and the person-as-her-body become?

In Ferenczi's essay on hysterical manifestations, he makes an analogy between "normal" children and hysterical adults: what the two have in common is this tendency toward reorganizing the body and a "habit of . . .

super-achievements . . . for instance, the individual control of muscles which ordinarily contract symmetrically, the voluntary control of the cardiac, gastric, and intestinal functions, of the muscles of the iris, etc., which they finally display as though endowed with some special gift." Children are trained to move beyond such feats since "a great part of the education of a child consists of breaking away from such tricks and acquiring others." Ferenczi does not say what these others are, but his description makes a place for the sword swallower to join the duo of child and hysteric. Perhaps in this way the circus is an implicitly nostalgic activity, that what we like about the circus is the chance to watch people perform from inside a "stage" (in more than one sense of the word) that we were jettisoned from by education; perhaps we experience a longing there for a relation to the body that we had to give up in order to accede to adulthood. The sword swallower, then, can be understood as repeating the tricks of and on the body, the kinds of tests we only began to indulge as children but never took anywhere before settling into the body's place and fit. The sword swallower continues to investigate that relationship.

To speak of *the* sword swallower misses the details, though, that distinguish Dan Meyer's work, its singularity and particularity.

Dan sometimes talks with the sword in his throat.

He often indulges in what is known as the drop: the performer holds the sword in his throat using only the muscles of the esophagus and then lets the sword drop further down the throat by relaxing the esophageal muscles.

After he has swallowed a sword, Dan bends forward with the hilt sticking out of his mouth, which makes him appear, to my mind at least, a cross between a mythical bird with a tongue of steel and a bodybuilder in the act of statuesque flexing, but in his case the gesture is an extreme alternative to a reflex and therefore not like any "flex" we may have seen before.

Dan has been known to swallow a sword after being dropped into a tank filled with sharks, which might make it seem as if he's gotten so good at swallowing swords that the challenge no longer entirely satisfies him. He often entrusts (and, let's also admit, dares) an audience member to experience a part of the act of swallowing a sword *with* him by giving someone the terrifying privilege of pulling the sword out. (On Dan's Web site, audience members can watch a video in which he has reserved this privilege for the world's smallest man.) "Nudge aside the heart" is a phrase he is fond of using when asked to explain what swallowing a sword entails, which makes me think one of the fantasies at work in his own performances is to bypass the organ most essential to the organism. The heart—so central, so over-riding, so necessary to life, our physiology's commander, so to speak—is taken down several pegs with that word "nudge," as if to say, I don't need you, you're in the way of something else this body is becoming. To "cram" or to "tickle," that is the question; to cram *so as* to tickle, to force *so as* to subdue. Oneself. Ah, but to tickle his tummy—this is what he is doing, he says, when swallowing a sword, and one can't help but imagine the parent or grandparent who might have loved/tortured him with tummy tickles as a child, but never knew it would lead to this.

To swallow a sword is to be entered into by different means, and I won-der if this can be applied to thought. How does one concoct the idea of swallowing a sword in the first place?—given that "concoct" means, first and foremost, to boil together, to prepare (*concoquere*), to cook (*coquere*); in the second place, to digest; and in the third place, to form and pre-pare in the mind? How does thought *enter in*? I like that sword swallow-ing helps me to wonder, what do I have to nudge aside to make room for the unthinkable? Various shapes hold me—they are my habits—and many others will never in my lifetime rise up inside of me, dawn on me, occur to me. Or does thought occur *in* me? Sword swallowing, hysterical swallow-ing, Chevalier Jackson's introduction of a rigid metal scope into an orifice: each of these acts is "preposterous": something has been turned around, a fundamental order undone—I almost wrote, "by these acts of upheaval," but even that word won't do—in these acts of literal down-heave-al.

In the disciplining required to swallow a sword, a new habit is intro-duced that undoes what we usually experience as habitual (the autonomic reflexes discussed earlier, for starters). Sword swallowing prefigures a radi-cal reformation of the body, but when we turn to the history of women who swallowed swords—and many have, though not nearly as many as men—the liberatory or transformational potential of the practice turns back, more often than not, into a familiar, if extreme, performance of female submissiveness.

Diane Arbus photographed Lady Sandra Reed, the albino sword swal-lower, and there was Vicki Pope, the sword-swallowing Fat Lady—both women obviously having to depend on more than one over-the-top ele-ment to complete her act. There are sword-swallowing belly dancers and contortionists, and women who swallow neon tubes. Lady Vivian, aka Miss Vivian Dunning, famous in the 1920s and 1930s, was known for swallowing a sword with a pistol mounted on the end. The pistol, when shot, would "ram the sword down her throat." Another, more contemporary sword swallower, Rhea Roma, is "blind-folded and a random audience member shoves a 22″ sword down her throat" in her famous Suicide Show. Edith Clifford, who learned to swallow swords at age thirteen in 1899, married Thomas Holmes, the Elastic Stretch Man of Barnum & Bailey Circus. Together, they performed as the Cliffords, with Holmes swallowing "razor blades, scissors, saw blades, and bayonets" while Edith "swallowed a bayonet that was shot down her throat with a gun." Houdini, seeing this stunt, claimed that "the sensation of her act was when the point of a bayonet 23½ inches long and fastened to the breech of a cannon was placed in her mouth and the cannon discharged with the recoil driving the bayonet down her throat." (All of this we learn on the Sword Swallower's Association International Web site.)

Women sword swallowers in these examples seem to be required to have the sword rammed, shoved, driven, or otherwise violently forced down their throats. No matter how expert they might be, there's no deft handling for them. They don't manipulate the sword but are manipulated by it, and all their training is in the service of a violating spectacle, a grotesque caricaturing of women as repository.

A silent film with a musical soundtrack made in the 1950s drives home the banal and predictable uses to which women sword swallowers have been put. Featuring Marie Cortez, *We Still Don't Believe It* has the performer wandering before a display of "Famous Historical Swords" in a made-up-sounding place called the Hollywood Museum. Numerous signs warn the viewer not to touch or handle the swords, and when she tries to ignore a sign by turning it around, she's confronted with another sign telling her to "cut it out." Each sword has a man's name attached to it, ranging from Ulysses S. Grant to Ali Hassam, and we watch, with keen lack of interest (the film is so boring!), Marie shrug like a doofus or pantomime like an idiot as she takes one sword, then another, down from its holder on the burlap wall, choosing and then rejecting one after another as she might a wooing swain. (Dan Meyer also performs this trope, which we might call the irony of choosing. In one of his homemade videos, he's in a hardware store looking for just the right pair of long-handled garden shears, but we soon discover they're not for trimming the shrubs.) Finally, Marie Cortez hits upon an acceptable sword, swallows it, and, as she does so, . . . a piece of her clothing falls off. Or rather, it *pops* off, as if the sword has made her burst out of her fulsome britches. With each new sword entered and removed, another piece of her clothing falls off, and at the end, left wearing nothing but her underwear, she throws up her hands in a kind of "Oops! What ya gonna do?" way.

There is another set of swords often reserved for women in circus settings: those long blades with the tasseled hilts that a magician thrusts into the sides of a box after enclosing a woman. We're made to imagine the worst—that she's been pierced and bloodied and that we're witnessing a murder—but the fantasy is soon dispelled by the emergence of the woman intact, unharmed. Sword swallowing for men seems practically like a sport, but when women are involved, I can't help but hear the word "tawdry" whispered behind the stage's velvet curtains. Neither as hip as go-go dancers nor as exotically erotic as belly dancers, the female sword swallowers, in the accounts that I've read, seem predestined for the strip clubs that Marie Cortez's film only hints at. Except that the sword swallower bypasses the tease and instead gives herself over to the act. She appears to inhabit a specific class position: the woman who will do (or is forced to do) anything for money, which may explain why "tawdry" seems apt. A strange word, it is derived from a syllabic merging of the name Saint Audrey in referring to St. Audrey's laces, women's neck pieces sold in the seventeenth century at Saint Audrey's Fair in Norwich, England, that came to be associated with a cheapening of character, the gaudy, showy, and sleazy.

Whether we consider sword swallowing bizarre, shocking, cheap, insane, or disgusting, we cannot deny the contribution of sword swallowers to the history of medicine (see figure 31). Partners of endoscopists from the start, sword swallowers are credited in numerous histories of gastroscopy as the "inspiration" (no pun intended) for the construction of the instruments that made possible the first successful esophagoscopies, since it was from the sword swallowers that physicians learned how the human mouth, throat, and neck could be safely positioned and manipulated to accommodate rigid rather than curved devices that would make possible diagnostic and other sorts of "views." In 1868, Adolf Kussmaul of Freiburg turned to a sword swallower as the perfect initial subject for the still precarious, untested and untried esophagoscopy, and thanks to his subject, was able to carry out what is considered the first successful pass with the instrument. Disappointed with the view his scope afforded (a method for adequately lighting the interior of the body through the scope had not yet been developed), he abandoned further research and never published the results. But Kussmaul's attempt was picked up decades later by students and other followers, including Müller, Killian, and von Mikulicz, who

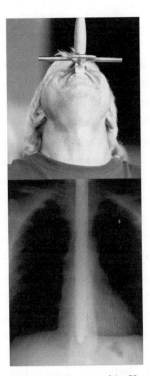

Fig. 31. Dan Meyer, sword swallower, mid-act and in X-ray. Used by permission of Dan Meyer, Sword Swallowers Association International (SSAI).

sought to determine if sword swallowing was the effect of abnormal anatomy or if normal folk could imitate the technique with what von Mikulicz, according to Eelco Huizinga, referred to as a "more innocent" straight instrument. Some sword swallowers refused to introduce the "clumsy experimental instruments," writes Dr. L. Walk in his "History of Gastroscopy." For the most part, though, sword swallowers agreed to serve as experimental accompanists, to provide the medical community with demonstrations, and generally to contribute to medicine the conditions of possibility for inspection of the human anatomy beyond the throat and into the stomach.

Chevalier Jackson would not have been able to be in the same room with someone as riskily assaulting of the human throat as Dan Meyer; or would he? How is a sword swallower's pursuit similar to or different from a scientist's or doctor's? It's well worth considering how doctors encountering sword swallowers in the street or theater or circus sideshow in their off-hours were excited enough by the act to use the sword swallower's body to think for them. "What can we do with this?" the doctor asks. "Let's see what we can make of this." But is endoscopy's what and why equivalent to sword swallowing's rationale and vice versa? I think not. The force of the idea forming within the sword swallower is different and unspoken: it is muted and bypassed by medicine's appropriation of the act at the same time that sword swallowing's psychosocial dimensions haunt endoscopy.

In my correspondence with Dan Meyer about an image of a child sword swallower from the 1890s that appears on his site, Meyer wrote that "it really seems highly illogical that a child that young (7? 8? 9 years old?) could have learned to swallow a sword so young, or that an adult would allow or try to teach a child that young to swallow a sword." Yet Chevalier Jackson taught children to swallow tubes that could aid in their recovery from stricture of the esophagus caused by lye poisoning, and apparently adults in the Jackson family scoped their children and possibly even taught them to scope themselves. In an oral history of Chevalier Jackson's granddaughter Joan Jackson Bugbee and her husband, Frank Bugbee, carried out in July 1991 by Phillip R. Seitz, the former director of the John Q. Adams Center for Otolaryngology, Joan recalls pleasant sensory memories of her grandfather roasting coffee beans, growing yellow variety tomatoes, teaching her woodworking, fishing in the mill pond, and cooking the fish that they caught. She also recalls his habit of waking at five A.M. and working for the better part of the day in his study, "where he was not to be disturbed" and where a "buzzer system alerted him to lunch." Joan described playing with casts of plaster hands that had real hair on them, her grandfather teaching her to play the flute, and undergoing six bronchoscopic examinations by her father, Chevalier L. Jackson, for persistent bad cough and sinus trouble. "They scoped me," as she puts it, and with that verb a whole new way of relating between humans is imagined, or at least a word is coined for a peculiar act turned average occurrence.

Meyer has written that "the act of swallowing a sword is not really a fun or 'pleasant' feeling itself" but "usually does not actually hurt terribly painfully"—though "it can sure feel *very* uncomfortable." Joan Jackson Bugbee reported that scopings "aren't bad at all," however. She said that Jackson's close associate Dr. Charles Norris had never been scoped, and that she believed all bronchoscopists should have the experience so they know what they are doing to their patients. Arlene Maloney, widow of Walter H. Maloney, who was a close colleague of both C.J. and C.L. (as they are called by those who knew them), told me in an interview that being scoped is definitely "uncomfortable," and offered, unprompted, a memory that contradicts Joan Bugbee's. "My husband had a bronchoscopy done on himself and he did one on Dr. Norris," she told me. "My husband developed a lot of allergies and he got asthma. He always felt as though something were caught, as though there was something caught. So Charlie said, 'Come on in and I'll scope you and see what gives.' Then Charlie got pneumonia, he wasn't getting over it, and he was bringing up all this gook, and he said, 'Walter, now it's your turn.' So they both knew exactly what it felt like." And then she added: "I don't know that C.L. ever scoped his father or that his father ever scoped him. Dr. Hollinger from Chicago, he had it done once, just to see what it felt like, but I don't remember any of the other residents doing the same thing. And there were quite a few. It was a very popular field for young doctors to go into. The Jacksons never had any problems getting residents or getting assistants, so they must have been doing something right."

For the Jacksons, "scoping" seems to have been a family tradition, and though Joan did not become a physician, she apparently did learn how to scope herself—which of course seems to be a kind of impossibility but is perhaps the logical next step, an amalgam of sword swallowing and scoping. Historian Louis Waddell, who also interviewed Joan Bugbee in 1991, wrote me that he "spent a fascinating morning with Frank and Joan Bugbee. . . . Mrs. Bugbee had fond memories to share and actually inserted one of CJ's tools into her throat." She might have been demonstrating how the instruments worked, but to actually insert a scope into one's own throat would require practice. We don't imagine doctors scoping themselves behind closed doors, even if they do—it'd be like a hairdresser trying to give himself a haircut—but the granddaughter of Chevalier Jackson demonstrated a mastery over an instrument that was part of her family legacy and, at the same time, unconsciously linked endoscopy with circus acts: endoscopy as stunt, endoscopy as performance. Late-nineteenth-century physicians thought that endoscopy never would evolve as a viable method for viewing and treating the stomach or the lungs because they assumed only sword swallowers would ever be able to withstand the insertion of the rigid tube. Joan Bugbee's grandfather and a generation of his patients proved otherwise, and a medical specialty was born.

Hardware. Swords. Scopes. Each act of self-penetration is in some sense also an act of (tabooed) self-investigation, a kind of (au)topsy-turvy in which a neat subject/object relation is undone, for, in each case, the doctor/operator is displaced, if not entirely usurped, and the distinction between doctor and patient is collapsed. Ingesting hardware. Swallowing swords. Self-scoping. These are operations performed on the self but without the alibi of healing, without treatment and cure as their reputed aim and end. Reclamations of the body, assertions of agency and will, they also seem violently to refigure the terms by which astonishment is generated inside the medical theater. The play of pulsating color that he glimpsed through his scope, that he held inside a deeply quiet yet highly orchestrated space, astonished Chevalier Jackson. The application of his instruments let awesome scenes unfold before the eye of a unique and privileged observer: the human body's live and lit interior. Hardware, swords, and scopes admit of astonishment too, but they replace quiet with cacophony; they insist a spectator into the place of an observer; they invite an audience in; they obliterate medicine's purchase on bodily interiority by—at least in the case of the sword swallower—enjoining viewers to watch a near self-evisceration. These acts aren't about seeing inside but about getting inside oneself; they're about controlling and testing one's own borders.

Meyer ingests a sword, and the audience responds with a deep intake of breath. They gasp. Some can't watch when the sword goes in. Others cover their faces and mouths. Some agree to remove the sword from his throat. A few pass out in the middle of the show, as happened in his 2009 performance at Cambridge University, a reaction that Meyer has termed his third "falling ovation."

I have never seen Dan Meyer perform live, but when I watch his videos, my reaction is to get "choked up." I experience vulnerability for him, and I'm afraid that one of these days he's going seriously to hurt himself. Maybe I identify in him my own sad relentlessness in having something to prove to fellow humans as a way of receiving love. Maybe I'm like Jackson in the way I, as a kid, wondered why so many families in my neighborhood gathered around the TV set in some summer in the 1970s to watch Evel Knievel tempt fate again. I wanted to stop it all, to talk Evel Knievel out of hurling himself and his motorcycle across impossible distances— gravity *does* exist, you *will* crash, why do you want us to watch you die?—to invite him out for a milkshake and supply the craven audience with blindfolds. Now I know these peculiar forms of human behavior can neither be stopped nor turned away from and that our enjoyment of, as well as our repulsion toward, such defiantly self-penetrating acts beg to be understood.

Reduced to speechlessness, beset by gawking, where will we find the words for understanding these phenomena and everything about them that's left unsaid? When the Human Ostrich was forced to swallow hard, sharp bits of the object world by a hungry crowd, he was, as it turns out, not simply sitting idly or innocently in a bar; he was in the middle of a performance of legerdemain, light-handedness or sleight of hand. He was opting to perform magic acts rather than traffic in the actual for a while. Thus his audience's violent reaction to him gains a layer, because it's hard to know what upset them more: That he was now tricking them when he had previously done something more daring? Or that seeing the magic act reminded them that he might have been tricking them when he swallowed all that stuff before? Somehow the Human Ostrich and his audience couldn't arrive at the mutual pact that makes performance possible—the trust that needs to exist in the medical domain *and* in the theater. Sword swallowing isn't magical, that's for sure; it can't be magical because it has no interest in grace. It's violent—as is Jackson's use of the word "stab" to refer to the use of his instrument in one of his earliest essays—and, in its way, totalizing, and entirely unsubtle. The Human Ostrich's audience was mad at him because he had given them something that was to their minds better than magic, and they wanted that again.

One human takes another human to a gasp-making pinnacle, like the story I don't know what to do with that appears in Poulet's tract in which a "step-mother, desiring to rid herself of a little daughter, made her swallow, at different times, a certain number of needles. After long suffering, these needles made their exit from different parts of the body of the child, and especially from her arms." Maybe a fiction writer on the order of Angela Carter could do something with this, to exploit its fairytale features toward feminist ends. Maybe a magical realist could find in it fascinating symbolism for unformed desire. But what could a compassionate thinker do with this? Did the (evil) stepmother mistake her daughter for a doll, and when the needles came out through the arms, was it alarming to the child, or did she experience it as a relief, a proof of life that made her stepmother faint?

Sometimes when I swallow, especially liquids, I have the feeling of what I've ingested trickling into some part of me that isn't the bronchus, but close. It must be a stray nerve ending at work when this happens, the same way referred pain occurs inside the human mouth especially. The going in *feels as though* it's going somewhere other than the stomach, like a cool spike across the ribcage, and it's not unsatisfying. It's temporary, this sensation, but for a moment, I am a series of estuaries rather than a chyme-producing organism. And something about that feeling I want to cultivate, or return to, or learn to like. Because there must be more than one way to take things in and give things out, to receive the world and answer to it, to enter others or oneself, to perform what there are no words for without exacting harm.

III.

WHAT *ARE* THESE THINGS?

In forty-seven cases of children the child was crying when the foreign body was inspirited. The natural purpose of the crying of children is to make a noise. In the usual forms of crying in children, the noisy phonation is kept up throughout a prolonged expiration. This is followed by sudden, deep, violent inspiration, the necessity being urgent to cut short the relatively silent inspiration, in order to resume the noisy phase as quickly as possible. This sudden, deep, violent inspiration seems to be one of the most common factors in the etiology of foreign bodies in the air passages of children. Crying is mentioned in only three of esophageal cases. (DAFP, 22)

When one has seen patients of 8 or 9 years of age climbing on to the operation table of their own accord, submitting to the washing out of a bronchiectatic cavity through a bronchoscope and irrigator, and then getting down and walking away smiling, one is brought to the conclusion that there is, in some cases, an advantage in using this comparatively peaceful method in place of the struggle and dread of a general anesthetic.

—V.E. NEGUS,
"The Course of Endoscopy in Chevalier Jackson's Service" (1924)

Fbdy #565, the Case of Margaret Derryberry: Objects Lost and Found and Lost Again

"We met in California, we were married in Mississippi, lived in Tennessee, and our kids were born in Kentucky." It could be the beginning of a song, starting in Pennsylvania, but it was part of a story that eighty-three-year-old Margaret Derryberry was telling me about how she and her husband had found one another, and about her life, which was, she explained, a series of blessings, including her finding a mate who proved to be "a perfect husband—as perfect as a person can be."

Margaret Derryberry and I hadn't literally met, but we crossed the threshold of the Mütter Museum coincidentally. I'd fantasized about the possibility of finding someone who was connected to one of the objects in the collection, someone still living who might have been treated by Jackson and who could share her experience with me. In the same week that I'd made one of my first official visits to the Mütter archives, I guess you could say I had been blessed, because that was the week Margaret called the museum in search of the hatpin she had aspirated in 1931, when she was eight years old.

At first I was incredulous—both her name, Margaret Derryberry, and her e-mail address, cobwob@aol.com, seemed made up. I couldn't even find "cobwob" in the OED, but, running a Google Books search, I struck upon a line in Alexander Pope's "Epistle to Dr. Arbuthnot, Being the Prologue to the Satires," in which it had appeared as an early variant of "cobweb": "Who shames a Scribbler! I break one cobwob thro'/He spins the slight self-pleasing thread anew." On second glance, applying a digital magnifier, I saw that Pope hadn't used the word "cobwob" after all. Nor did Samuel Butler, Robert Burns, or the many other presumed cobwobbers sited by Google Books, but the search tool consistently mis-read some early typefaces' nearly closed "e's" as "o's." Searching and finding, losing and searching again, Margaret Derryberry (who was Margaret Billig when she had her foreign-body accident) and I formed a fast familiarity with one another.

"Sincerely." "With fond regards." "Forever thankfully yours." I don't know at what precise point we started to sign our letters with the word "Love," because our conversation had begun with the simple sharing of a story, the recounting of an accident, the production of a ghost:

> We were visiting friends in Catawissa, Pennsylvania, where we had once lived. And the girl was about my age, and she had this bunch of hatpins, I don't know why. And we were playing with them, we were up in the bedroom. And my mother wanted me to go across the bridge and play with the children while she went shopping with the mother. And I was very unhappy about that, and I started to cry. And Mom was firm, she said no, you're going with your sisters across and play. But I cried so hard, and I put my hands up to my face. I sobbed, hard. One little cough. And I was standing there looking at my hands, and mother asked me, what was wrong? And I said, I had a hatpin in my hands and it's not there now. . . . I didn't feel it, I didn't know it was down there. I just knew I did that little cough. . . . Everybody was down on their hands and knees except Mother and me looking for the

pin in the rugs . . . but they took me over to Danville and they X-rayed me
and they saw where it was and they said they couldn't do it, and they sent us
to the University of Pennsylvania.

The firmness of a mother meets the inspiration of a child gulping air in
protest of a leave-taking. Is it out of politeness or an attempt at self-comfort,
this tendency to bring our hands up to our faces or up to our mouths when
we cry?

This is what Margaret Derryberry remembers: root-beer floats. A carton of milk. A baby doll. The other kids were promised root-beer floats for
the trip but not Margaret. A carton of milk soured in the car without her
having any, and she didn't understand why she wasn't allowed to eat or why
the car had to be driven to Philadelphia so slowly, avoiding any bumps. She
knew the pin had disappeared, but because she could not feel it inside her,
it was almost as though nothing at all had occurred: nothing at all, and yet
something potentially grave.

I don't know if Margaret had been wearing her play shirt or a favorite
check dress with matching translucent apron when she was driven from
her friend and their playful interlude, driven all the way to Philadelphia,
but she remembers that it must have been summertime because she was
in short sleeves and ankle socks (see figure 32). Her mother knew Margaret to be honest and good—she believed her, while the others had re-
verted to all fours, searching out the pin inside a carpet—but she was also
exasperated: "I can't take you anywhere!" In response to that global pro-
nouncement, Margaret remembered thinking, "I don't remember going
anywhere and causing trouble." Margaret vividly recalls certain impres-
sions from her experience in one of Jackson's clinics, while other things
she only remembers being told in the experience's aftermath, and she ret-
rospectively understands some details anew because she grew up to be a
nurse, which was another blessing: it was a line of work she'd fallen into but
grew entirely to love.

A white sheet, the glint of silver metal. Bits and pieces waft back from
the recovery room that Margaret remembers sharing with a little baby who
had a cast on "because she had congenital dislocation of the hips," and
a girl who was strapped to a board a couple of times a day with her head
down while a doctor slapped her on the back. "And I think now, she probably had cystic fibrosis. You know, that was postural drainage," Margaret
explains. "Bless her heart, she felt so important . . . how she strutted! . . .
I don't imagine she's with us now." Margaret remembers being told that it

Fig. 32. Margaret Derryberry (née Billig) about the age she was when she accidentally inhaled the hatpin that was removed from her bronchus in one of Jackson's clinics. Photo courtesy of Margaret Derryberry and her daughter, Peggy Derryberry Gould.

was because of Chevalier Jackson that her life had been saved—he had just recently designed the particular bronchoscope his assistant used to retrieve the pin, without anesthesia. Otherwise they would have had to perform a bronchotomy. Jackson didn't actually perform the procedure; her family was told he was in Europe at the time. She remembers her mother asking for the pin afterwards: "I think after everything was over and done with, she was so relieved that she wanted the pin to show to people what I had inhaled. And they told her, I don't know how they told her, I'm sure they told her in a nice way, that they would like to keep it for the display case."

At the center of Margaret Derryberry's interview with me, the recurring pivot point of our conversation is not so much memory's scattered remnants, however instructive or delightful they might be. What Margaret *can't* remember is the keynote of what she shares with me, what she entirely cannot get over, a gap and an absence that she desperately wishes to understand, and to which she repeatedly returns, and that is the fact that she cannot remember being at all afraid. "Because you know something else strange about this? Never did I have a minute of fear or anxiety," she tells me early on, and then repeats at numerous junctures in our talk:

"I can't understand *not* being afraid."

"But I just can't get over the fact that I wasn't even slightly alarmed."

"And I think I'd have a memory of it. You know, something like that would stick with me."

"But what impressed me overall was the fact that I can't remember any fear at all. And I thought, if I had had anesthetic, you know I could understand it a little. But no fear at all."

"I just cannot remember anything frightening about it."

This gap or lapse or absence of feeling might explain another conundrum: why, after all these years, did Margaret go looking for that once aspirated hatpin? What motivates anyone blithely, resignedly, to give up the goods to the Jackson clinics or insist on keeping their foreign body Thing? Margaret's mother certainly understood the newfound importance of the object she wasn't allowed to keep: she kept a duplicate pinned inside the lining of her purse, which she brought out for visitors from time to time to show them what Margaret had survived. Eventually, she discarded it—or, as Margaret put it, she "finally got rid of it"—but only after a number of years had passed. "She'd bring it out and show it to people . . . like it was some kind of an achievement," Margaret jokes.

Margaret's own search for the pin wasn't something that occurred to her during her training as a nurse at Geisinger Hospital, where she might have gone looking for the X-ray. It was the computer that prompted her search, she tells me, though in recent years she had mused with her daughter about whatever might have happened to that pin. Yet I suspect what may really have necessitated Margaret's quest was the incompleteness, the indecipherable missing link, the gap between what she must have experienced but couldn't recall that is the defining matrix of trauma. Margaret had been in search of the evidence of her experience—her embodiment and her survival, the mark of her having lived, not died, the trace of peril and salvation. She hadn't felt the pin go in; one minute it was there, and the next minute it was gone, a part of her. Nor did she see it coming out. Though it was lost inside her body, she could not feel it there. Even when it was removed, she didn't see it and does not remember feeling what would have been an appropriate reaction—fear. Did the pin even exist? The X-ray said it did. The clinicians should have thought to show her the pin.

Many years hence, in trauma's aftermath, perhaps the pin could tell her how to feel. The pin as the mark of having been happened to, having been acted upon, having felt fear and longing and sadness too (that sob).

"I was crying so hard," she said, "and when I cry hard, I sob hard." She went on: "And you know something, this might not interest you, but on the way home, my mother brought my baby doll. And I was sitting in the backseat of the car, and I was undressing my doll, and dressing her. And I took the little pin out of the back of her dress and put it in my mouth, and started to undress her. And I could remember Mother turning around, she didn't say a word, she reached back slowly and yanked that pin. So I guess I did give her problems I can't remember!"

In only a matter of months, my correspondence with Margaret Derry-berry had become frequent and fascinating and gemlike; I was caught up in it, as I was with all of my new discoveries about Jackson. I couldn't quite believe I'd found her, or she me, and we considered our meeting something that was strangely destined. But trauma is more swift-footed than our attempts to keep it at bay, it takes us out of ourselves and it takes us off guard, so I didn't tell Margaret right away when, just two months after our first interview, I found a lump in my breast and had to be ushered into a full and long-term treatment regime for cancer. My diagnosis was in June, but I waited until late July to craft a letter to her. "If you don't hear from me, then, it's only because I've been temporarily required to take un unexpected turn in life's labyrnthe (a word I've suddenly forgotten how to spell)," I tried to joke as I drew my letter to her to a close. I told her that I thought the cancer, instead of throwing me entirely off course, might deepen my relationship to the medical matters I'd be contemplating in my work on Jackson, because "cancer, after all, is a sort of 'foreign body,' isn't it?" I asked.

What had Margaret felt when she saw her foreign body for the first time after seventy-five years of missing it? The Mütter Museum's educational director had miraculously managed to locate Margaret's pin and generously photographed it alongside a penny to give her a sense of its size. Jackson's accompanying foreign-body grid was meticulous and thorough at the level of technique and in describing the problem the case presented, but it did not include identifying details like the date or the name of the patient. For those details, one would need access to the case report, which, in Margaret Derryberry's case was, as far as I could tell, no longer extant. Did Margaret finally feel that long-deferred fear? I hadn't thought to ask her exactly what she felt when she found her pin, perhaps because I hadn't yet had the experience of a foreign body myself. The moment was ghoulish when, teetering and out of it, I was asked if I'd like to see the X-ray that had just been taken of my chest, complete with a foreign body inside: the chemotherapy port and its accompanying spaghetti-string catheter that had been implanted in my chest. My stitches were fresh and I was still woozy from pain medication when I was brought to stand like a drunk before a kind of mirror (and yet not quite a mirror) and gaze at an image that was so familiar from my work on Jackson: the upper torso spookily interrupted by an object breaking its horizon. Though I felt far from grandiose, there was something martyrlike about the scenario, as though I'd been punished for studying foreign-body ingestion by captors who forced one inside me and then made me look: "You want to see a foreign body? *Here*'s a foreign body!" Much later, upon its removal, the surgeon exclaimed how beautiful the pouch was that my body had formed to accommodate the port. I did not see the pouch, but I asked to keep the port.

Cancer made me aware of a new foreign-body calculus, because even if we haven't ingested a foreign body, my work and my life were teaching me that none of us is immune. Can cancer be understood as a foreign body produced by the body? The body made alien to itself? Is cancer's genesis the effect of having ingested or aspirated something foreign to the body, something that it could not assimilate? Cancer offered a new lesson about my conception of that which is alien to the body: so long as it is still excisable, it can be understood as a foreign body inside the body, but once it becomes more fully constitutive of the body, it is no longer foreign, and *therefore* deadly. In this sense, the "foreign" of "foreign bodies" is still compatible with the body; it's when the distinction collapses that the body does as well. By this account, a thing's foreignness to the body isn't what makes it threatening, but its ability to confuse itself with the body and thus cease to be foreign: to become the body. Or its ability to simulate the body and therefore displace it. A tumor is a foreign body with a blood supply.

I shared my news, such as it was, with Margaret on July 21, and looking back on it, it appears I strutted: "I'm sorry to have to share such news with you, but the main thing I wish for you to know is that my book on Chevalier Jackson *will* get written, and it will get published. I have no doubt about that." Once I was lost, and now I was found. This wasn't how I felt in cancer's wake. It was more like once I knew things, and now I know nothing, even though the sentence I wrote to Margaret seems so insistent and in control. When I met Margaret, I was knowledgeable but innocent, and in a few months, I was wise because truly, admittedly dumb.

What I couldn't know (so much that I can never know) and did not know was that I had waited too long to write my letter, because on July 19, Margaret had fallen and broken her hip, and on August 4, her daughter wrote to tell me that she had died: "Margaret went peacefully." And I sobbed and sobbed. How could my conversation with her not continue, especially now, when I needed her most? How had I missed the chance to give her a parting message or gift? How could I go into the operating room as a patient the next day with the knowledge that my new friend was no longer in the world?

When Margaret Derryberry found her lost object, she didn't just recover a particle of the vast universe of matter; she imagined having found, in a sense, her self. "*We're* in drawer number seventy. *We're* item 565 in drawer number seventy" was how she put it to me. She marked "the pin that's mine," "my pin I circled in red." When Margaret was alive, I tried to discover more information relating to her case to give to her, but I came up short every time I went digging and sifting through the extant case studies in all of the archives I had explored. Wanting to bring the pin back and back and back—and no doubt Margaret, too—I recently looked for the description of the case in Jackson's *Diseases of the Air and Food Passages of Foreign-Body Origin*. Using one of Jackson's guides is always gratifying for the way this fits into that and that fits into this. You bring your finger to the index, find case number 565, go to page 13, and read: the patient was eight years old, the head of the pin had been in the left main bronchus for two days, a 7mm tube had been used with no anaesthetic, the point was buried in the tracheal wall, a side-curved forceps was called upon in the case, the extraction took all of one minute and sixteen seconds. The grid also noted "a hemorrhage from pin-point puncture" that Margaret had no memory of—chalking it up, again, to the miracle-working acts of the Jackson clinic. But this time I noticed something I hadn't noticed at the beginning of my research: a small-case parenthetical note that read: "Fig. 5, Plate 1." I gasped: Jackson had illustrated Margaret's case for this book. I imagined how thrilled Margaret would have been to know this—to see her eight-year-old insides, complete with fbdy, as depicted by the master himself; I imagined writing her family even before I'd flipped to the page. I couldn't wait to read what Jackson had to say about this case. I yelped to see that he made not just one but two illustrations of it: illustrations number five and number ten, placed one above the other, distinguished by the streak of blood that ran like a rivulet past the vocal cords from the point of puncture (see figure 33). "Girl aged eight years," his notation read, "steel shawl-pin with head in left main bronchus, the point in tracheal wall above orifice of right bronchus. A tiny stream of blood is seen to be carried by the cilia toward the posterior wall of the trachea. Peroral bronchoscopic removal. Cure" (description of plate 1, *DAFP*).

No sooner had I felt the astonishment of finding Jackson's own illustrations of Margaret's case than I realized something that felt terribly sad— I remembered what Margaret remembered so well, that Jackson had not treated her, and if he hadn't treated her, he could not have illustrated her case. He only illustrated what he was present to have seen—those views through his scopes. The pin in drawer 70, case #565, I hated to admit, probably couldn't have been Margaret's. That would explain why she did not remember hemorrhaging. Because she hadn't hemorrhaged, and hemorrhaging, according to the illustration, was the major feature of this case.

Margaret Derryberry was right: she had always been keen to stress to me that what she had inhaled was a hatpin, while case #565 described a shawl

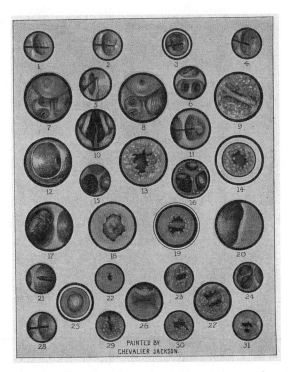

Fig. 33. Illustrations in oils of bronchoscopic, esophagoscopic, and gastroscopic views. Case #565 (what had been thought to be the case of Margaret Derryberry) is represented by figures 5 and 10 (DAFP, 124).

pin. And Chevalier Jackson was never wrong. It hadn't been a shawl pin; it had been a hatpin, so this wasn't her pin. Margaret knew quite well what she inhaled, but the collection failed to confirm her knowledge. It cannot do that for a person. Try as we might, it is quite unlikely that we will find ourselves in this cabinet, safe, secure. Margaret's hatpin is irrecoverable.

We seek to find ourselves, to be individuated by and through an object, especially if that object was at one time inside us or a threat to our lives. But the objects inside the fbdy collection blur into one another as they coalesce into a singular subject: their author. Once again, a living former patient's reclamation of experience inside the clinic hinged more on the absence or presence of Chevalier Jackson than on the absence or presence of the object or of the patient. You can't blame the educational director, because it *is* hard to believe that more than one—in fact, a multitude—of eight-year-olds might have come to Jackson's clinics with hatpins in their lungs. What are the chances of finding one's own pin inside a sea of pins?

People, myself included, wish to make the fbdy collection less anonymous. One of the greatest aftereffects of the fbdy collection may in fact be the twists and turns, the truly labyrinthine routes, that people with a connection to the collection might take to find themselves therein even if arrival is futile. The spring 2009 issue of the newsletter of the American Broncho-Esophagological Association (ABEA), the organization that Jackson founded, shows this individuating impulse at work. The presidential guest of honor at the organization's proceedings is a Mr. Pepa, who is distinguished by the claim that he is Chevalier Jackson's "oldest living patient," who "will speak briefly about his experience being a patient of Dr. Jackson and present photos from his time in the tracheotomy ward." Also featured in the newsletter is a story recounted by Dr. Wayne Hellman about his grandfather Rudolph Hellman, whom Jackson had rescued from a potentially fatal brass cap in 1916 when Hellman was a boy. Dr. Hellman quotes a note written in 1999 from the Mütter Museum's late curator Gretchen Worden: "I have never met anyone or heard of anyone with a personal interest in our Jackson collection." Including this note seems to suggest that he is the only living person to have a personal relationship to the collection, itself an example of someone's desire to individualize the otherwise indiscriminate mass of Things. The impossibility of using the collection this way, however, is strangely a consequence of Jackson's own doing. His hope for the collection was to create what he called "canned experience" for future practitioners. Did this mean that only his experience was original, and everyone after him was to be a copycat? "A parallel can be found for almost any case encountered," he explained in *Diseases of the Air and Food Passages of Foreign-Body Origin*. In other words, what the collection offers the practitioner is a duplicate, a double of the case before him so he can work by example. There are no unique *you*s to be found inside examples; the power to duplicate exacts an erasure of the individual and of the individuating.

The pin inside the frame of case #565 *is* Margaret Derryberry's in this sense: she found it. And lavished attention on it. And it found her. And I found her, through it, she found me: the object was lost but the story was found. Whatever happened to the original pin, we'll never know. Was it carried across the lane in a beaker, carried away on the wind, a sad sliver lost to the crack in a sidewalk? What remains is an intimacy forged across the drawer of one of Jackson's objects in his cabinet of curiosity. Because Margaret and I shared a *fascination*, which doesn't mean together we form a coterie.

Margaret led me to learn something of the history of hatpins and their relationship to the history of women. The period between the 1880s and the 1920s marked their heyday, a period during which women were liberated from their ribbon-tied bonnets and freed to display a range of hats better suited to new and daring hairstyles. So linked with women's power were they that, in the early twentieth century, various laws were passed limiting the length that a woman's hatpin could be. According to the American Hatpin Society's Web site, the pins were considered deadly weapons. The phrase "pin money" has curiously complicated origins around consumption and production (and desire). It may refer to an early-nineteenth-century edict in England that restricted the sale of hat and other dress pins from France to two days out of the year, January 1 and 2. Women, saving their money in anticipation of those days, were accumulating "pin money." Or it may refer to Queen Victoria's taxing her subjects at the beginning of each year in order to pay for her own fancy pins.

See that hatpin with adjustable ends for swiveling its glittering stone, or this elaborate model with a screw-on container for holding smelling salts, a tiny mirror, or a powder puff. The pin that Margaret and her friend were playing with was simple, she had told me, not ornate, but even a simple hatpin is equal to a complex material culture and a replete personal history—a history, in fact, of the body. Of course there is power in the evidentiary, but an object—and here's the twist—may not be reducible to its material trace. Margaret Derryberry's pin *materialized* in our conversations. Together we found it, and made from it affection, and now I stow it in this chapter drawer.

It's hard to acknowledge that, at the beginning of our relationship with one another, Margaret was coming to the end of her life, and that she knew it. Margaret knew what no one wished to. She'd asked if I'd been able to find any other still-living patients of Chevalier Jackson and then added, "You're going to think this is terrible, Mary, but when you suggested times for calling, I thought to myself, 'Better do it now, you might not be here Thursday!' "

According to our ongoing e-mail correspondence, there had been no spring either in Providence, Rhode Island, or Frankfort, Kentucky, in May 2007. I complained that the new shoots in my garden were met with the stifling air of late summer rather than the temperate breezes of spring; she reported that where she lived it had gotten very warm, and "new growth appeared and then we had a hard frost. Consequently, things got nipped. I now have a green and yellow hedge out front . . . which I can't trim because cardinals are raising a second family in it."

We know a child body can sob, but can it gasp, or is that something only adult bodies do? Margaret Derryberry led me to Alexander Pope, and left me with Gerard Manley Hopkins. To a poem filled with oddly tilting lilts and backward-turning breaks, with heightened silences and mysterious measures. Now I find, and lose, and find again that verse called "Spring and Fall"; it is Mar-ga-ret I mourn for, with an emphasis on each hale syllable of her name.

Instrumentality and Instruments as Things

It seems necessary from the outset to state that this presentation is from the author's individual viewpoint, which means that of one who metaphorically, as well as actually, sees narrowly through a small tube.
                    —CHEVALIER JACKSON, "Discussion on Overlooked Cases of
                            Foreign Body in the Air and Food Passages" (1925)

Lightness of touch was one of his hobbies.
                            —Chevalier Jackson's handwritten notes
                        for his autobiography, Smithsonian Institute

I must move on now before age overtakes me and makes my hand tremble.
(LCJ, *209*)

In spite of Chevalier Jackson's hopeful and instructive legacy, peanuts, coins, and safety pins still top the charts of most frequently identified foreign bodies, Christmas tree ornaments continue to appear (no other holiday detritus seems to enter people's bodies so unceasingly), and so do jacks, yet fbdy cases are still treated by some physicians as anomalous firsts. Consider the man who recently inhaled a "fast-food foreign object." Though fast food hadn't been invented in Chevalier Jackson's day, plenty of plastic had already been inhaled, yet this recent case of a North Carolina man beset by fits of coughing and undiagnosed respiratory distress was met with bafflement and surprise. Doctors eventually determined that the patient's lung was harboring a foreign body, but according to newspaper reports, "they couldn't figure out what it was or the best way to retrieve it." One doctor suggested that the easiest strategy would be to remove the man's lung entirely! Fortunately, the case came to the attention of a pulmonologist at Duke who, more regularly engaged in removing cancerous tumors from people's airways, suggested he could attempt to remove the fbdy using a rigid bronchoscope—that is, the "à la Jackson way." Waiting to see what might be lurking inside the man's lung, the operating team was amazed when a plastic fragment of a Wendy's eating utensil came to light. "We're as quizzed by the whole situation as everyone is," the doctor reported. "This is quite a surprise that this could even happen."

The patient's admitted tendency to gulp down his Wendy's (fast) food aside, what intrigued the operators even more was that the fbdy bore a message. Realizing that the fbdy had letters on it, the operating staff began to read aloud: "A-M-B-U-R-G-E-R." The idea of carrying around an object that bears part of the Wendy's motto—"Old Fashioned Hamburgers"— is more tantalizing than a bit of actual stuck hamburger would be. Foreign bodies that need to be read command a special place in fbdy lore, as though things caught in bodies are more fascinating if they bear a secret-seeming message, issued from who knows where. Message-bearing fbdies take on special meaning, like things first hidden and later found, like messages in bottles with their singular allure.

The beauty of the seaborne bottle is that it can bob perpetually and traverse vast distances without the aid of any transport system except the currents of the sea; the riddle of it is how long it will take to be found—if it ever will be found—and where in the world it will next show up. A pin enters a knee and comes out through the chest; another begins inside the gullet and emerges from behind the ear; a third goes in at the mouth and exits through a calf. (The three examples taken together offered more than enough fodder for a 1937 article in *Popular Science*, "Strange Things

That Roam Through the Body.") A bottled message is dropped off the coast of Brazil and arrives on a beach in Africa, enters the Southern Indian Ocean to arrive at the west coast of Australia, is deposited in Rhode Island's Narragansett Bay and washes up in southwest England, or begins in the Baltic Sea and resurfaces in San Francisco. We're intrigued by these strange meanderings, and it's not always clear if we want to solve, or to predict, the body's currents or the sea's, or if we're simply happier not to know: to entertain the latitudes of wayward sojourns that we, ourselves, are loath to take. Wherever it arrives, the message in a bottle culminates with its recipient. Do you smash the bottle or fish the message out? If the bottle is plastic, do you cut the bottle open or try to preserve the vessel intact? Is the message, once read, bound to have a lesser yield than the fact of the bottle itself, as though to read it and receive it is to break its spell?

Think of all the precious objects washed up on the shores of yard sales! A mirrored cabinet; a leaf-pressed bowl; a three-legged stool with the face of a gargoyle. On one occasion, a small wooden box marked "50 cents" with a scene inlaid on its lid. For fifty cents, it might make sense that the box, when you carried it, threw up a rattling sound as though a broken-off piece were stuck inside it. But for fifty cents, you wouldn't imagine that the sound was made by an object, not broken off but secreted inside. How to access the thing, that is the question, and the minute you ask this, you discover that the box has camouflaged movable parts—it's not just any box, but a Japanese puzzle box. The pleasure in cracking the box's code is unspeakable. The primitive back and forth, give and take, here and gone, of being oneself puzzled, and solving the puzzle in turn. The detail of one part of the box requiring the shifting of a moveable miniature book, like the feeling of finding a life-size library's hidden door, and then the revelation of the Thing inside: a tiny, eminently swallowable key.

How a person goes at the box is revelatory too, and Jackson's methodology is the best example of this. Can you tackle the thing without breaking it? Do you favor your eyes or your touch in the process? Do you palpate or knock? Do you examine or notice or do you just bite into it? Do you pry? Do you spin the box on an axis, hoping for a lucky pointer in a game of chance, or visualize its openings and calculate its angles, preserving its integrity, in turn? Each of our methods of resolution tells us something about ourselves, our temperaments, our interest in and our patience with an object, our aptitude for curiosity.

From John Kirkup's *The Evolution of Surgical Instruments*, we learn that the production of the earliest surgical tools was driven by the need to remove foreign bodies—splinters, thorns, and bodily intruders that needed plucking out—and that the human hand and the human mouth, which were used to suck out or otherwise remove foreign bodies, served as these instruments' prototypes. Devising special tools to extract bodily invaders is as old as humankind, but this doesn't mean that such instruments were applied with elegance or aplomb. In fact, the results of inserting instruments into the mouth, throat, stomach, or lungs were pretty uniformly dismal before Chevalier Jackson introduced his unique array of scopes and forceps, his adept and thorough instruction, and his incomparable technique.

In his illustrations for one of countless sets of "endoscopic views illustrating mechanical problems encountered in cases of foreign bodies in the lungs," Jackson remains dumbfounded by the fact that his "predecessor in the case stated that he had grasped the foreign body and had pulled as hard as he dared" (*NMP*, 91). In a record of remarks from a 1921 article on new mechanical problems in bronchoscopy, a Dr. William B. Chamberlin of Cleveland, Ohio, uses a metaphor that likens doctors to overeager, testosteroned killers, whose "haste and zeal to seize a foreign body was similar to what hunters called 'buck fever,' they were so anxious to shoot that they missed." Dr. Louis Clerf, in his 1952 address "Historical Aspects of Foreign Bodies in the Air and Food Passages," revisits some of the cruder forms of removal and the transition from outmoded methods toward supposed technical improvements in the mid-nineteenth century:

> Until [Samuel] Gross presented his views on the subject it was of common occurrence to use some form of bougie to push the offender downward into the stomach. In fact in one of the very early cases reported from India, a certain gentleman used his cane to aid the progress of a mass of meat on its way to the stomach. Gross advocated the use of curved forceps, blunt metallic hooks, a piece of wire formed in a noose or with a piece of whale bone or a gum elastic catheter furnished with a stylet or having a piece of sponge, or linen ball or something similar attached to its lower extremity. A number of ingenious instruments were devised, notably the Gross probang and the Graefe coin catcher.

I'm not sure why Clerf describes these instruments as ingenious, since they seem mainly to have been ingeniously fatal. "Mishaps," followed by the patient "succumbing," seem to have been the order of these instruments' day. Jackson's predecessors as well as his contemporaries were responsible for blind graspings and jabbings until the fbdy was lost; they attempted to remove tacks without first disengaging the point; they "morcellated" peanut kernels, thus leaving the patient with a scattering of peanut bits trapped in the airway, which led to fatal abscessing; they suffocated patients by compressing the trachea with instruments whose bulk, together with the size of the fbdy, were too great or that, in combination with general anaesthesia, suppressed the patient's ability to breathe; they overshot the fbdy with their scopes, relying on what Jackson called "injudicious traction"; they dragged the foreign body forward and took human tissue with it; they pulled, they tore, they lacerated. The history of endoscopy is riddled with practitioners heading out into the terra incognita of the throat, the stomach, or the airway, stalling petrified before the entryway, entering in successfully, but then inciting an "accident" on subsequent attempts and closing up shop altogether, abandoning further development of the instrumentarium.

It's an early winter day in Brooklyn; no doubt everyone else's hands are chafed except for dainty, cared-for Jackson's when he delivers his lecture and lantern demonstration to the Kings County Medical Society on December 19, 1911. "It is one of the sad duties of the oesophagoscopist to see little children brought in dying or seriously ill from rough, unjustifiable, brutal attempts to remove a foreign body by such relics of obsolete surgery as the Graefe basket, the coin catcher, Bond's forceps, bristle probangs, etc.," Jackson opines, but then backtracks slightly as if to rescue the work of his peers, at least partially: "It may be thought that the bristle probang should not be included here. Possibly its use may not be very dangerous in the adult, but in infants it is, to my certain knowledge, often fatal. The only safe method is to proceed only under the guidance of the eye, as in modern oesophagoscopy."

Reliably safe entry of instruments required a euphemistic "trial and error" period, but even after a technique for entering in was mastered, there still remained "the mechanical problems of the disentanglement, disimpaction or version of foreign bodies" (NMP, 51): the art of endoscopy had been mistakenly reduced to the (formidable) introduction of the instruments, according to Jackson, with little or no attention paid to the type of foreign body and the mechanical problem it represented. As an example, Jackson describes an experienced endoscopist proceeding with the illusory sense that a coin could simply be "lifted out" without recourse to a study of the mechanical principles that attended its residence inside the upper torso, thus failing to retrieve the coin with the patient under ether for an hour.

In an attempt to drive home the necessity of treating each presentation of a fbdy as a new mechanical problem, Jackson asked his colleagues to think about the foreign body as they might a human infant, an analogy that is more interesting than it is accurate, since of course a fetus isn't exactly stuck inside a uterus, childbirth needn't rely on instruments, and a foreign body isn't a living thing. (Or is it?) Just as an obstetrician would not attempt to deliver a baby without "studying . . . the position of the foetus and every part of its anatomy in relation to the material pelvis just so must the endoscopist study the position of the foreign body and the relation to its every part to the invaded bronchus or oesophagus," Jackson urged. And "just as the obstetrician depends upon abdominal palpation to aid him in his interpretation of the presentation, so the endoscopist studies the roentgenogram" (*NMP*, 54).

Perhaps obstetrics does apply to Jackson's endoscopic work in this: his refinement of otherwise vulgar techniques was life-giving, but insofar as his technical virtuosity set him apart, it was impossible to forge analogies; instead, it risked separating him from the gang of his peers. Not wanting to claim a fame built on the failure of others, Jackson decided that when he bequeathed his fbdy collection to the College of Physicians of Philadelphia in 1924, he would not include the details of the history of damage performed by instruments, their makers, and practitioners. Explaining how to apply his grid as a field guide to fbdy prototypes in *Foreign Bodies in the Air and Food Passages (Charted Experience in Cases from No. 631 to No. 1155)*, he concludes with what he has chosen *not* to include:

> As we could not always distinguish with certainty the instrumental trauma of our predecessors from the trauma inflicted by the foreign body itself, we deemed it best to omit mention even of the obviously instrumental trauma inflicted by our predecessors. This trauma, along with the resultant pathology, enormously increased our difficulties and in some instances added to our mortality. In about 40 per cent of the cases here tabulated removal had been attempted before the patients were sent to us. All mention of this has been omitted. We have recorded in each case our own work only.

How an instrument is introduced into medical practice, how it enters into common usage and becomes eclipsed or is rendered obsolete, no doubt has as much to do with the history of attention to a particular body part, to one kind of medicine gaining ascendancy over another, to ways of seeing or touching, to diagnostic protocol and epistemic paradigm shifts as it does with economies and politics, both inside and outside the medical profession. Medical historian James Edmonson reminds us that the "technical advance of instrumentation did not always proceed in a unilinear fashion," that the "standardization of instrumentation remains an elusive ideal," and that "important changes in instrumentation have been prompted by technical advances occurring outside the recognized domain of gastrointestinal endoscopy, and even beyond medicine per se."

Edmonson delineates three phases of gastroscopic development: the "rigid endoscope" era that began as early as 1805 and ended in 1932 (these were the instruments that Jackson used); the "semi-flexible endoscope or Schindler era" running from 1932 to 1957; and from 1957 to the present, "the 'fiberoptic' era." He cites L. Walk's work in further identifying three principal kinds of endoscopes that vied for attention during the decades of the late nineteenth and early twentieth centuries, when Jackson's work would have been coming into prominence: "straight open tubes without lenses" (it was this type that Jackson used), partially pliant endoscopes, and "rigid straight tubes with optical systems."

There is much that is vexing about this history, and some of its less-than-unilinear aspects are counterintuitive. For example, while flexibility might seem like an advance over rigidity, pliancy sometimes made for less visibility, and while flexibility seemed to guarantee easier entry into the body, it sometimes led to "instrument impaction," as when the Hirschowitz Fiberscope "doubled back on itself to form a J within the stomach." While fiber optics is the state of the art that we all have heard of and can't imagine modern medicine without, fiberscopes, Edmonson explains, were slow to enter into actual practice because of client loyalty to particular endoscopic instrument companies.

Where foreign-body work in particular is concerned, it seems to me that endoscopic methodology has moved in backward-turning ways. Chevalier Jackson would be appalled to know that the average duration of an endoscopic procedure to remove a foreign body is forty-six minutes, with anaesthesia; the procedure ranges from 5 to 260 minutes; operators use baskets and retrieval nets; surgery is often called upon; and the statistics on fatalities remain high—according to a group-authored article from 2008, "Foreign-body Ingestion: Characteristics and Outcomes in a Lower Socioeconomic Population with Predominantly Intentional Ingestion," approximately 1,500 fatalities per year are attributed to fbdy ingestion in the United States. Current treatment modalities include the return to bougies to push foreign bodies further into the stomach, with the hope of a patient passing it via peristalsis, and the use of Foley catheters administered transnasally. The flexible, tubular device, which includes a balloon at one end, is inserted through the nose and into the esophagus in a procedure usually carried out by a radiologist. The aim is to push the catheter and its balloon past the esophageal foreign body and then inflate the balloon, which, when pulled back through the esophagus, retracts the foreign body into the upper throat, at which point the patient is instructed to spit it out. I can't think of a procedure more foreign (forgiving the pun) to Chevalier Jackson's exacting formulae and care.

Transnasal esophagoscopy is described by Dr. Jonathan E. Aviv as the current state of the art for examination of the esophagus, but transnasal approaches to fbdy extraction using a Foley catheter as described elsewhere in the literature seem crude and potentially unsafe compared to Jackson's meticulous protocols. The history that Aviv traces is telling. Esophagoscopies performed in Jackson's clinics were usually carried out with the patient neither sedated nor anesthetized. Topical anesthesia and intramuscular sedation were practiced from the 1940s to the 1960s, while "transoral rigid esophagoscopy has been routinely performed in the operating room with the patient under general anesthesia" since the 1960s. Even though the new transnasal examination method seems convincingly safer, even "complication-free," contemporary physicians might still lack the skill and confidence to attempt to view the esophagus of an unsedated patient. Is it possible that the ability to absent the patient anesthetically encouraged operators to be less careful than Jackson? While newfangled objects would pose fresh mechanical problems to Jackson—for example, the case of a patient swallowing five AA batteries and an audiocassette—history confirms that no one before or since Chevalier Jackson had the patience, mechanical genius, dexterity, fixity of purpose, and single-mindedness of mission to be able to remove foreign bodies with the consistently good results that he had. By his own account, he never made a single accidental perforation with one of his esophagoscopes, so adept was he in its use.

Jackson's instruments had no mirrors or prisms (Schindler's early scope had twenty-six lenses), and while other esophagoscopists inflated the stomach in order to inspect it, according to L. Walk, Jackson rested content with the view afforded by his scopes, which varied from "one third of the stomach to a complete view." The bronchoscope does not magnify like a microscope or telescope, Jackson explains in a 1938 radio talk sponsored by Philadelphia's Franklin Institute, but it does afford a direct view of the regions below the vocal cords that makes it possible to manipulate obstructing tissues out of the way and to bring others into the line of sight. The instrument had been specially designed "to facilitate its introduction; to provide a good view; to prevent injury to the tissues; and most important of all, to avoid asphyxiating the patient by shutting off all his airway." It was nothing more than a hollow brass tube slanted at its distal end with a handle at "its proximal or ocular extremity," Jackson wrote in *Bronchoscopy and Esophagoscopy: A Manual of Peroral Endoscopy*. It featured an auxiliary canal on its undersurface containing the light carrier, and numerous perforations at the end "to allow air to enter from other bronchi when the tube-mouth is inserted into one whose aerating function may be impaired." The slant of the tube helps to introduce the instrument into a canal, but if the instrument is designed with too pronounced a slant, it will perforate what it enters. Nothing is standard about these scopes, but an esophagoscope nine millimeters wide by forty-five-centimeters long reaches the stomach of most adults. The tube itself has one kind of handle, which some commentators liken to a pistol grip, and the forceps that are inserted into the tube have another kind of handle resembling the handles on a pair of scissors. Because the bronchi and esophagus cannot be dilated—"rupture or even overdistension of a bronchus or of the thoracic esophagus is almost invariably fatal" (*B&E*, 17)—Jackson designed tubes of different sizes to meet the demands of bodies at different stages of development.

"How can a straight and rigid tube be passed into, and through, the crooked passages from the lips to the bottom of the lung?" Jackson asked his radio audience in 1938, and he answered with a series of analogies. First was an ear speculum: the canal leading into the ear is crooked, and, in order to examine it, the physician "straightens the crooked canal by putting in a little funnel-shaped tube so he can look straight in to the region of the drumhead." Or these specula work on the same principle as an arm when it straightens a "bent and crumpled coat sleeve." Scores of forceps were designed to suit the nature of the foreign body, including forward-grasping, rotation, alligator, side-curved, square-built, long-jawed, spoon, and beaklike forceps. The method depended on one endoscopist accompanied by a team of assistants: one who held the patient's head, one who attended the instruments, one who held the patient's arms, and another who changed the endoscopist's glasses when they became spattered with sputum backing up through the tube. But this isn't surgery per se, and this is not exactly a surgical team: where surgery is bimanual and binocular,

Jackson stressed time and again that bronchoscopy in the service of fbdy removal is "a monocular, depth-gauging procedure handicapped by limitations due to the smallness of the bronchi and the length and slenderness of the instruments" (*NMP*, 24).

Training the eyes to work in uncommon ways, Jackson recommends that the operator proceed with both eyes open and with his right eye against the tube mouth. The scenario calls for a darkened, backlit room to help the operator ignore what he sees through his left eye and to prevent reflections from forming on the surface of his protective glasses. When these spectacles become fogged or spattered, they are immediately replaced by another pair that stand at the ready in a pan of heated water. Hand in hand with the eye of the tube mouth (see how the perceptual metaphors intersect and overlap), the mounted X-rays of the patient made by radiographer Willis F. Manges supply an indispensable visual field (Jackson places them upside down in a shadow box for a better conception of the relations in the recumbent patient). Jackson always credited Manges as a co-author in the development of the field of upper-bronchial work.

The body's interior fills up the doctor's eye before the tube—it is all that there is in the world for that moment—and yet he enjoys a severely compromised view since he only sees what appears directly in front of him inside a contracting and expanding circumference. The doctor's eyes are of the essence, as is his ability to project his knowledge of physiology into and through and down the scope, to see what he manipulates through *his mind's eye.* But touch is not diminished—rather, it is heightened as the operator feels his way in, sensing rigidities and resistances in the body, sensing the intensity and direction of the instrument's insertion, gauging depth so as not to go too deep, watching for collapsing walls and clamping folds. The eye must not mistake one opening for another, of course, but Jackson trained his students to feel anatomical parts, chinks, and byways with the distal end of the tube, and with practice to acquire what he called a "nerve-cell habit" in his fingers until manipulating human anatomy with these instruments is "made subconsciously as with the knife and fork in eating," using forceps designed by him to "permit of the delicacy of touch of a violin bow" (*B&E*, 30, 32).

Jackson attributes his tactile sensitivity to his practice as a toddler of patiently twisting slender strips of paper into lamplighters for the family. But from where did he derive his reassuring whisper, his voice's soothing patter, the calming method (truly an instrument) of his modulated tones? He removed foreign bodies with singular dexterity, but he also subtracted fear from the equation with his voice. Movement and struggle in a fbdy case can cause the fbdy to move inside the patient, and that accidental displacement can have disastrous effects. The power of Jackson's voice to still people must have been more than merely distracting; it must have been hypnotic. In Arlene Maloney's recollection, the pair of Chevalier Jacksons, both the father and the son, had this ability that everyone tried to emulate: "They didn't force it, they just took it easy, keeping up a sound of softly talking even if it was a little baby, they just kept on talking . . . if the secretary was taking notes . . . they never raised their voices, and the secretary just took down what they were saying."

A secretary is riveted by the voice; a patient is made drowsy. Where touch fails, sight enters in, and where sight fails, touch deftly registers. Voice acts as a support for the working of both, and all three serve a set of instruments as their extension inside another human body. To turn the pages of Jackson's numerous guides to the application of these instruments is to be perpetually confronted with different orders of awe. First, where bronchoscopy is concerned, there is the awesomeness of the bronchial tree's spontaneous movement, seemingly making the insertion of a rigid instrument impossible. Jackson's account shows that, to the contrary, the instrument and a host of correlative bodily responses governing inspiration and expiration work as aids to one another. "The normal movements of the trachea and bronchi are respiratory, pulsatory, bechic, and deglutitory," his account of the complex physiology of breathing begins. "The two former are rhythmic while the two latter are intermittently noted during bronchoscopy." The breathing apparatus and windpipe serve a "respiratory" function, or, medically speaking, perform a ventilating movement; they work by way of a rhythmic vibration ("pulsatory"); they are protected by the cough ("bechic") reflex; and they serve as an aid to the swallowing ("deglutitory") process. Moreover, making things both more difficult and more amenable to the introduction of an instrument:

> It is readily observed that the bronchi elongate and expand during inspiration while during expiration they shorten and contract. The bronchoscopist must learn to work in spite of the fact that the bronchi dilate, contract, elongate, shorten, kink, and are dinged and pushed this way and that. It is this resiliency and movability that make bronchoscopy possible. The inspiratory enlargement of lumen opens up the forceps spaces, and the facile bronchoscopist avails himself of the opportunity to seize the foreign body. (*B&E*, 57)

That the bronchoscopist who does fbdy work must recognize forceps spaces or create them (in other words, to gauge the amount of "wiggle room" around the fbdy) amps up the difficulty of his work. Previous doctors' ignorance of the need to allow for or create a forceps space around the fbdy could cause bleeding that obscured their view, the loss of the fbdy, and fatal harm to the patient. Physicians' tendency to "futilely jam the forceps into the mucosa in an effort to force the forceps onto a foreign body" shows them losing sight of the human body as a three-dimensional plane. "With the jaws opening sagittally," Jackson explains, they ignore "the lateral forceps spaces that would have facilitated grasping had the forceps been turned so the jaws would open in the coronal plane" (*NMP*, 55). The bronchi open and close in an immediate, not a gradual, way; nevertheless, the bronchoscopist has to intuit the start of the inspiratory phase and then and only then "promptly, though gently" insert the forceps jaws into the forceps spaces as they gape. He goes on: "the prompt collapse of the bronchial walls at the beginning of inspiration renders it necessary to start the insertion of the forceps jaws at the beginning of the inspiratory phase. If later, the jaws will be met and stopped by the collapsing walls" (*B&E*, 55).

Bronchoscopy—and esophagoscopy, too—is a matter of timing; it's a choreography of space and time that, while it might allow for invention, never allows for improvisation. Just as an athlete trains his body to move and reach in unimaginable ways, just as the sword swallower spends years practicing toward a habituation of seemingly impossible entry, Chevalier Jackson went to extraordinary lengths to make his fingers into receptors of vital information. The extent to which the athlete or sword swallower comes to know something as a result of his training is hard to judge, though it is clear that he learns to do something. For Jackson, repetition produced new knowledge as well as technique—but what was the nature of this knowledge? Jackson practiced and studied in order to know by touch exactly how much pressure a peanut kernel could withstand without being crushed, and he recommended that "the man who expects to be successful in removing peanut kernels" use "a delicate forceps well-oiled and working smoothly in his possession" to "crush a few quarts of peanut kernels to acquire the sense of tactile differentiation between the degree of forceps-pressure necessary securely to hold a peanut kernel during its withdrawal through the glottis and the degree of pressure that will crush it. This is a purely manual thing to be acquired only by feeling the peanuts crush and then feeling others against the tube-mouth while being withdrawn"

(*NMP*, 72). He studied grains of maize to determine exactly how to avoid fragmentation, noticing that kernels of corn "usually present the germ end, the center of which is soft. If this germ is grasped it will come away leaving the 'mouse-gnawed' grain behind" (*NMP*, 74). He suggested that the grain be grasped at its midpoint rather than at its tip, using special forceps he had designed for the purpose that guaranteed a combination of "gentleness of grasp with sufficient holding power" (*NMP*, 74).

For every attitude, disposition, presentation, type, and fbdy scenario, Chevalier Jackson seems to have designed a special instrument. He generally worked inductively rather than deductively, letting the fbdy dictate the choice of instrument rather than force an already existing instrument to fit the particular fbdy. Thus, a special bronchoscope was created with an oval end to accommodate both points of a swallowed staple (of which there were many in his clinics). For the rare but still occasional instance of a fbdy lodged in an upper bronchus, he designed a forceps that could reach around a corner; if the fbdy is hollow, a forceps that can fit inside the fbdy and then expand before making traction is required. The instruments must be well made—a well-made forceps, for example, hugs a fbdy, whereas a faulty forceps precariously balances upon it. All of these instruments are rendered useless if not properly cared for—and the degrees of mastery involved in Jackson's practice multiply.

How exactly does Jackson free the points of a jackstone or remove a collar button without exacting harm? (See figures 34 and 35.) What made him so capable of retrieving safety pins? In dealing endoscopically with an open safety pin, lodged point upward, you don't move forward until first determining seven essential things:

1. The size of the pin.
2. The greatest spread from the point to the keeper.
3. The exact plane of this greatest spread.
4. The direction of the point.
5. The precise location of the point, the keeper, and the spring.
6. The degree to which each of the two branches of the pin deviates from the vertical axis of the patient's thorax.
7. Bends, breaks, kinks, or other imperfections of the pin. (*NMP*, 68)

The problem of the safety pin is often solved by using the forceps first to seize and then to rotate the pointed branch of the pin. Then this branch must be enclosed inside the instrument's tube. The keeper remains outside

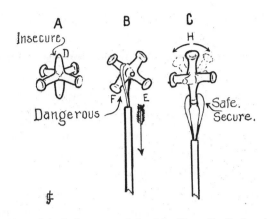

Fig. 34. The problem of the jackstone explained in Chevalier Jackson's "New Mechanical Problems in the Bronchoscopic Extraction of Foreign Bodies from the Lungs and Esophagus," Transactions of the American Laryngological, Rhinological, and Otolaryngological Society 27 (1921). *Courtesy of Thomas Jefferson University, Archives and Special Collections.*

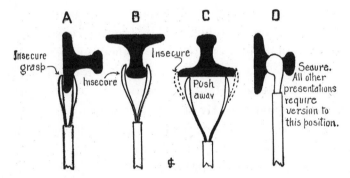

Fig. 35. Solving the mechanical problems associated with retrieval of collar buttons in the upper torso as it appears in Chevalier Jackson's "New Mechanical Problems in the Bronchoscopic Extraction of Foreign Bodies from the Lungs and Esophagus," Transactions of the American Laryngological, Rhinological, and Otolaryngological Society 27 (1921). *Courtesy of Thomas Jefferson University, Archives and Special Collections.*

the tube, and the entire ensemble slides harmlessly out through the windpipe or esophagus.

All that we cannot anticipate or imagine is literally within Chevalier Jackson's grasp in his solution to these Gordian knots, and it's neither miraculous, nor stupendous, nor transcendent: it's the effect of the application of a quality of mind—"unbefogged by alcohol," he'd be quick to add—reliant on a fundamental life-defining paradox: that nothing in the world is reliable (there are no safety nets, you're sure to fall through the rabbit hole, other people can't be trusted) and that every fbdy problem can be solved.

A splayed hairpin points upward in the esophagus. The bent part of the hairpin—its "dart"—lies lodged in the direction of the stomach while its two ends, like crinkled wings, threaten to pierce the esophageal wall on either side. Simply to grasp the dart with the forceps and attempt to pull the hairpin out could cause fatal trauma; it had done so in the past. Jackson's carefully worked-out solution shows him disengaging each point one at a time or, more literally, lifting each pin out of its crevice by placing the forceps behind the pin and then rotating each point inward using a side-curved forceps in order finally to draw both ends into the tube.

Jackson might at first resemble a watchmaker, but on further consideration, it's clear that he is a time-bomb detonator, a defuser of explosives, because his solutions depend on his figuring out a way to disengage and manipulate the fbdy against its intention to do the most harm. "It is sometimes desired to make traction on an irregularly shaped foreign body, and yet to allow the object to turn into the line of least resistance while traction is being made," he wrote in his 1922 guide to bronchoscopy and esophagoscopy. Fbdy removal begins to sound like a method from which a system of thought, a set of spiritual principles, or a philosophy could be born. Call it the chi of bronchoscopy because the operator has to be sensitive to the simultaneity of yin and yang. He must be able to activate or instigate two opposed tendencies at once. Better yet, he must allow for a slackening, give himself over to it, and exert force at the same time. Giving himself over to accidents and mistakes, admitting that forces militate against such an arsenal of skill and foresight, and accepting that error could be occasioned by the instrumentarium itself was harder, and it is especially painful to encounter, in spite of Jackson's unimaginable application and devotion and ingenuity, freak accidents to which he was not immune and (albeit rare) missteps.

In his 1908 report on some of the earliest cases in his tracheo-bronchoscopic practice, Jackson documents a fiendishly unpredictable series of events by which, working in reverse, a fbdy trapped the broncho-scope inside the patient's body, the effect of the slits in the sides of the bronchoscope being placed too near its lower end. The patient coughed as the scope was inserted, and the pin that Jackson was attempting to remove made its way into one opening in the side of the scope and out the other, so that it was lodged like a crossbar inside the instrument, trapping it inside a bronchial wall. The pin, in effect, spiked the scope into position, rigidly fixing it in place and making it impossible for the instrument to be withdrawn. Jackson was forced to break the fbdy into three pieces, two of which were withdrawn and one of which was lost. It must have been a particularly bad day, because Jackson also explains that his protective glasses had broken, and the patient had coughed cocaine (used as a local anesthetic) into his naked eye, thus leaving it to Dr. Edith Waldie to make a careful, though unsuccessful, search for the remaining bit of pin. Jackson confidently concluded that the small remaining point was lost in the secretions withdrawn with the tube and noted the child's perfect recovery, but we are left to wonder.

Jackson was an instruments man, no question. People who visited him at Old Sunrise Mills commented on the rich instrumentarium he laid out before a turkey he aimed to carve. He was both an instruments man and a doctor, and the combination of two in one (or three or four or five) helped distinguish him. Jackson was an instrument designer and a practitioner who made prototypes of his instruments on the metal lathe in his mill, and he enjoyed a lifelong relationship with the Philadelphia-based Pilling Company, which manufactured instruments for him en masse. James Edmonson concludes his short history of gastroscopy's instrumentarium by remarking upon "the central importance of the vital, creative alliance of physician and instrument maker." The two roles did not always exist so peacefully: in the mid-nineteenth century Dr. Maximilian Nitze and Josef Leiter, a leading instrument maker in Vienna, collaborated to make improvements upon the cystoscope but parted ways when "each claimed personal credit" for its design and success. Johann von Mikulicz and Josef Leiter proved a more successful team, even though their efforts were initially hampered by something Jackson criticized: they tried to use an instrument meant for one part of the body—the urethra and urinary bladder—on the very different conditions found inside the stomach. In the person of Chevalier Jackson, the physician and the instrument maker came together.

Chevalier Jackson was an artisan. A skilled laborer. An artist whose instruments are practical devices and works of art. The instruments might be part of a matrix of forces and formulae, working at the crossroads of a physician-body and a patient-body that define the practice of endoscopy, but they are also (especially when they are encountered in an archive) aesthetically charged; even more than beautiful, they are gorgeous Things.

A black tray and white gloves against instruments silvery, pristine, and absolutely clean—nothing mars them—lain against a backdrop of velvety green cloth. Down, down, down inside the Mütter Museum's basement, inside the drawers inside the moving cases inside the vaults, lay seven light carriers that seem as though they could be plucked, so truly do they resemble violin strings. If you didn't know that these were instruments of medicine, you'd suspect the tubes were musical instruments because of what resembles a mouthpiece, a spout that arcs out of the top, and the delicate holes at the bottom—surely, this is a cross between a clarinet and flute. Not really, though, because the spout is actually a hose attachment for supplying oxygen, the distal slits are drainage holes, and the tiniest hole at the top is the diminutive manhole cover that a person clings to for dear life, clings to from the underside, entire biological systems plus a soul tethered to an opening the size of a dot.

The scopes are of different diameters: one the size of a drinking straw, the other the size of a pipe, and all absolutely rigid. At the top of each is a part like a thumb or a wing that you use to hold the instrument when it is inserted. What "part" is the aperture the operator looks through? I look down through it and experience an eye within an eye, an iris within an iris. Two scopes show the same view, and a third an utterly different view. One has a wide opening at the top and two spigots fanning out like tulip heads, while the grasper is shaped like a knob, a pawn. At the base of one, a valve. Consider how tiny the circumference of the hole at the base is, and then what Jackson saw there, and what he depicted there. Now place your hand atop the cast made from his hand—the flat thumb, the knuckly, swollen joints, the slightly crooked little finger—after all this time spent imagining the fingers to be delicate and long (see figure 36). This hand, cut out, cut off, mounted, seems to perch on a bit of imaginary beach, drifting; tentacles detached from mind feel for disappearing things—the waxing and waning of inspiration, of expiration.

A seven-year-old girl stares wistfully at a glass of water. She hasn't been able to swallow even a drop of water for a week. It's amazing that she is still alive. When she tries to swallow, the water comes back through her nose and her mouth. The girl had been found on the floor of a coal miner's shanty, where her three-year-old brother was attempting to feed her water with a tin cup from a tin pail. But the water fell out of her mouth and onto her clothes, soaking her, because she could not swallow it. One of countless children who were victims of lye (see figure 37), the girl was brought to Chevalier Jackson, who passed his esophagoscope down the girl's throat and discovered a nearly closed esophagus, scars left by the lye

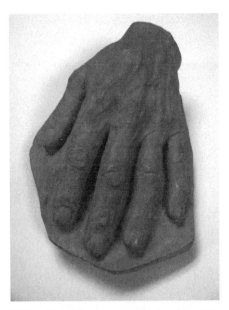

Fig. 36. Plaster cast of Chevalier Jackson's hand. Collection of the Mütter Museum, The College of Physicians of Philadelphia.

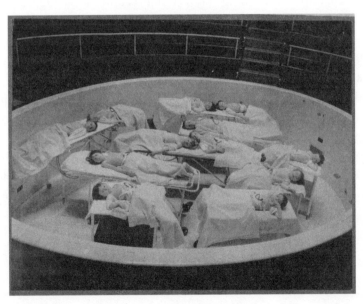

Fig. 37. Children treated for ingestion of lye in the medical amphitheater of one of Jackson's clinics. Chevalier Jackson Papers, 1890–1964, MS C 292, Modern Manuscripts Collection, History of Medicine Division, National Library of Medicine, Bethesda, Maryland.

that hadn't entirely sealed the passage, and a cork-like plug of gray matter. He removed the plug with delicate forceps:

> After removal of the instrument the child was given a glass of water. She took a small sip expecting it to choke her and come back up. It went slowly down; she took another sip, and it went down. Then she gently moved aside the glass of water in the nurse's hand, took hold of my hand, and kissed it. She took more water and a glass of milk.

At the end of two years, following dilation of the strictured esophagus with Jackson's scope, the girl "could swallow any kind of food in a perfectly normal way; she grew well and strong" (*LCJ*, 107).

Astonished that she could swallow once again, and grateful for it, the girl pauses to choreograph a search: holding aside the liquid, without which none of us can live, she seeks the hand that saved her and brings it to her lips to kiss. There's no utterance to speak of, but just this relay of lips and hands: to swallow, to kiss, to swallow again.

What are these Things? we might ask of Chevalier Jackson's instruments. What are these Things but art objects and life-saving devices; on both counts, the product of his hands (see figure 38).

Modernist Portals and Secular Tabernacles: Chevalier Jackson Meets Joseph Cornell

On a brilliant spring day in 1930, members of the French Academy of Medicine sat in a darkened room. Changes were aloft in the Parisian fashion world—white dinner jackets, banjo sleeves, wide shoulder pads, and the color shocking pink had been introduced—but these French doctors stayed inside, clamoring for a place inside an amphitheater on whose screen was projected a compelling cartoon. The animated motion picture

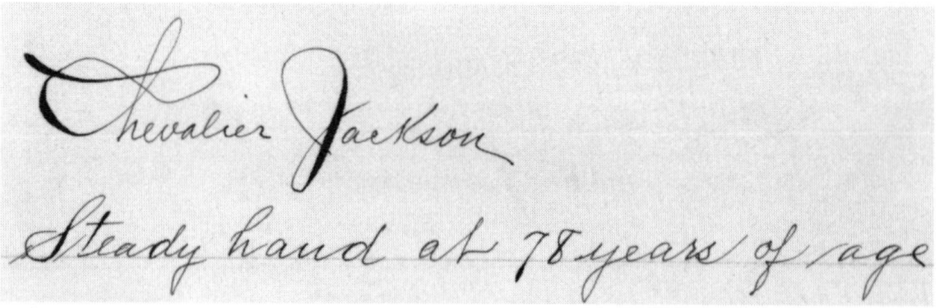

Fig. 38 Chevalier Jackson's signature with note. Chevalier Jackson Papers, 1890–1964, MS C 292, Modern Manuscripts Collection, History of Medicine Division, National Library of Medicine, Bethesda, Maryland.

illustrated, in step-by-step fashion, a bronchoscopic method for treating abscesses of the lung that the film's producer, Dr. Soulas, had learned from Chevalier Jackson.

Meanwhile, back in Philadelphia, Jackson's audiences remained steadfast in their fascination with his demonstrative method, the never merely illustrative but *embodied* visual performances for which he was known. Those students who attended Jackson's famous on-the-spot ambidextrous "chalk talks" went away dazzled and changed by the rare opportunity to bear witness, in a sense, to Jackson in repeated acts of first seeing and then remaking what he saw through his scopes in the forms of many-times-magnified chalk-pastel renderings. In this way, Jackson "worked up" the bodies that he treated, but not in the sense that medicine uses that phrase now. This was not a stats-gathering procedure, a collation, or a keeping of tabs. As if by magic, he brought the body's insides to light, as light. Jackson's hands were his imaging technology and they made for a unique pedagogical encounter irreducible to what we now think of as proplike visual "aids." The Jacksonian chalk talks exerted a curiously hands-on seeing-feeling identification between student and teacher that was impossible to reproduce, for its emphasis was on medical practice not simply as a way of seeing bodies or acting upon bodies, ill or well, but of *making* bodies.

"Dr. Jackson First Wooed Muse of Art: Bronchoscope Inventor Wields Brush."

That was the headline for a 1928 *Evening Public Ledger* article in which Jackson said the only thing that kept him from pursuing art professionally was the fear of failure, starvation, and subsequent hunger. But Jackson's art-making was not opposed to or exclusive of his medical practice. Jackson understood the manual dexterity required by painting to be in every way commensurate with the training of the hands and eyes called for by his endoscopic work. It was inextricable from and essential to his profession.

One of Jackson's "how-to" illustrations might show a physician-reader the placement of the neck and head in what came to be known as the Boyce position (named for Dr. John W. Boyce); or it might resemble pictures in an instruction manual, diagrammed with arrows and marked with letters of the alphabet as pointers. (These sorts of pictures aren't exactly suitable for framing, though one can imagine a collector of instruction manual art being intrigued by them.) Inside the same article or book, Jackson called upon a different order of art reserved for rendering the fbdy solo, unadorned by explication, there for the showy fact of it. Such illustrations don't subordinate themselves to any text but stand on their own, rendered with the exactitude and flair of a natural historian. In place of an endangered species, a cockatoo, blue jay, or red-capped sparrow, in lieu of an unfurling fern or an arboreal taxonomy of leaves, we find a tack, nail, or button, voluble, nearly embossed, so true even in black and white that we feel as though we might be able to lift it from the page.

Chevalier Jackson's offices were starkly utilitarian and fbdy-bedecked, but in the midst of that clinical coolness, one of Jackson's ochre- or hay-colored oil paintings might appear, of his home on the Ohio River, where he recovered from his first bout of tuberculosis, or of sinewy old apple trees, the gold afterglow of Old Sunrise Mills, or Alice's sewing basket. In his studio, poised before an easel of an afternoon, Jackson painted land-scapes, "A Woodland Path" of "sycamores in fall foliage, Arroyo, Pasadena, morning effect." Less often, he painted portraits—for example, of a girl named Yvonne in which the shadows from the forest make up the patches on the Sargent-like patterns of her robe (see figures 39 and 40). Are those morning glories or thin-as-paper roses of Sharon in various stages of open-ing in the undulating tapestry that is her dress? And her walnut-shaped eyes? Did they see into Chevalier Jackson's heart? Did they glimpse his woodland brights and darks?

The art that we find Jackson making in his studio with colorful palettes, sifting light inside a thicket of shapes, shows him to have been a minor mas-ter worthy of a midlife portrait of himself by himself. Instead of applying makeup, he daubs flesh tones from a palette to form a cheek on the canvas set before him. He lends himself vigor and authority, like Bozzini before him crafting a self-portrait—endoscopists as anachronistic Renaissance men—or like an Emersonian self-reliant man whose becoming a doctor is most fully realized in becoming an artist who can picture himself as such. He could be Velázquez in his studio in a photo taken at Old Sunrise Mills, or Vermeer with one modern accoutrement—a telephone (see figure 41). In the photograph, Jackson wears one kind of collar, the kerchief of an art-ist, and paints himself wearing another kind of collar, the starched formal-wear of the accomplished man. He reserved for in-person encounters the less subdued purple collar of his lab coat, the color of a priesthood: it's the regal hue of those inducted into the French Legion of Honor.

In his autobiography, Jackson broaches the possibility of an aesthetic philosophy whereby "nature and art are diametrically opposed to each other" (*LCJ*, 197). The kind of fascination produced by an encounter with the natural world, he concludes, cannot be reproduced in a painting, and when a viewer "appreciates" a landscape painting, it's not the infinitude of

Fig. 39. One of numerous black-and-white photographs of Chevalier Jackson's oil paint-ings donated to the Smithsonian Institution by Jackson's granddaughter Joan Jackson Bugbee. In Jackson's handwriting, on verso: "A Woodland Path, Sycamores in fall fol-liage [sic] Morning Effect, Arroyo, Pasadena, 25 × 30." Smithsonian Institution, National Museum of American History.

nature that astounds him but something that he does not go on to describe or to name. To say that art can only approximate nature is one thing, but to say that art and nature are "diametrically opposed" presumes that they cancel out or negate one another. Jackson may have believed this where his landscape painting was concerned—that it was a poor imitation of a finitude—but then his landscape painting doesn't venture much by way of the sublime: one step away from conventional genre painting, his land-scapes are usually resolved, balanced, flatly harmonious, and even quaint. They are indeed, "appreciations" of nature rather than investigations of it. Art and nature are allowed to overlap, whether Jackson knew it or not, in the marvelously weird medical illustrations—sometimes in charcoal, other times pastel, often in oil—that he made of the views through his scopes.

This strictly endoscopic art (see figures 7, 8, 11, and 33) is a kind of genre painting all its own and of a moment. The first acceptable color pho-tographs of the insides of the stomach weren't produced until 1937. This was about the time of Jackson's formal retirement; insofar as he remained active for the next twenty years, he continued to work by way of the naked eye rather than the camera eye, the hand that draws the body forth rather than the camera that records what it sees. Yet his illustrations in some cases

Fig. 40. From a black-and-white photograph donated to the Smithsonian Institution by Jackson's granddaughter Joan Jackson Bugbee. In Jackson's handwriting, on verso: "Yvonne, Portrait of my daughter when 12 year old, painted in 1922. 25 × 32." Smithsonian Institution, National Museum of American History.

can be compared to the first medical photographs of any kind: the microscopic daguerreotypes made by Dr. Alfred Donné of Paris in 1839, later improved upon by Dr. Joseph Janvier Woodward of Philadelphia and assistant surgeon Edward Curtis during the Civil War, described by Gretchen Worden in her introduction to the book *Mütter Museum: Historical Medical Photographs,* in which exquisite examples appear.

Rather than attaching a camera to the microscope, Woodward and Curtis made the microscope into a camera. The room was dimmed save for a thread of sunlight that streamed through a tiny hole they drilled into a shuttered window. Directing this beam through the scope and focusing it on a photosensitive plate, they coaxed along a finely tuned alchemical process that they timed with a metronome set to strike at one-second intervals. Much like Jackson, photomicrographers would magnify the images of what they saw microscopically but maintain the perfect circle or aperture as the picture's frame so as to accentuate the specialized vantage afforded by the technology, as if to remind a viewer that, from inside the furtive purchase of a peephole, the world is not what it seems.

Fig. 41. Chevalier Jackson at work on a self-portrait in the summer kitchen at Old Sunrise Mills. Courtesy of Parks and Heritage Services, County of Montgomery, Norristown, Pennsylvania.

Presented with a photomicrograph, you first think what you are seeing is a bit of the natural world—a beautiful landscape painting of delicate boughs interspersed with trunks through a break in the clouds—only to learn that this is a magnified micrographic image of the blood vessels of the human retina injected with silver nitrate. From the vantage of the photomicrograph and of Jackson's endoscopic illustrations, art and nature do not oppose each other but meet, and they do so at the threshold of the body. When the effect of the photomicrograph or the medical illustration is to confuse anatomy with nature, Jackson's aesthetic dictum must be revised, because art in these instances does not oppose nature but interprets nature. Here it locates nature inside the human body. In both cases, the technology creates affiliations and likenesses, tempting us to imagine, if not believe, that human anatomy at its minutest level mimics the sublime arrangements of forms found in nature and faithfully depicted in landscape painting. Through portals that display human physiology as a kind of "nature scene," fascination bests appreciation; or art hints at an infinitude reserved for nature at the threshold of the body.

Take, for example, a typical set of illustrations of the larynx (and a few of the bronchus) rendered by Jackson in black and white, each image set at the exact same distance apart and arranged in rows of *a, b, c,* and *d.* In every case, it is the same feature represented, and not the same feature; in each case, it is the same bit of physiology, and not the same bit of physiology (see figure 42). Something is altered, something is changed, something is distinctly different and yet the same, and we glimpse it in the interval between each image as though we were watching seriated film stills. It is clear from the protuberances and suppurations apparent in every still that we are being made to look at symptoms of disease—to remark, "This is what disease looks like"—yet it's impossible not to see each image *as* an image, see each depiction *as* art, and beautiful as such. As each image departs in this way from one kind of knowledge and toward another, it seems imitative, familiar. From another point of view, these images also look like pathways into mines into which a coal cart could enter at any time. These black-and-white illustrations are studies in vibrating shadows. What is it about them that makes them seem so much more than detached parts? Pulsing, each becomes an organism unto itself—part of a self, yes, but more than a self. Other. If, in one image, arteries resemble branches rising toward the horizon, exactly what kind of scape are we seeing through the scope? Endoscopic art is made of images that make the eye want to peer inside, to

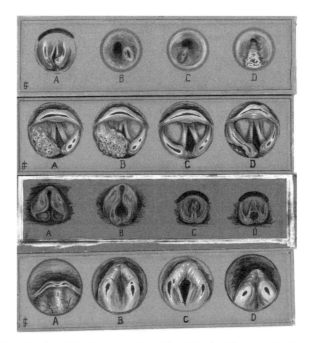

Fig. 42. Seriated endoscopic views, mostly of the (diseased) larynx, black-and-white media, by Chevalier Jackson. Collection of the Mütter Museum, The College of Physicians of Philadelphia.

look inside, to find something there, to look for what is lurking beyond the throat and into the stomach, anatomy's (or nature's?) mysterious keyhole.

After day of typical futility shaved and put on a good pair of trousers to go over to Fort Totten waterfront to find some glasses for sand boxes washed in from the Sound. . . . Some fine pieces of jetsam—one especially a toy metal horse beautifully corroded, lead with green and reddish coloring after the sea change . . .

—JOSEPH CORNELL, diary entry, October 5, 1945

Creative filing
Creative arranging
As poetics
As joyous creation

—JOSEPH CORNELL, diary entry, March 9, 1959

Inserting Chevalier Jackson into a history of art, we might think immediately to pair him with his near-contemporary, the Philadelphia realist par excellence and depicter of Samuel Gross in his famous clinic, the painter-anatomist Thomas Eakins. The artist whom his work and even his life most echoes, though, is not Eakins, but the modernist master of portals and maker of assemblages: the American visionary, untrained artist, woodworker, collector, metaphysician of ephemera, and box-maker Joseph Cornell.

The ur-scene of a Cornellian art opens onto an Alice in Wonderland playspace—a party at which the cake is more than it seems. It's edible and inedible, tantalizing and secretive, enchanting and surprising, more lasting than icing or sugar-shaped flowers. It leaves each child with an object to cherish. It marks each child as separate and distinct, and makes each child feel part of a whole. It's not a cake at all, in fact, but a pie—the Little Jack Horner pie (a specialty of Cornell's mother, according to his biographer Deborah Solomon), which is nothing more than a paper box filled with tissue-wrapped favors: "a colorful ribbon led from each plate to the gift-filled 'pie,' so that everyone at the table could become the Jack Horner of the age-old nursery rhyme, pulling out a plum." Bullied as a child, Chevalier Jackson would claim as an adult to eschew such sport. He would be horrified by a device that encourages the immanence of objects in appetite—*all things are secretly edible*—even if his own pleasing arrangement of swallowed Things is just such a pie for any visitor who opens its drawers in Philadelphia's Mütter Museum.

Cornell delivered gift packages to children in hospitals that were filled with assortments of "dimestore *objets*" and designed the last exhibit of his art for children: he set the boxes at a child's height and served cherry soda instead of champagne. Child-identified Cornell thought like a child, according to the filmmaker Marjorie Keller, revisiting childhood games, investigating the special nature of the object that is the toy—especially the toy that has been forgotten, abandoned, no longer played with, the toy sans child as remnant. The Cornell box is a toy that museums don't allow adults (or children) to handle but only to view.

Joseph Cornell and Chevalier Jackson meet for dinner as adults—not really, because neither went in much for dinner or for socializing. They meet for sweets. They both existed on food reserved for childhood—in Cornell's case, a diet of cookies and pies, pudding and donuts, Jell-O and chocolate éclairs; in Jackson's, according to Alice in a letter to his mother, "fried mush with bacon fat and brown sugar like he used to eat when a little boy. He still gets his angel cake with the candy icing." Is artistic genius dependent on a sweet tooth, or a refusal fully to "grow up"?

Like Jackson, Cornell started out as a collector of objects but soon became a maker of objects, as he called most of his early work, and then a maker of boxes inside which he arranged said objects in marvelous ways. "Sculptor" doesn't describe Cornell, nor "painter," but "assembler," whose foragings and arrangements made mere objects into Things that delicately dramatized states of being. Like Jackson, Cornell might have been an artist, but he regularly described his studio as a laboratory.

Are those bingo chips amid the birds inside of a box? What kinship can be struck between bingo chip and bird? Is that box a bird-gullet inside of which bingo chips are stuck? Inside a Cornell box, bingo chips and birds discuss the difference between tumbling and flying; they relate at the level of gravity. In a Cornell box, someone has made art out of what was thrown up by the sea onto the shore—bits of coral, driftwood, and glass. Those objects that Cornell or Jackson collected, studied, framed, cherished, rescued, and arranged can only be so big. They can only be as big as a human stomach can handle.

Both Jackson and Cornell were ascetic accumulators whose self-denial only attenuated their sensuous gifts rather than tamping them down. They were both obsessive cross-indexers. Cornell's work has been compared to the music of Debussy and Charles Ives, the poetry of Gérard de Nerval and Mallarmé, and the visual art of Ernst and Duchamp. Jackson has been compared to no one, but he should be compared to Joseph Cornell.

While best known for his boxes, Cornell also made collages. A letter from him might take the form of an intricate enfolding—a translucent envelope with the word "tinsel" inside but visible from the outside, and on the outside, the message "no need to open." Cornell witnessed "acts of sudden grace" and gathered "blue dense," bits of glass in his favorite color. He produced extensions and explorations, dossiers and constellations—a concept borrowed from Mallarmé, an infinitely expandable file box of items focused on a single burning issue, a group of trivial items linked to a grander philosophical system—in Dore Ashton's words, "the centripetal force of a topic spreading out into luminous expansion." Jackson's three-ring binders with Naugahyde covers, mechanical workbooks, and fbdy X-ray albums—might they be his own brand of dossier?

Jackson places a teddy bear eye next to a tiny hinge, which lies next to a foreign coin inside a series of frames inside a drawer (see figure 21). Cornell fills a chest with tiny blue-capped bottles containing, according to a list on the box's inside lid, watchmaker's sweepings, juggling acts, souvenirs of Monte Carlo, chimney sweeper's relics, Mayan panthers, white landscapes, and Venetian maps. Or is it "Venetian naps"? Each is a manuscript found in a bottle, à la Poe, or the deposit of castaways on a sand-swept shore, though Cornell calls the box a Museum. Of course, questions of containability are at the heart of Cornell's work, of diminution and expansion, of dream logic and an investigatory faculty.

It's too simple a thing to conclude that objects are trapped in Jackson's assemblages and liberated in Cornell's, but the status of jackstones (aka jacks) offers an interesting case in point. You put a coin into a machine and it delivers a prize. You drop a penny into a slot, crank a handle, and watch a moving picture show. The penny arcades of New York inspired a series of gamelike boxes for Cornell, many of which feature the images of Renaissance boys and girls, members of the Medici family in particular. Often enough, a jack appears in the drawer or in the unswept corner of such a box.

Jackson's work featured a jack-in-lung and Cornell's a jack-in-drawer; Jackson studied the sounds that lungs make while Cornell, filling a drawer with ball bearings and springs, invited a meditation on the sound a drawer's mechanics produces, the sound of drawers as such. Filling a drawer with sand, he invited a listening to the sound of the objects nestled inside drawers rattling and hissing, shifting and sifting when the drawer was opened. Opening a drawer is like opening a mouth, and the question of whether silence or language will issue therefrom is an either/or that invites more possibility than the tight-lipped terror of a knobless drawer (of which there are some). A jack jostles inside a drawer or gleams silver and red like a chocolate kiss seen through a tiny window. They orient a Renaissance boy at points to the right and left of his box.

A part of a jack in Jackson's images is caught in the undertow of the alimentary canal. It's a jack that can't be burped up or coughed up but sticks like a stubborn weapon, in place. Inside Jackson's drawers, a jack resists its fixed placement: it's difficult to sew one in place with its points splayed in all directions (see figure 21). Here's where Jackson departs from Cornell, because our doctor places in order to secure. Consequently, his objects are stripped of their threat but not of their menace: to pin them down is to bestow them with a vague and ambient danger, an auratic if not literal power inside a boundless fascinational field.

The prototypes of jackstones or "chackstones" (stones to be tossed) have been found in the prehistoric caves of ancient Greece and Ukraine, but before the six-pronged iron types, they were fashioned from the knucklebones of animals. Jackson's jackstones seem nearer to those jacks made from cartilage, tinged with physiology and then shuffled like stacks of skulls in an ossuary, whereas Cornell's jacks have the hand and the eye and the movement in mind of the game from which jacks hail, a game in which one act must be completed while another is suspended in midair.

Consider the uncanny likeness between the plates that figure in Jackson's *Diseases of the Air and Food Passages of Foreign-Body Origin* and a box made by Cornell categorized as a *Forgotten Game*, circa 1949 (see figures 33 and 43). Jackson's portals arranged inside a boxlike frame, his medical illustrations of caught fbdies, certainly seem like versions of Cornell's rows of bird-filled circles—or is it the other way around? In place of vocal cords or cartilaginous bridges, Cornell places perches made of tiny dowels; every hole exposes not the view through a bodily canal but a nut-hatch, enclosing the sound an animal makes inside walls, the sound of contained fluttering. Cornell's circles telescope down, as the images they capture grow more vast. They wend large to small to large again. They dilate incrementally, like a harmonic or mathematical order, whereas Jackson's circles are like soap bubbles of different sizes, a menagerie ascending and descending in size, seemingly haphazard. Jackson's circles are marked with numbers that seem arbitrarily out of order except that this same exact idiosyncratic numbering sequence (1, 2, 3, 4, 7, 5, 8, 6, 9) repeats in other illustration plates in the book. This could recommend the numbered cups on a Skee-Ball machine—that game of part skill, part luck—or a pattern that only he can master.

Jackson's illustration is accompanied by an explanatory text, while Cornell's title calls forth a narrative that we can only make up. In what sense is the game to which Cornell's box refers "forgotten"? Is it forgotten because it has been abandoned, and do we therefore apprehend a halo of loss and neglect around the box, the unplayed game, stripped now of its original pleasure? Or is the game forgotten because this kind of fun, this sort of pleasure-making device, has gone out of style? Is it forgotten because amnesia has set in around a particular form of violence—the violence of the shooting gallery as a stand-in for some other form of 1940s violence (notice that the shooter seems to have hit and missed, shattering the glass in the game's lower right corner). Or forgotten because we've forgotten what birds can tell us about weather—an impending storm, say. *Forgotten Game* cross-references Cornell's Dovecote series, although it also fits squarely inside the Slot Machine or Penny Arcade series, which in turn cross-references the Aviaries and Hotels series.

The Dovecote boxes unleash a host of romantic associations (remember Proust? "Just as she would sooner have rented an estate on which there was a Gothic dovecote or another of those old things that exercise such a happy influence on the mind by filling it with longing for impossible

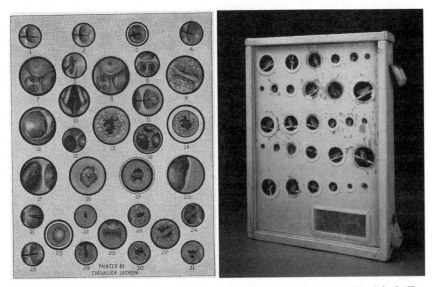

Fig. 33 (left: see caption on page 201). Fig. 43 (right). Joseph Cornell, Untitled (Forgotten Game), *c. 1949, box construction, 21⅛ × 15 × 3⅞ inches, Lindy and Edwin Bergman Joseph Cornell Collection, 1982. The Art Institute of Chicago, catalog no. 1852.*

voyages through time"), and their origin is a kind of cabinet of curiosity in which the specimens are alive. Call them pigeon chambers. Cornell's Dovecote boxes enabled him to arrive at some of his most gorgeous forms, as in the famous all-white dovecote in which small wooden balls stand in for birds, their placement both still and verging, about to roll, casting a kind of magnetic glow across the box, creating the idea of the bird not quite arrived, the bird not quite departed.

What Jackson's medical illustrations and Cornell's boxes have in common is a preoccupation with portals, leaving us to wonder what either man's work asks us to see through its holes. From the outside, the body has but a few sets of openings, but there are openings inside as well, openings within openings, and Chevalier Jackson's illustrations almost always begin at the inside portal, the mouth of a cave that is the back of the throat, just as Cornell, going inside the Dovecote, proves that it's not just a beautiful building from without.

You stand in line and wait your turn to discover why everyone is gasping, laughing, or awestruck before an aperture inside a Piranesian square atop a hillside in Rome. The hole is small, but it gives way to a resplendent view of the Vatican with long rows of cypress trees on either side. The tunneling effect is part of the gasp-making pleasure of the view because a tunnel masks off everything else in the world—but that only tells half the story, because the tunnel that is an aperture limits and opens up vision simultaneously, just as pigeonholes aren't narrowing biases but concurrent worlds, white forms and their shadows, part of a complex geometry, each distinct.

Among Cornell's earliest boxes were pillboxes, remade. In place of pills in a bottle labeled "Sure Cure for That Tired Feeling," Cornell supplied his own idea of a cure-all, according to Solomon: "tiny shells, sequins, red ground glass, rhinestones, beads, black thread, scraps of blue paper— a mix of natural and theatrical ephemera that hint at a very personal prescription for well-being." Chevalier Jackson, we will recall, was not a medicine-giving doctor but one who gave his art to cure. "Sure Cure for That Tired Feeling?" Try that collection of Chevalier Jackson's swallowed Things. While Cornell was seeking access to a glorious metaphysic, Jackson always held the human body in view. The "physick," the body preeminent: in one case, the audacity of repeating compasses, numerous rows of the same thing arranged inside a box; in the other, the audacity of getting to draw vaginas and call them larynxes again and again and again.

IV.

MYSTERY BONES AND THE UNRECOVERED BOY

Microscopical mounts and lantern slides also sent were unfortunately not received through some failure in the mail.

—Footnote to Chevalier Q. Jackson,
"The Bacillus of Leprosy: A Microscopical
Study of Its Morphological Characteristics"

The hand must have been beautiful and was certainly exacting that dipped a pen into India ink and addressed Chevalier Jackson as "My dear Doctor." The ink was fine, the sentiments heartfelt and unfading in the letter sent on December 9, 1923. But words tell only part of the tale of their author's affection for Chevalier Jackson, because, in the corner of each missive that he sends, this writer gifts to Jackson a watercolor illustration. In grades of red and blue and brown, of black, chartreuse, and whitening inside a shade, the artist performs a sketch that feels like magic: who is this boyish figure that he draws, and what is this pose reclining? (See figure 44.)

His head is given body with the paintbrush, as if to say you'll know him by his dark and curly locks. His legs are crossed as he leans both back and forward, bent intensely toward an instrument he seems to play. The boy's right arm outstretched reaches further into space than any real arm could command, and his bow, a mythic bronchoscope, is alarmingly sleek and long. It passes through the figure's other arm and rests beneath no hand but a form more nearly resembling the tail of a sea creature. Or perhaps it *is* a hand, limp-wristed. Into the upper torso, the painter has seen fit to pencil in the prospect of an inner anatomy not exactly X-rayed but conceived. "You are a Greek god," the image would say if it could, "and you play the bronchoscope for me, playing it upon your own body."

The same line that urges the bronchoscope into space marks the field of a pregnant pause inside the letter, a long-drawn blank or gasp, and later crosses the first letter of the writer's last name, F, with a flourish, as well

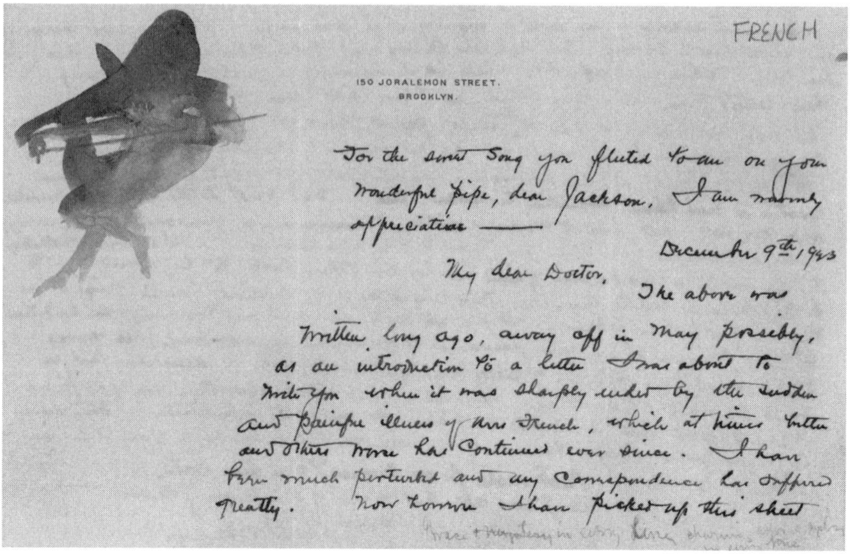

FRENCH

150 JORALEMON STREET.
BROOKLYN.

For the sweet Song you fluted to me on your wonderful pipe, dear Jackson, I am warmly appreciative ——

December 9th, 1923

My dear Doctor,

The above was written long ago, away off in May possibly, as an introduction to a letter I was about to write you when it was sharply ended by the sudden and painful illness of Mrs French, which at times better and others worse has continued ever since. I have been much perturbed and my correspondence has suffered greatly. Now however I have picked up this sheet

Fig. 44. Letter from fellow laryngologist Thomas R. French to Chevalier Jackson with illustration and the caption "For the sweet Song you fluted to me on your wonderful pipe, dear Jackson, I am warmly appreciative." Chevalier Jackson Papers, 1890–1964, MS C 292, Modern Manuscripts Collection, History of Medicine Division, National Library of Medicine, Bethesda, Maryland.

as, in other notes, the bar atop the J in Jackson. Alongside the image, the writer pens a caption that gives the gift the feel of an illuminated manuscript. It reads: "For the sweet Song you fluted to me on your wonderful pipe, dear Jackson, I am warmly appreciative————"

What is the nature of this gold among the dross, so marvelous? For how many years have these exquisite letters, rendered by a fellow doctor/artist, been lodged inside the archive's endless gullet, lost inside interstices of mail we might call junk? In the National Library of Medicine, I put in a thumb, and pulled out a plum, in the corner of which I found another watercolor view of wizard Jackson from the side and from behind. It's nearly cubist. His diaphanous outfit is a dazzle of wings, a conductor's tuxedo tails, a cape, as he poises the instrument to enter no body but amorphous space, the pool of light that is the origin of color. From the corner of another piece of stationery, a polar bear looks back toward a world outside the edges of the alphabet, having emerged from an inkblot of ice to which he might return. The caption in red ink to offset the letter's black, dated April 9, 1926, is full of whimsy: "Going far North? / Very fashionable just now! / If you head that way early in June / Don't forget to stop off in

Montreal where your presence would be welcomed and inspiring." The letter itself then begins in the writer's voice: "My dear Doctor Jackson, The blot-of-a-bear having had his say I'll take the floor for a minute or two to say to you that we are grateful for you because you are developing a new and better form of medicine, in physiology, in anatomy and in therapeutics."

The letters from this admirer almost always begin with words of praise beneath illustrations rendered ever more elaborate, as in "My dear Doctor Jackson, A man who can perform such magic in the passages of humans as your good self must possess other gifts which express themselves in artistic form." At this crossroads of art transmuting into doctoring transmuting into art, the writer inscribes a biblical-seeming figure, barefoot and sandaled in shepherd's garb who wrestles an unidentifiable creature, part dog. The caption explains, "As our modern Cyclops / Strangles disease in the / lower airways of Man." But the pièce de résistance inside these letters comes in the form of a drama wrought in lovingly crafted miniature, a world within a world upon the page (see figure 45).

The paintbrush must have been hewn to a point fine as any embroidery needle that enabled Jackson's friend to tease open the imagined cabin of a boat, sagittally, and bring to life an entire narrative therein. An American

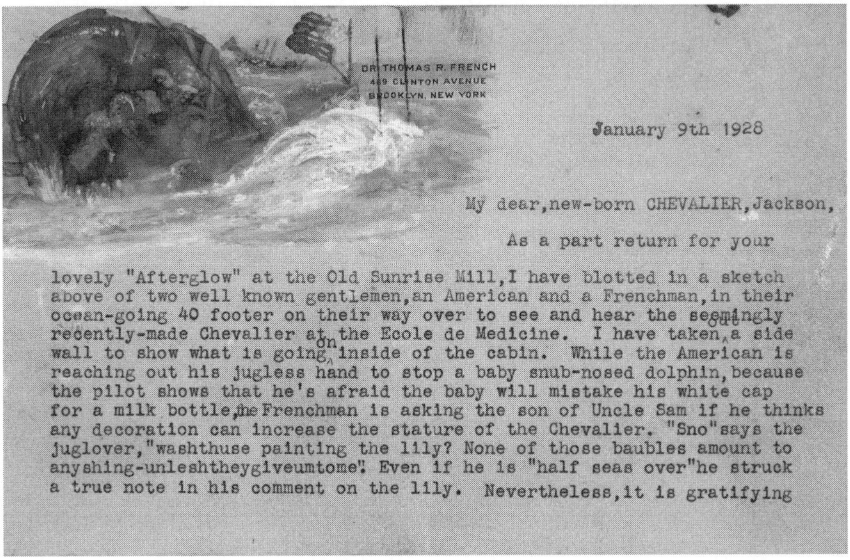
DR THOMAS R. FRENCH
489 CLINTON AVENUE
BROOKLYN, NEW YORK

January 9th 1928

My dear, new-born CHEVALIER, Jackson,

As a part return for your lovely "Afterglow" at the Old Sunrise Mill, I have blotted in a sketch above of two well known gentlemen, an American and a Frenchman, in their ocean-going 40 footer on their way over to see and hear the seemingly recently-made Chevalier at the Ecole de Medicine. I have taken out a side wall to show what is going on inside of the cabin. While the American is reaching out his jugless hand to stop a baby snub-nosed dolphin, because the pilot shows that he's afraid the baby will mistake his white cap for a milk bottle, the Frenchman is asking the son of Uncle Sam if he thinks any decoration can increase the stature of the Chevalier. "Sno" says the juglover, "washthuse painting the lily? None of those baubles amount to anyshing-unleshtheygiveumtome". Even if he is "half seas over" he struck a true note in his comment on the lily. Nevertheless, it is gratifying

Fig. 45. Illustrated letter of congratulations from Thomas R. French to Chevalier Jackson upon his receipt of the French Legion of Honor. Chevalier Jackson Papers, 1890–1964, MS C 292, Modern Manuscripts Collection, History of Medicine Division, National Library of Medicine, Bethesda, Maryland.

and Frenchman, he explains, are en route to France "to see and hear the seemingly recently-made Chevalier at the Ecole de Medicine"—his point being that Jackson, about to receive the Legion of Honor, and thus to be dubbed Chevalier, is already a Chevalier, both literally and figuratively. He doesn't need an award for us to know his worth—"washtheuse painting the lily," the fictional American "half seas over" asks, while the writer gifts to Jackson the vivid wheel by which one steers the ship, a flag upon a mast, even other boats upon the horizon tucked into the corner of a letter. The white blue froth of ocean water meets the shore of these words in red: "My dear, new-born CHEVALIER Jackson." The figures in his painting evince a drama that can keep Jackson company on his trip to receive his medal, and to thank him for the image he had sent through the mail, a reproduction of a painting of the Mill titled *Afterglow*.

One wonders if Jackson appreciated the humor here—if imagining the American's being drunk ("half seas over" and beset by slurring words) betrays how much or how little the writer knew his addressee—but whereas Jackson sent him copies of his work (as he did to many people around the new year and holidays), this doctor/artist sent originals: the painting *was* a letter, a correspondence meant for Jackson, and him alone.

The man who writes these letters and paints these pictures is a fellow laryngologist named Thomas R. French. He is seventy-eight years old when he writes this particular letter to Jackson, who is sixty-three, but he addresses Jackson as a "boy" in a correspondence that doesn't shy away from being amorous. "When you told me of the two supreme honors I felt that I too had been decorated, for the swords touched the shoulders of my friend," he writes, and then, relying on the power of a pause, he adds: "For, dear boy, I have learned to love you."

French's *New York Times* obituary, which appears exactly one year following this letter, describes him as a "noted Physician," a specialist of the throat and nose and a professor of laryngology at the Long Island Hospital who was still practicing up until the moment of his death from pneumonia at age eighty. No children from his marriage to Helen M. Wilson (a cousin of Woodrow Wilson) appear among his survivors. French was at one time the president of the American Laryngological Association and had recently completed a study on the pathology and diagnosis of disease of the tonsils; he was a prolific physician/researcher whose articles from the 1890s focused on methods of photographing the larynx—"Laryngeal and Postnasal Photography with the Aid of the Arc Light" and "On a Perfected

Method of Photographing the Larynx"—and other subjects reflective of the then-burgeoning medical specialty. Among my favorites are "Action of the Glottis in Singing," "Lymphoid Growths in the Vault of the Pharynx," "Mouth Breathing: Its Cause, Effects and Treatment," and "Two Voices and a Double Epiglottis," about a singer and contortionist who was able to command two entirely distinct voices: one a high falsetto, and the other low. "He uses either according to habit or association, and asserts that many of his friends are not aware that he has two voices," though he was apt to use the high voice with his family and reserve the low voice for business. High and low come together in performance when he, starting out low, suddenly breaks into falsetto "to produce a sensation." According to one of Jackson's textbooks, *Peroral Endoscopy and Laryngeal Surgery*, French had designed an operating table that bore his name and that Jackson preferred at the time to all others. In a discussion of the endoscopic tables then available, Jackson notes that "in an emergency any sort of table can be used, but where a special table is to be provided, the best one to be obtained is that of Dr. T.R. French designed especially for nasal and throat operations."

Dr. French's letters, things of beauty in themselves, discuss the status of a patient in common, new forms of laryngeal illuminations, French's progress on a chapter in a forthcoming textbook edited by Jackson—professional matters all, but marked by an exquisite intimacy in every way, and one can't help but notice how French, even in the shortest letter, even if he must go in through the back door of his narrative's logic, never misses an opportunity to tell Chevalier Jackson how much he loves him.

Their patient in common, a Miss King, is evidently special—"one of the loveliest human beings it has been [French's] good fortune to know," leaving him "distressed not only because of her condition but also because [French is] not privileged to serve her in any way." But this is just a prelude to the tones he wishes to play upon his pipe for Jackson:

> A world whose inhabitants were all of Miss King's type would look so delectable that we would all want to go there. If such a world should exist then my good friend I should expect that you would be picked for one of its inhabitants. This world is however much richer because of the use you have made of your life and brilliant powers.

"There's a Place for Us" might be Dr. French's theme song, and even when he's seeming paternal, there's a touch of Greek-derived eros to be found, as in these lines from his letter of congratulations to the newly born "Chevalier":

> The Athenian fathers in the time of Pericles advised their sons to live in such a way that the world would be the better for their having lived in it. Strife for such a mark is to me the essence of greatness. You have always aimed high and have hit the mark. I am not a Chauvinist. Napoleon never appealed to me. A cause is never lost if the aim is for something higher than oneself. The Creator made a fine man when he made you, and in your work you are a class by yourself.

French uses language lushly and caringly, telling Jackson how impressed he is with "the splendor of his laryngostasis and laryngostat which marks a brilliant advance in work about the vocal bands." He refers to Jackson's articles animatedly as "wonderful stories," for which he thanks him, and compares his scholarly presentations to "chapters from the Arabian nights." He sends Jackson a "laryngeal photograph" which, he tells him, "looked worthy enough to live in your den," but he's convinced it must have "missed" Jackson because he's sent it to his Philadelphia office rather than to Old Sunrise Mills. Did the photo sent by American Express get lost in the mail, or did Chevalier Jackson not acknowledge it swiftly enough for Thomas French's taste?

Is it possible to find the contours of a personality etched inside the sentences that cluster inside a thin layering of leaves called "letters"? French uses language robustly and with kindness ("with best wishes for a gladsome year"); he appears a generous and buoyant personality; and he continuously exerts a desire to be closer to Chevalier Jackson: if he will send Jackson a work "to live" in his den, he describes the reproduction of one of Jackson's paintings, in turn, as "beautiful . . . it will be good to live with." These things you send me, he seems to say, I don't just acquire them and then throw them in a drawer. What you give me lives with me, and what I send you, I expect will fuel the fire of your living too.

A letter describing the death of Mrs. French is the only one among this slender ream of correspondence that is, understandably, without an illustration. French's description of Helen Wilson's passing is heartbreakingly loving, but this does not preclude his taking the opportunity offered by thanking Jackson for his sympathy to tell Jackson once again the extent to which he has, in a sense, pierced him:

August 8, 1924

My dear Jackson,

It was good to get your [illegible: word? hand?] of sympathy. It shows the man and expresses real feeling with great simplicity of language. It would serve as a key to your success in writing. And yet, bless you, you say: "words are useless anyway." That's too true for many but not for you, for these from your hand are like meat to me.

I tried hard to keep Mrs. French longer—she so wished to live—but her call had come; a call which could not be deferred, and so in her unconscious state, and it may be from the far away hazy shore, she saluted with a smile and took wing. Somehow your personality has worked itself into me and I hold you dear,

Your friend————

And the line pierces through the name, French.

Book reviews, obituaries, and presumed "tributes" to Chevalier Jackson picture him as a friendless loner. "He never had an intimate friend, never a confidante," one colleague, Dr. John W. Boyce, bluntly declared. Another, the Scottish laryngologist James McCrae, remarking on Jackson's unfailing generosity and helpfulness but personal detachment said, "He is the warmest-hearted cold-blooded man I ever met" (*LCJ*, 169). In a posthumous tribute, Louis Clerf described him as having "no intimate friends or confidante," as never accepting a social invitation, "feeling that life was too short to waste the time." At the meetings of the various professional societies at which he spoke, we're told he appeared only at the scientific session and never at the social hour or banquet. Leave it to some sifting in the archives, an accidental bobbing to the surface of a many-paneled wave, to prove the myth untrue—for, in the letters of Thomas R. French to Chevalier Jackson, we find the presence both of confidante and friend. Which is not to say that the relationship does not remain in some essential way mysterious, or that Jackson's reticence was a cover for a deeply social man. Jackson may have encouraged a perception of himself as friendless, but it seems more likely that what he truly was was quiet, private. He kept his friends to himself. Friends and admirers abound in the documents that shape the archive, as do, in equal measure, mysterious relations, missing parts, and unsolvable riddles.

Jackson clearly had a beloved close friend in Angelique Piquenias, a Breton from Quimper, whom, the story goes, he "discovered" on one of his trips to his beloved France. She traveled with him back to the United States as early as 1920 and worked as his close and formidable personal secretary until the end of his career. "My aunts have learned to love you and pray for you in gratitude for what you have done for me," she writes on one of sixteen separate postcards sent to Jackson on a trip back home to Brittany in 1935. Fellow laryngologist Gabriel Tucker, also onetime president of the American Laryngological Association, admired Jackson so much that he named one of his sons after him. Even today, according to Chevalier Jackson's great-grandson Frank Bugbee Jr., admirers of Jackson—including people who as children were saved by him—seek out Frank to share their admiration for his ancestor, like the anesthesiologist from Texas whom Jackson treated as a boy and who called Frank to say that he keeps a shrine to Chevalier Jackson in his living room.

Novels could be written from the sundry untold details of a lifetime of relationships left ajar that startle, refuse to square, or deserve more mention. Who was the unnamed bachelor responsible for paying young Jackson's passage to Europe in order that he might study with Morell Mackenzie? The "bachelor," who suffered from a chronic throat ailment, funded this key moment in Jackson's career in exchange for the promise that Jackson would treat his throat for the rest of his life. What were the circumstances of the suicide of the Pittsburgh laryngologist who helped Jackson establish his early practice there? Dr. William H. Daly, another in the line of presidents of the American Laryngological Association, had been despondent since the death of his wife several years prior and was "suffering from melancholia" when he killed himself, according to the 1901 *New York Medical Journal*. How did Jackson weather the loss of this important colleague, whose aid and generosity Jackson found as "invaluable" in the early, lean years of his entry into the profession (*LCJ*, 87)? What could explain the remoteness that Chevalier L. Jackson seemed to exhibit toward his father even as they shared a profession and worked nearly side by side until his untimely death just a few years after Jackson's? If Jackson's son was absent—C.L. was traveling in Brazil when his father died, a situation that Jackson anticipated in his own instructions about his funeral arrangements—who was the girl that Jackson painted in 1922 named Yvonne (see figure 40), described on the back of a photograph of the painting as "portrait of my daughter when 12 years old." Descendents of Jackson to whom I've spoken do not know who she is, but the painting is clearly Jackson's and the handwriting unmistakably his, yet we know he had no daughter. Perhaps she was a metaphorical daughter: she was some-one whom he loved enough to paint.

Chevalier Jackson was not friendless: *that* mystery is solved. Thomas Rushmore French. Chevalier Quixote Jackson. Two men with middle names monumental and seemingly "made up." "[A]nd now that my pen is running on paper for you": if Thomas French's heart did not bleed for Chevalier Jackson, at least his pen ran for him. In what might have been the last letter French would write to him—French's closing words seem so final: "With best wishes for a gladsome year and life, Cordially yours, my friend Jackson, As always, TFrench" (with the T and F written as one)—French mentions a paperweight he is working on for Jackson. It's not clear by his language if this is a commissioned task or a gift from a friend long in the making:

> A heavy demand upon my time has forced me to delay the making over of the inscription on your paper-weight. I am, however, sending it now with this. It goes by express. The red in the lettering got scared when the fixa-tive was dropped upon it, and ran. I was about to make another when it oc-curred to me that as it was a relief to the flat white and black, a little dressy I thought, you might prefer it. If you don't like it, I'll do it over any time.

Once again, Thomas French's ink runs for Jackson; Thomas French, like a gentle kinsman, incites Chevalier Jackson to be more venturesome; to admit his love of "dressiness" in lieu of a reputation for self-denial.

Closing a folder feels like ending a chapter, and there's something sad about returning the letters to their position of a needle inside the haystack that is an archive. Perhaps my finding French will lead to a fresh display—has his unabashed expression of affection found its time? I can see these letters featured now inside a glassed case or cabinet of curiosity for the story that they tell of perfect correspondences: of doctors who are also artists; or of unremarked Americans who had a knack for painting and design. But wait: I can't quite put the letters back and tucked away because a heedless scrawl draws my eye. Someone else has scribbled something at the bottom of one of Thomas French's letters to Chevalier Jackson in faint pencil. A sentence at the bottom of an otherwise pristine letter reads: "Grace and ~~mystery~~ in every Line, charming color and [a word that might be "mystery"] in every tone." Who was the man or woman who wrote that line? Possibly a friend, of mine.

•   •   •

Philadelphia was his workplace, but when he traversed the distance back to Old Sunrise Mills each day, Chevalier Jackson entered into a deeply quiet, rural space, ascending climbs and steeps with views of promontories, past totemlike power lines. Come June, the roadways of Montgomery County are lush, and the highway en route is pebbly and jagged, braced on either side by those brown-black rock climbs that could pass for the Pennsylvania Rockies. Clumps of low-lying trees and bushes contract space on the back roads that open just as dramatically into fields. The barn and mill and bridge, the walls and archways, the house on the hillside overlooking the wide-bottomed pond rely on rough-hewn stone and carefully planed dark wood for their construction, and one expects the damp hush of a monastery, birdsong rustling the somnolent shade, a haven that was no doubt the closest Chevalier Jackson could get to the idea of a country house in France.

"This was a very private place," Arlene Maloney reiterates about Old Sunrise Mills, and we're reminded of the eccentric touches that Jackson impressed upon it that made it his, like the inclusion of a stove on his small boat to cook the fish he caught; the stand of automobile batteries that he lined up inside the mill and charged with running millstones for electricity; or his habit of buying old barns that extended outward from the property, taking down the top part of these barns, and using the material to make new houses.

I'm in the final, final archive when I find the article, a tiny news clipping really, about the size of three postage stamps laid end to end, floating inside a folder bulging with miscellany in the name of "biographical material on Chevalier Jackson and family." The archive is one of the last repositories I had to visit, the Chevalier Jackson Postcard Collection in the Conwellana-Templana Collection at Temple University.

Foul Play Ruled Out in Case of Mystery Bones

The Evening Bulletin, May 17, 1974

Two Montgomery County workmen were startled yesterday while inspecting the county's pre–Revolutionary War Sunrise grist mill on Neiffer road in Upper Frederick Township, Pa.

In the Mill's dark and dusty third floor, they came across an old cardboard box filled with human bones. They called state police who called Dr. John Hoffa, Montgomery County coroner.

The bones, wrapped in a June 18, 1926, edition of *The Public Ledger*, included a skull, jaw, pelvis, arm, and fingers.

Dr. Hoffa ruled out foul play and called the bones "a beautiful work of dissection, done by a professional."

The box of bones probably was left there by Dr. Chevalier Jackson, a physician who owned the mill before it was acquired by the county some years ago, Dr. Hoffa said.

Chevalier Jackson worked in Philadelphia but he lived and worked at Old Sunrise Mills. Did he even read the *Public Ledger*? After all, he had an aversion to newspapers and their men. One doesn't picture him reading the paper even though he often appeared in it as one of the city's stars. Instead, he uses the paper to wrap an assortment of human bones that he stows in an attic on his property. He doesn't bury the bones beneath a floorboard like a crazed character from Poe; nor need we imagine him throwing back his head with the delight of a mad scientist as he wraps and stows his human specimens, laughing a throaty laugh into the surrounding silence. It's not as though he was hiding something when he wrapped and stored the bones, and yet one imagines he would not have been happy with their coming to light in the way they did, via a sensational-seeming story run in a newspaper many decades after he deposited them there.

Foul play versus beautiful handiwork versus stabs, jabs, and cuts administered "professionally" rather than with homicidal intent of malice: the assumptions are beguiling. If the dismemberment is a hatchet job, something sinister transpired; if, however, the disassemblage of the human skeleton shows signs of clean cuts, there is no reason to presume criminality and therefore no mystery to be explored, investigated, or solved. "Foul Play Ruled Out"—well, it depends on how you define foul play and if you don't wish to investigate the criminal element that attended the anatomy class for centuries before legislation was introduced, i.e., body snatching, grave robbing, and the use of human cadavers without consent. Ruling out "foul play"—the word the coroner opposed it to was "beautiful"—presumes that all murderers are bunglers and that all doctors work methodically, though of course some doctors are butchers and some murderers are masterminds. What's more sinister? A methodical dissection or one carried out in a fit of irrational, irascible rage? We might need to bring Poe back in to answer that; we might need to consider how the most truly perfect crimes are those that have science as their alibi. But is it possible that the article was trying to say that the bones showed no signs of violence done against a *living* body but only some act performed upon a *dead* one?

"Mystery bones": methodology does not render the bones any less "mysterious" even if the newspaper article would like to dismiss any query attaching to its wonderfully evocative phrase. Attics are mysterious, as are archives, and bones recovered in either place more mysterious still. I expect bones to be placed in a resting ground marked with a memorial to the person to whom they once belonged, not wrapped in newspaper and placed in an attic alongside the Christmas ornaments and grandfather's broken violin. An attic is the place where we put things that we have no room for anymore but that we need to keep, the things that are part of a house's inhabitants' collective unconscious.

What act or set of acts do these bones hark back to in the life of Chevalier Jackson? To whom did they belong? Do the particular parts hold significance? How were the bones disposed of following their discovery in the 1970s? What were they doing in Chevalier Jackson's attic wrapped in newspaper? Cadavers were shared by students in anatomy classes in the nineteenth century, and it's likely that these bones date back to Jackson's classes at Jefferson—that a cadaver was assigned to a group of physicians-in-training, and parts of it distributed among them. Integrity is hardly paramount, as I learn from osteologist and current curator of the Mütter Museum, Anna Dhody, who explains that there is a definite possibility that the bones did not all come from the same individual but were collected over a number of years from multiple dissections. The skull and pelvis were used by ethnologists as indicators of gender and of race; they were considered the parts of the human skeleton from which the most information could be gleaned about a person's "identity." Possibly this collection constituted Jackson's teaching specimens and there is nothing untoward about the fact of their existence.

"Oh those bones, oh those bones, oh those skeleton bones. Oh those bones, oh those bones, oh those skeleton bones. Oh those bones, oh those bones, oh those skeleton bones. Oh mercy how they scare!" The famous spiritual "Dem Dry Bones," with music composed by James Weldon Johnson, is used to teach young children about anatomy, as it moves on in its second jaunty stanza to connect all the parts—the leg bone connected to the knee bone, the knee bone connected to the thigh bone, etc.—but the fright implicit in the song might serve as a reminder that the people most often *anatomized* in the history of medicine were the disenfranchised:

suicides, executed felons, paupers, and, in the United States, African Americans. To unlock the mystery of the bones held in Chevalier Jackson's attic is to acknowledge the fact that these bones were probably those of one or more persons of color. John Harley Warner explains in *Dissection: Photographs of a Rite of Passage in American Medicine, 1880–1930,* that not only were most of the bodies used for dissection in Jefferson Medical College in the nineteenth century procured from the African American burial ground, Lebanon Cemetery, but racism and murderous intent ran high when the secret practices of the anatomy class were exposed:

> When the demonstrator of anatomy at Jefferson Medical College in Philadelphia was indicted in 1882 on charges of conspiring with body snatchers to steal cadavers from Lebanon Cemetery, student solidarity seemed only to redouble. Jefferson students heralded the resumption of classes by breaking into a parody chorus of the abolitionist anthem "John Brown's Body," calling with racist epithets for black subjects to be brought in for anatomical demonstration, and demanding that the reporter who had broken the story be lynched. "We might have some fun, the *Philadelphia Press* quoted one student. "We might make a few fresh stiffs, too."

In his discussion of the phenomenon of a burgeoning tradition of dissecting-room photographs, particularly those in which medical students pose with their cadavers, Warner notes a shared history with "commemorative" photographs of lynchings; in fact, "some professional photographers made part of their living taking *both* lynching and dissection photographic portraits."

Does dissection provide indispensable knowledge of the human body that cannot be acquired otherwise, or is its main purpose to socialize doctors as a breed apart and stage a rite of passage that secures a doctor's entry into the profession? Numerous historians of medicine are currently willing to consider how these questions are implicated in each other, and *Dissection* brings into broad daylight the terms and conditions of a profoundly powerful medical taboo.

"Dem bones, Dem Dry Bones" returns us to the Old Testament's valley of death, whose bones Ezekiel's faith in God is meant to re-inspire with life: "The hand of the Lord was upon me, and he brought me out by the Spirit of the Lord and set me in the middle of a valley; it was full of bones. He led me back and forth among them, and I saw a great many bones on the floor of the valley, bones that were very dry. He asked me, "Son of man, can these bones live?" I said, "O Sovereign Lord, you alone know" (*Ezekiel* 37:1–3, New International Version). The song, the spiritual, is not merely an anatomy lesson but an attempt to reassemble the disarticulated bones of slavery's history, which includes the history of racist medical practice. Bones do speak; they report the history of a body and of a life lived, not merely the virtuosity of the medical student who severed and studied them as a means to secure his professional identity. Jackson's attic contained a skull that once harbored a brain and a personality, a physiognomy, a nod; a hand that held or wrote; a pelvis that may have conceived; a jawbone that moved to speak, to chew, to grind, to clench, to open (willingly or no), to swallow. And who knows what particular aspects of the people's lives to whom the bones once belonged were visible *on* the bones, as in the case of an eighteenth-century Connecticut slave named Fortune who was dissected by his owner, a man with the unbelievable name of Dr. Preserved Porter.

Pamela Espeland's annotations to poet Marilyn Nelson's *Fortune's Bones: The Manumission Requiem* explain that Porter "rendered" Fortune's bones, and inscribed them with their anatomical names with the aim of passing the skeleton down to his sons (also doctors) and grandchildren as a hands-on learning tool. A team of anthropologists, archaeologists, and historians has recently traced the skeleton, whose identity was mistaken, forgotten, and altered over time (at one point, the skeleton was called Larry), back to Fortune and determined that his bones spoke of a life of continual labor and forms of injury that include a once-broken back.

The bones that were found in Chevalier Jackson's attic are, as far as I know, nowhere to be found. Did the workmen keep one each as a souvenir of their discovery, or did the coroner dispose of the bones, or inter or burn them, or . . . ? It's anybody's guess. What redoubles their mystery is that Chevalier Jackson *saved* them though not every student of medicine does. Writing to his father in 1886, Jackson distinguished himself from his peers as someone who was more interested in knowledge than they were. As a student, Jackson carefully saved human pathological specimens, microscopical preparations, and bones:

> The bones are sawn at each side of the joint so as to avoid carrying unnecessary bones. The majority of students don't seem to care whether they get through with any practical knowledge or not but they never interfere

with anybody that does want to learn. It looks as if they wanted to get a smattering of knowledge to make a display and hoodwink the people by a semblance of knowledge. They are the dudes.

If you wished not to be classified as a "dude"—a term newly coined in the late nineteenth century to describe a dandy, a foppish man, a man affecting an exaggerated fastidiousness in dress, speech, and deportment, in effect, the kind of man Chevalier Jackson no doubt was—if you truly wished to gain knowledge of the human body and not merely appear to have done so, you must keep dem bones, you must render specimens, or so Jackson was convinced:

> Dear Father,
>   . . . I have had to make a pretty large expenditure. It was however for the best. The professor of anatomy said by all means to save the ligaments on the joints in dissection of a part and preserve them in alcohol. He said that was the only way any person would ever know them. I went to him afterward and asked him about it. He said he never could induce students to save them and consequently they never learned them and that they were of the utmost importance as relating to anatomy of dislocation. He said to economize in other directions and buy the bones if necessary. I thought the matter over and concluded to take his advice.

Hereafter he describes "skirmishing" about town in search of undiluted alcohol and a 2.5 gallon jug: "I obeyed the professor's injunction not to add water as it would macerate the specimens to such an extent that when I most wanted them they would be worthless and would tear apart like paper." Jackson had quite a supply of bones, judging from these letters, the bones found in the attic, and his description in his autobiography of having had to sell "a fine, dissected, dried and anatomical specimen [he] had made during the winter months in the dissecting room" to a wealthy medical student. "The nine dollars would just barely pay my train fare home," he wrote (*LCJ*, 62).

Yet his "mystery bones" distinguish him again in this: they bring out the kernel around which his life's energies rallied, the terms of his own defining crisis, that complex preoccupation with a need to save oneself or the desire to save others, that confusion whereby keeping and saving come to be thought of as one and the same. At the center of Chevalier Jackson's life story—whether we locate that in the autobiography or in the acts that constituted his life—is the sense that he needed to reckon with a feeling that he must save himself, both from other people, and by himself. Of course all saving is relational; no one truly saves, liberates, protects, rescues, or redeems himself without the help of others. Jackson knew this better than anyone; he knew that other people relied on him to save their lives every day. But the sign of his conviction that no one could save *him* manifests in his collecting—the compulsion to take pleasure in saving Things, to rescue and then to keep Things as a repetition of self-saving. Jackson's mystery bones are another form of self-preservation, another genre of keepsake, a sign of his fervent desire to protect himself, to perform a secular, fetishized redemption.

"I dread leaving Alice to get through life's affairs. Otherwise, the cardiac failure that is getting worse steadily does not worry me." Chevalier Jackson did not keep a personal diary, so it's especially poignant to come upon a calendar book in the National Library of Medicine from 1952 in which he monitors a feeling of failing health inside the square of each new day: "heartrate up"; "slight vertigo after going up stairs"; "edema"; "dyspnea"; "suffocation attacks at night"; "fatigue noticeable but can render it less conspicuous by activity." Also: "Tuesday, November 4th, went to Poll to vote. This is my 87th birthday anniversary"; "Christmas Day. Father died suddenly on Christmas Day 1889, 63 years ago." Alice predeceased Jackson by one year.

Around 1952, several years before his death, Jackson took care of details that he did not trust to others. He knew, nearly a decade in advance of his actual demise, that his son would be too busy to attend to his father's death notice. "My son might be away on one of a series of meeting trips and confusion of many accumulated things on his return might cause delay," he noted in materials that he left for his secretary, which included the letter she was to send to the American Medical Association upon his death. It began, "Dr. Chevalier Jackson passed away yesterday," gave his CV, and advised reading his autobiography for further details.

Was "Chevalier Jackson passed away today" too difficult a sentence to write of one's own passing? Does "yesterday," putting it in the past, confer a distance on it while imbuing that detail with an aura? Is this Chevalier Jackson's self-hewn headline? It's Jackson "taking care" of Things and then some; it's Jackson speaking from beyond the grave.

With great care, intent on saving, Chevalier Jackson wrapped each part of what remained of a human in a piece of newspaper—the June 18, 1926, edition of the *Public Ledger*, to be exact. The bones are a product of an anatomist's work—that is what made them worth *saving*—and perhaps Jackson hoped to *keep* them that way, pure, unmarked, unspeaking. But the newspaper as casing enfolded the bones with stories and therefore with many more mysteries, unplumbed; it pinned them to a moment of time even if, archivally, the time is not their own.

Wrapped around a jawbone: Miss Pauline Bell won the National Spelling Bee for spelling the word "cerise"; Babe Ruth failed to connect in four times at bat in a 6 to 2 setback against the Sox; and the "Human Fly" thrilled thousands in Camden: "For more than ten minutes last night a 'human fly' hung from the cornice of the Camden courthouse, endeavoring to swing himself over the ledge. He finally made it. Then he stood on his head on the cornice, climbed the dome and sat on the nob at the peak."

Cradling a hand: sesquicentennial celebrations continue with an episodic spectacle depicting ancient Rome, medieval Venice, Florence, and modern Italy; Celestino Madeiros has admitted to the murder "world famous radicals" Sacco and Vanzetti are accused of committing.

Crimped at the corners of a skull: the newspaper's *Lost and Found*, mostly lost:

- small black suitcase
- pin: diamond and pearly crescent
- eyeglasses
- handbag
- package from "Night Comfort Garment"—reward
- naturalization papers no. 49538 in the name of Aaron Miller, 818 N. 7th, reward if returned
- dog, Pekingese, answers to name Chin Chow.

Chevalier Jackson was caught up in the furtive occupation of preserving his handiwork; it was a rainy day, according to the *Public Ledger*'s weather report, and this was a rainy-day project, so he probably did not pause to read the scantest outline of a tragic tale that must belong to realms of fable. One headline gives a general sense of the story—"Ends Life When Horse Dies"—while another, in a smaller font, yields more particular details: "Farmer Hangs Self with Rope Which Caused Animal's Death." In smaller lettering still, the tale is told:

Kansas City

Misaji Kawahara, a Japanese truck farmer living near this city, hanged himself today when he learned that his horse, to which he was much attached, was dead. The horse became excited during a thunderstorm last night and choked itself to death in an effort to break away from a tree to which it was tied. Using the rope from the halter, Kawahara hanged himself from the tree.

Chevalier Jackson would have felt a deep affinity for Misaji Kawahara, whose love for and identification with an animal inspired so extreme an act. Or maybe not: maybe he'd blame the farmer for his carelessness. The farmer loved the horse too much to live without it; the horse's death became an impasse beyond which the farmer found it impossible to live. The death of the horse by desperation and strangulation, the pathos of the horse's suffering and struggle, the idea that it might have been the farmer's fault for tying him there, the sense that this horse was all the farmer had—the condensed story invents its own details. With nothing but these bare and extreme details, Kawahara's life gives way to a grand narrative whose pivot point is the fact of something dying by trying to get free. Less mysteriously, the life could gain some scaffolding. Such as: a Japanese farmer in 1926 travels from crop to crop without the chance to own. He barely gets to eat the food he cultivates. A Japanese farmer is a source of hatred in 1926, as witnessed by the 1922 court case that declared all Japanese people ineligible for citizenship and enacted more enduringly by the anti-Japanese immigration act of 1924 disbarring Japanese from emigrating to the United States for another twenty-eight years. Misaji Kawahara had no naturalization papers to lose. Who was that man? A "suicide." An immigrant. A victim of a lynching? Where would they bury him? Where are his bones?

Such bones as these are here, disarticulated, detached, inside a cardboard box inside a famous doctor's attic; stowed high, high up, high as a human fly could stray, arcane as a French word for bright crimson, mysterious as buried treasure, waiting for some unassuming laborer to find them. To disturb them, create a ruckus, and cry out.

The life and work of Chevalier Jackson is its own genre, a grand narrative made up of three distinguishing parts: it begins with something quotidian and banal—an object; it requires some form of handicraft and invention—the instrument; and it often entails a pilgrimage. The instrument, like a magic wand, may cure or calm the tale's bewitching parts, but it's also bewitching on its own. The pilgrimage is the tale's religious aspect.

Arlene Maloney's mother "never really told too many stories," Arlene remarks, but there was one she liked to tell. Arlene, now nearing ninety, remembers hearing it in her own early childhood. Her Pennsylvania Dutch grandfather took her mother out of school in eighth grade and sent her to work for an Orthodox Jewish family in Allentown. This family "made her read" and sent her back to school, supplying her daily with a fresh batch of newspapers and magazines to hone her skills. One day at a picnic, a young cousin of hers was "chomping on an ear of corn" when he hiccoughed and aspirated a kernel into his lung. The boy became sicker and sicker until he developed pneumonia. "I know somebody who removes things": the sentence falls like magic onto her aunt's and uncle's ears as Arlene's mother tells them she read an article in the *Allentown Morning Call* about a Philadelphia bronchoscopist named Chevalier Jackson. The family entrusts the teenaged girl to make the pilgrimage with their son, who by now has developed an abscess. She's the one who read about him, so she should be the one to meet him—maybe this is how they thought about it. She and her cousin took the hour-and-a-half trolley ride—"they still have that trolley, by the way"—from Allentown to Philadelphia, where "Jackson was to expect them." Arriving in the lobby of the clinic, she says, "I'm here to see Chevalier Jackson." The reply is obvious but unforgettable: "He's waiting for you." Arlene's mother stays with her cousin during the day; in the evening, she sleeps in a boardinghouse across the street from the hospital. Jackson removes the kernel, and, within thirty-six hours, she and the boy are on their way back home. He'd recovered completely and was never thereafter affected by the accident. Looking back on the tale, Arlene sees it as having— why not indulge the pun?—a kernel of destiny since her nursing career takes her to Philadelphia, where she meets her bronchoscopist husband and even works as a circulating nurse in Jackson's Temple University clinic.

Before I make my journey to the Jackson homestead and Old Sunrise Mills, the assistant administrator of nearby Pennypacker Mills advises me: "The Sunrise Mill property is not open to the public and is quite hilly, so bring comfortable shoes." I don't generally wear high heels to archives, but I guess I could feel inspired to dress up for this particular trip, marked as it is by the power of the dwelling place.

Prior to my arriving, the administrator tells me that they have some "items" relative to Jackson stored off-site—things donated by his grand-daughter Joan, window shades, some wicker furniture, a coat. "We have his coat," the administrator reiterates in a phone conversation in which he haltingly describes, in slowly unfolding bits and pieces, the types of Jacksoniana I might see. Unless it's his lab coat, one would be hard-pressed to know why the coat was saved. *The* coat. *A* coat. *Your* coat, *my* coat. What will happen to any of our coats after we die? "Mainly I'm struck by the idea of my making a pilgrimage to a coat," I write a friend, "because in some weird way that's what I'm doing."

My guide is generous, and his tour of the grounds' tree-lined roads backlit by forest is resplendent. The mill's perfectly square windows are calming, maybe for the way they offset the mill's heavy and irregular rocks, maybe for the way they sing of measure alongside the rushing waters of the millpond's falls. There are confirmations ("Ah, I know this") and surprises ("I could have never imagined that!"), while all the time we are accompanied by a yellow butterfly striped in black that sometimes flies behind us and sometimes leads. We stroll as we roam, until the afternoon promises to swallow us up, when the administrator reminds me of the storeroom they are in the process of creating. It's in another location, at one of the Montgomery County parks, and there are boxes there, and other Things that had only recently been found in an attic or in the barn. "The box of letters is about eight inches thick," the administrator had earlier written me. "I hope to have them cleaned and all the rusted paperclips removed by Thursday. Many are patient reports, some relate to his speeches and are his notes and some deal with speaking engagements in Madrid and Paris."

The storage room, itself an attic, only awaits cabinets to store this stuff, most of which strikes me as so much detritus. Scattered across an expanse of floor and neatly stacked in piles are cords of magazines that Chevalier Jackson had subscribed to, a box of dried-up paint supplies, assorted broken-off bits of pottery, and a many-layers-deep supply of surplus reproductions of the images Jackson sent each year as Christmas cards. Donning the white gloves that always accompany archival boxes, I leaf and rifle through what I can't believe continues to exist as a paper trail. I've been through umpteen boxes and countless case studies in the major repositories of Jackson's life and work. How could more papers at this late date have been found in the attic or barn? How could there be anything left over, left behind, undug, and only recently dusted off? I force myself to race against the clock and read even though I know I don't have room in the metaphorical box that is my book for any new discoveries, and I don't expect to make any. Still, I let myself settle down and pause before one case history. It's lengthy and it's moving and it's harsh—it describes a boy who did not survive—and though I'm not sure why, I decide I want a copy for my files, so I ask the curator to Xerox it for me before I go.

Back home, I take in slowly the difficult details of this case, involving a ten-year-old boy and a silver half-dollar, but I'm mostly preoccupied with the frustration of groping in the dark. One of the archives I've relied on for illustrations has closed because of budget problems, so I've gone back to the drawing board by ordering a range of Jackson's textbooks through my library to see if I could possibly find some vaguely proximate images in the public domain. I'm blindly browsing, not really reading, when I come upon a photograph of a boy. He's perched at the end of a long gurney and pictured from the side. His hair is matted with sweat, his eyebrow arched, his face marked by the pain that sitting upright obviously causes him. A linen panel crosses his thighs and genitals, but otherwise his too-thin body is unclothed. He dangles there, as though his body is the subject of a lettering system that holds his abnormality in place: an A and arrow point toward his back, and a B labels his front (see figure 46). The only fat on the boy is to be found in the protuberance that the letters mean to mark. The protrusion is in fact so prominent that the boy seems as though he's been devoured by a foreign body—that his own body has become its host, and there is hardly anything left of him except as casement for the thing. The book in which the image appears was a contribution to the *Annals of Roentgenology: A Series of Monographic Atlases* published in 1934, and Jackson's caption reads:

> A large subcutaneous purulent accumulation (A) in a boy, aged ten years, an extension of pulmonary abscess due to a coin (half-dollar) overlooked in the esophagus (not bronchus) for six years. A similar purulent accumulation had been evacuated before admission and the fistula (B) was still discharging at the site of evacuation. The coin did not follow the pus. An epithelialized fistula had been established by the coin between the esophagus and the left bronchus.

In layman's terms, the boy was subject to a swallowed coin that, stuck in one of his body's passageways, the foodway, now protruded into another, an airway, where a serious infection had subsequently taken hold. The A and B seemed so misplaced alongside the child's live and emaciated body. Even an untrained eye could see the growth that protruded from his back and the hole in his front from which the wound was draining. Why did Chevalier Jackson feel the need additionally to point?

In a sudden gasp of apprehension, I realize that I know this boy. I have been knowing him and not knowing why, but it's him whose case study I'd stumbled upon in the unfinished storage room and felt compelled to save. This is the boy I had brought home from the attic, from the barn. Encountering these photos with the boy's case history in hand is like finding someone's soul, and for long moments I swear I feel him with me (does it matter it's an attic study from which I write?). I feel him with me, but I don't mean by this that I'd concocted something mystical in the convergence of photo with life story. It was more like fitting part to whole and, in the accidental rediscovery, being given the chance to remember the boy, to whom medicine might have done a great injustice, differently. To demystify him as a figure of amorphous pain and wasting, to fulfill a request that was obvious and pure: to close my story of Chevalier Jackson with his own.

Yes, it's clear. I've seen this boy before this and not seen him at all. I reopen Jackson's *Autobiography*. He's there. I open the textbook tome I've most relied on— *Diseases of the Air and Food Passages of Foreign-Body Origin*— and he's in there too, always in the form of a photograph and its blithely instructional caption. In the autobiography, he is lying on his back, supine, and his arms, so thin, look too long for his small body. They've blotted out his eyes in the way that students in the dissecting room cover the face of their cadaver while they work so as not to be reminded of the status of the body as a person or a personality. Did they shield his eyes, already pained from squinting, from the flash of the photo, or instruct him (as so many medical procedures do) to hold his breath and stay stock still? The point of all of these photographs of this terribly suffering patient seems to be to demonstrate how hopelessly sick he is.

But who was that boy, the living boy, and how can we regard and re-inspire him with the aid of the case history? All of the great names populate the pages of the case—Chevalier Jackson, L.H. Clerf, T.A. Shallow, and eminent radiologist Willis Manges—they were *on* it, while the boy himself is given three differently spelled last names. The son of Polish immigrants, the boy appears to have a last name that begins either with Ch or H and ends either with an a or an e. His first name is always Michael. He entered Jefferson Hospital on January 26, 1926, and died there on February 18, 1926. The diary account of his decline is dominated by references to a "fluctuating mass" and its drainage, and temporary relief for the boy as indicated by phrases and sentences such as "considerable improvement" and "patient's condition seems to be definitely improved," only to yield in the days that follow to "quite serious" and what was already anticipated— "Death"—as a result of an infection of the pleura and subsequent formation of pus termed *empyema necessitas.*

"Examination is difficult because of pain complained of by the patient when chest is percussed," Clerf notes on his initial observations of the boy, and his is just one of several meticulous accountings of the examination of the boy's body. Manges describes the attempt by numerous X-rays to create a detailed map of the location of the coin, and after gaining permission to have the boy swallow some bismuth so as to yield a clearer picture, Manges is able to conclude that the coin had indeed "eroded through the esophageal wall, the pleura and into the left main bronchus." An autopsy report

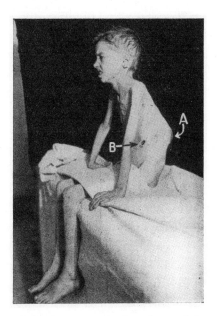

Fig. 46. Michael H., who died as a result of an ingested American half-dollar that numerous doctors failed to believe in and that therefore went untreated from the time that Michael was four until the time of his death, at age ten. Foreign Body in Air and Food Passages: Roentgeneologically Considered, with Two Hundred and Thirty-six Roentgen-Ray Studies and Ten Clinical Illustrations *(1934).*

reveals an "American half-dollar embedded in the coronal plane of the esophagus"; it determines that the heart weighs 110 grams, and measures $8 \times 6.5 \times 3.5$ cm; describes "the little fellow's body[as] pale and wasted"; and adds to the list of death's causes "gangrene of the lung."

Extensive descriptions of the particulars of the damage done by the coin to the boy's body in an age before antibiotics can't really help the boy and seem like failed efforts to fill the gaping holes left by misinterpretation and disbelief. The story of Michael's life after he swallowed the coin—from the time he was four-and-a-half years old to the time he arrived in the Jackson clinics at age ten—is one of repeated attempts by himself and his father to convince numerous doctors of the presence of a fbdy in his throat. A Polish doctor in New Britain, Connecticut, where the family lived, had been consulted immediately after Michael swallowed the coin. X-rays failed to reveal the coin, and the doctor "told father that he did not believe child swallowed the coin; if he did, it would cause no harm." Soon thereafter, they visited another doctor, named Zwick, whose further X-rays also did not confirm the boy's admission of a swallowed coin. Afterward, "this child was seen by a number of physicians, all of whom laughed at the father for believing the presence of the coin was the cause of his child's illness." The child had difficulty swallowing solid food, his growth was stunted, and he suffered from a constant cough, often accompanied by regurgitation and vomiting. At ten years old, the boy was diagnosed with consumption by yet another doctor. The doctor told the father that the "coin was not present and not the cause of the trouble."

Failure is the keynote of this narrative, and finally a schoolteacher sent a truant officer to the boy's home "because of the child's failure to attend school." The officer, finding Michael to be quite ill, took him to a hospital in New Britain where "fluoroscopic examination shows the coin to be present, in the mid-line of thorax, about 3 inches above diaphragm. It was believed to be in the lung having ulcerated through into the lung." Just as father and son returned to Dr. Zwick with the new diagnosis, more than five years overdue, Michael developed what his father called a boil over his left lower chest; the doctor attributed it to "poison in the child's system due to the presence of the coin." Zwick performed an operation of some sort to relieve the boil and wanted to "remove the coin" at the same time, but the father would not permit it, and "Dr. Zwick gave up the case." Then the father visited another doctor who, upon seeing the X-ray, advised him to bring the child to Jefferson Hospital.

I don't know if Michael had much of a childhood—if, on some clear days, he played with a puzzle or dangled a piece of yarn in front of his cat; if he caught things in nets or read storybooks; if he waited by a window for the snow to fall, or rolled down small hills the way apples languidly drop then roll out from beneath the shade of their trees. The fifty-cent piece was always there, throbbing, blocking, inarticulable to a child, yet truly felt. The problem with the fbdy was that it stayed lodged, but the body was still growing, and its growth could not accommodate it. Here's what we don't know: the circumstances by which Michael swallowed the coin. Here's what we do know: his and his father's command of English must have been impeccable for their story to have been recorded. Here's what the case study shows: Michael had been in life, and in death, carefully examined, but he had never been understood.

How did Michael swallow the coin that eventually made him so ill beyond imagining? Was it the effect of an "expression of emotion," or was it attributable to the "properties of the foreign body itself"? Was he not properly watched over because of being poor? The sundry visits to numerous doctors imply that his family did not live in poverty. Had he been "taking a deep breath to cough or sneeze," or had he been in the habit of imitating conjuring tricks with coins? Was he surprised by how large the coin was—about the diameter of a dollop of ice cream—and did he wish to determine if he could fit his mouth around it? Was his swallowing the half dollar an untoward afterward of "recumbency," "running or jumping," or "sobbing, laughing or whistling"? Certainly he wasn't drunk.

In the caption underneath the patient's picture in his *Autobiography*, Jackson is so frustrated by the case that he becomes nearly heartless, returning quite predictably to "carelessness":

> A boy nearly dead and emaciated almost to a skeleton from abscesses in his lung due to prolonged sojourn of a coin he had swallowed. Had he been taken to any hospital promptly, the abscesses could have been prevented by esophagoscopic removal of the coin. Better still, such an accident could have been avoided if the coin had not been put in the mouth.

What Jackson subtracts is the fact that Michael's father *had* taken him to a doctor "immediately," and that an "X-ray examination was made at a hospital in New Britain which failed to reveal the coin." Michael's case was a very special one to Chevalier Jackson in this way: it was a case that Jackson could not solve, before which he was left to feel helpless. No attempt was made to remove the coin at Jefferson Hospital because, I surmise, by the time the coin had been believed in, and therefore looked for and finally discovered, the boy was already too seriously ill and the coin had done too much damage for any endoscopic procedure to be safely carried out.

In yet another caption attached to Michael's photo, in the earlier *Diseases of the Air and Food Passages of Foreign-Body Origin*, Jackson used the case to prove a more relevant cardinal rule of his, namely that the

> chief etiologic factor in all the pulmonary pathology present in this boy was the over-looking of the foreign body. Had an early diagnosis been made there would have been no pathology; the foreign body could have been removed by esophagoscopy and there would have been prompt recovery, or, rather, as in the patient shown in Fig. 5, there would have been no illness from which to recover.

Had Jackson lost the documents in his attic by the time he wrote the *Autobiography*, when he used the photo to tell an entirely different, finger-wagging tale? It's as though Jackson suffers from selective amnesia. Had he detached the photo from the case notes and, with nothing but the appalling figure of the boy to contemplate (a human being reduced to a pile of bones), felt overcome by the feeling that the horror it depicted was not his fault? In *Diseases of the Air and Food Passages of Foreign-Body Origin*, he used Michael to exemplify part of the gospel he had preached throughout his life: foreign bodies must not be thought of as curiosities but must reside in the realm of the possible, the ordinary, the likely, and the real. Convincing fellow doctors of fbdies as commonplace was part of Chevalier Jackson's crusade, but his tendency to save, his need to keep, his collection rarified them yet again. The Chevalier Jackson Foreign Body Collection does not necessarily encourage fellow doctors to look for foreign bodies, believe in them as likely, and expect them at the door of each new cough. Instead it leaves them, mouths agape, in awe of a master; it permits a certain lolling and retreat; it festoons the imagination and dots the crenellations of a dream.

Is the Chevalier Jackson dreamspace his self-reward for an allegiance to precision? Arlene Maloney reminds me that endoscopy with rigid instruments is an exacting science—a hairbreadth off with the position, direction, or pulsion of the instrument and you could ruin a person's larynx or inflict a fatal injury. Chevalier Jackson never searches for a fbdy without a map of the body that he already knows like the back of his own ambidextrous hands. With newfangled search engines at my disposal in the year 2009, I expect my journey to find Chevalier Jackson to be easy. I've set a Google alert for him so that, whenever a new piece of knowledge attaching to his name appears, I'll find it. Rarely does anything turn up, though occasionally the inexacting, lumbering World Wide Web alerts me to an article on Michael Jackson.

One of these times, unwilling to feel lonely or betrayed by my research, I click on a link to the more famous figure with that surname. It pulls up a video of Jackson in a live performance of "I'll Be There," which has resurfaced after Jackson's untimely death. Rising toward the performance's final fever pitch, Jackson throws his head back, far back, as though he's preparing to swallow a sword, if only an imaginary one. Really, he's preparing the back of his throat to produce a sound more exquisite than silver, more porous and more fluent than steel. He holds his hands atop his mouth to hold the note, cupping them around an invisible rope or bar of something going into him and something going out of him.

On another occasion, across several years of life with Chevalier Jackson in which his name appears in my alerts, I'm directed to the place where his bones are interred. I've never thought to make a pilgrimage to Jackson's grave—is this because it would mean my work was over?—but here I can visit his "resting place" by way of a virtual tour. Laurel Hill and its sister cemetery, West Laurel Hill, where Chevalier Jackson is buried, "is more than just a cemetery," the Web site for these burial grounds assures. "It is an outdoor sculptural garden, a horticultural gem, and a truly unique historical resource. It also happens to be one of the few cemeteries in the United States to be honored with the designation of National Historic Landmark." As a burial ground unrivaled in its "peace, beauty, and splendor" since its founding by Quaker Joseph Jay Smith in 1836, it can't even be considered the rich relative of once plunderable (and later condemned) Lebanon Cemetery. It seems, instead, to exist in a world apart, its citizens' bodies invested with great value worthy of undisturbed, inviolable, and hallowed ground.

If I click on LOCATE, I can find "Chevalier Jackson, MD," his name affixed to a virtual flag attached to a pushpin that points to the place where his bones reside. From this bird's-eye cartographic view, set to the left of the Schuylkill Expressway, which resembles from this height an esophagus, to the right of which runs the Schuylkill River (as trachea), it would appear that Chevalier Jackson's resting place is a lung. Chevalier Jackson is here, the flag insists, indexically; and if you want, by clicking on another part of the site, you can also see the mausoleum in which he is buried and details of its stain-glassed windows, carved with angels that watch over him.

The burial site as Web site has also provided an alphabetized list of dead "notables," but Chevalier Jackson does not appear among them. You can find a biographical sketch of him here, but, at the time of this writing, he is not searchable as noteworthy inside the index that highlights the inventor of Campbell's condensed soup; the founder of Mother's Day; John B. Stetson, the hat manufacturer; Alexander Calder, artist; Loren Eiseley, naturalist; the father of professional baseball; a survivor (in a manner of speaking) of the *Titanic*; and the father of scientific management himself, Frederick Winslow Taylor.

I won't be visiting Chevalier Jackson's grave, because I know, and you know, that he's not to be found there. His story and his legacy are housed in a collection of fbdies in the center of Philadelphia, in the Mütter Museum, where he also resides. But I have, as I have said, made a pilgrimage to his coat. I'd almost forgotten about it and was leaving, and the historian who'd been my guide, he too was bringing his workday to a close when I reminded him, "I'm sorry, but you said you had a coat of his? Might I see the coat before I leave?"

"Ah, the coat, of course you can see the coat," the keeper of the artifacts replies. And, from some place I cannot see, he brings out a black wool overcoat that he holds before me on a hanger. I don't dare touch it; I stand before its bodiless mien and feel myself held inside a stillness it beholds as me.

"So *that*'s the coat that once contained the body of the man," I think. And then I really see it, because the thing about this coat is that it's tiny, and Chevalier Jackson ordered his clothes two sizes too large. It's not really a man's coat at all; it's a coat, cinched a bit at the waist, and shapely, a little dressy, suited to the contours of a boy.

SELECT BIBLIOGRAPHY

Abraham, Benjamin, and Adekola O. Alao. "An Unusual Foreign Body Ingestion in a Schizophrenic Patient: Case Report." *International Journal of Psychiatry in Medicine* 35, no. 3 (2005): 313–18.

Adityanjee, Yekeen, A. Aderibigbe, D. Theodoridis, and W. Victor R. Vieweg. "Dementia Praecox to Schizophrenia: The First 100 Years." *Psychiatry and Clinical Neurosciences* 53, no. 4 (1999): 437–48.

American Broncho-Esophagological Association. *ABEA Spring 2009 Newsletter*, www.abea.net/website/news/newsletter/index.html (accessed June 1, 2009).

"American Epic of Attainment." *Etude* 57 (Jan. 1939): 5–6.

Armstrong, Tim. *Modernism, Technology and the Body: A Cultural Study.* London: Cambridge University Press, 1998.

Ashton, Dore. *A Joseph Cornell Album.* New York: Da Capo Press, 1974.

"Automobile Cancer Cause?" *Science News-Letter* 12, no. 332 (Aug. 20, 1927): 121.

Aviv, Jonathan F. "Transnasal Esophagoscopy: State of the Art." *Otolaryngology— Head and Neck Surgery* 153, no. 4 (October 2006): 616–19

Bachman, J.P., Jr. "Where Miracles of Science are Commonplace: A Thousand Paths Converge at Dr. Jackson's World-Famous Bronchoscopic Clinic, An Interview with Dr. Chevalier Jackson." *Revenue: The Magazine of Light*, June 1930, 18–20.

Baltzell, William. Interview by Andrew Spector, M.D., John Q. Adams Center for the History of Otolaryngology—Head and Neck Surgery, Philadelphia, PA, Nov. 18, 2004.

Barnie, Doris D. "Twenty-Five Years Revisited." *Gastroenterology Nursing* 23, no. 1 (2000): 10–14.

Barnhill, John Finch. "Introduction of the Living Ex-Presidents of the American Laryngological, Rhinological and Otological Society, Used in Introducing Each at a Dinner in their Honor." *Transactions of the American Laryngological, Rhinological, and Otological Society* 34 (1928).

Barta, Caroline M. "Peroral Endoscopy." *American Journal of Nursing* 37, no. 11 (Nov. 1937): 1243–46.

Bergner, Gwen. *Taboo Subjects: Race, Sex, and Psychoanalysis.* Minneapolis: University of Minnesota Press, 2005.

Bigelow, F.S. "Why the Doctor Was So Sure." *Saturday Evening Post* 208 (Aug. 1935).

Black, R.E., D.G. Johnson, and M.E. Matlak. "Bronchoscopic Removal of Foreign Bodies in Children." *Journal of Pediatric Surgery* 29 (1994): 682–84.

Blakely, Robert L., and Judith M. Harrington, eds. *Bones in the Basement: Postmortem Racism in Nineteenth-Century Medical Training.* Washington: Smithsonian Institution Press, 1997.

Blakeslee, Howard W. "Folks from All Over World Who've 'Swallowed Something' Beat a Path Here to Dr. Chevalier Jackson, 71-Year-Old Master of the Bronchoscope," *Philadelphia Bulletin,* 1936.

Blinder, Barton J., and Christina Salama. "An Update on Pica: Prevalence, Contributing Causes, and Treatment." *Psychiatric Times* 25, no. 6 (May 1, 2008), www.psychiatrictimes.com/display/article/10168 (accessed May 10, 2010).

Bondeson, Jan. *The Two-Headed Boy and Other Medical Marvels.* Ithaca: Cornell University Press, 2000.

Botoman, V. Alin, and Maureen Botoman. "The First Dilation of a 60 Year Old Stricture: The Legacy of Chevalier Jackson—America's First Endoscopist." *Abstracts of the Proceedings of the American College of Gastroenterology 70th Annual Scientific Meeting,* 2005.

Boyd, Arthur D. "Chevalier Jackson: The Father of American Bronchoesophagoscopy." *Annals of Thoracic Surgery* 57 (Feb. 1994): 502–5.

Brandt, Doug. "Curiouser and Curiouser." *American Journal of Nursing* 106, no. 8 (Aug. 2006): 37.

Brody, Jane E. "For Some, All Food Is Hard to Swallow," *Spokane Chronicle,* Jan. 23, 1989.

———. "When Swallowing Food Becomes a Problem." *New York Times,* July 20, 2004.

"Bronchoscopist." *Time,* June 1936.

"Bronchoscopist Jackson Retrieves Things Careless People Swallow." *Life,* June 13, 1938.

Bugbee, Joan Jackson, and Frank Bugbee. Interview conducted by Phillip R. Seitz, for John Q. Adams Center for the History of Otolaryngology—Head and Neck Surgery, Schwenksville, PA, July 31, 1991.

Bulgakov, Mikhail. "The Steel Windpipe." In *A Country Doctor's Notebook,* 27–37. London: Harvill Press, 1995.

Bundy, A.D. "Death from the Introduction of a Stomach Tube." *Medical Record* 26 (1884): 504–5.

Butler, Judith. *Giving an Account of Oneself.* New York: Fordham University Press, 2005.

Byard, R.W., L. Moore, and A.J. Bourne. "Sudden and Unexpected Death—a Late Effect of Occult Intraesophageal Foreign Body." *Pediatric Pathology* 10 (1990): 837–41.

Calvo, Luz. "Racial Fantasies and the Primal Scene of Miscegenation." *International Journal of Psychoanalysis* 89, no. 1 (Feb. 2008): 55–70.

Cartwright, Samuel A. "Diseases and Peculiarities of the Negro Race." *DeBow's Review Southern and Western States* 11 (1851).

Caws, Mary Ann. *Joseph Cornell's Theater of the Mind: Selected Diaries, Letters and Files.* New York: Thames and Hudson, 1993.

Chesnutt, Charles W. *The Marrow of Tradition* (1901). Ann Arbor: University of Michigan Press, 1969.

Clark, Stanley G. "Foreign Bodies in the Esophagus; Specimen; Illustration." *Brooklyn Medical Journal* 14 (1900): 987–90.

Clerf, Louis H. "Historical Aspects of Foreign Bodies in the Air and Food Passages." *Annals of Otology, Rhinology, and Laryngology* 61, no. 1 (Mar. 1952): 5–17.

———. "Historical Vignette: Chevalier Jackson." *Archives of Otolaryngology* 83 (Mar. 1966): 124–28.

———. "Memoir of Chevalier Jackson (1865–1958)." *Transactions and Studies of the College of Physicians of Philadelphia* 27, no. 4 (1959–60): 190–91.

Cohen, Eleanor. "From Solitary Vice to Split Mind: Psychiatric Discourses of Male Sexuality and Coming of Age, 1918–1938." *Australian Historical Studies* 112 (1999): 79–95.

Collins, Lauren. "Choke Artist." *New Yorker,* May 8, 2006.

Cooper, P.R., and St. Clair Thomson. "Tranquil Tracheotomy." *British Medical Journal* 2, no. 3069 (Oct. 25, 1919): 545–46.

Crary, Jonathan. *Techniques of the Observer: On Vision and Modernity in the Nineteenth Century.* Cambridge, MA: MIT Press, 1990.

Crozier, Lucille B. *Medical Pioneers in Pittsburgh.* 1959.

Crysdale, W.S., K.S. Sendi, and J. Yoo. "Esophageal Foreign Bodies in Children: 15-year Review of 484 Cases." *Annals of Otology, Rhinology and Laryngology* 100 (1991): 320–24.

Covey, Herbert C. *African American Slave Medicine: Herbal and Non-Herbal Treatments.* Lanham, MD: Lexington Books, 2007.

Daily Telegraph, "Under the Knife: Woman Eats Cutlery Set." Oct. 29, 2009.

Damrau, Frederic. "Strange Things That Roam Through the Body." *Popular Science,* May 1937.

Danford, Darla E., and Agnes M. Huber. "Pica Among Mentally Retarded Adults." *American Journal of Mental Deficiency* 87, no. 2 (Sept. 1982): 141–46.

Davis, Robyn L. "In Minnesota, a Museum of Madness." *Washington Post,* Apr. 4, 1999.

Dawlatly, E.E., A.L. al-Arfaj, and M.A. al-Azizi. "Pediatric Foreign Bodies: The Lessons of Failure and Near Misses." *Journal of Laryngology and Otology* 105 (1991): 755–79.

Dickens, Charles. "The Haunted Man." In *Christmas Books.* Oxford: Oxford University Press, 1954.

"Dinner to Chevalier Jackson," *British Medical Journal* 2, no. 3645 (Nov. 15, 1930): 836.

"Doctor Removes Plastic Fragment Lodged in Lung." *CBS 2 Chicago,* Sept. 19, 2009. http://cbs2chicago.com/watercooler/John.Manley.surgery.2.1194891 .html (accessed May 2010).

"Down the Hatch." *Self,* April 1993.

"Dr. Jackson Draws a Nyle Out of Kelvin Rodgers." *Newsweek,* July 1936.

Edmonson, James M. "History of the Instruments for Gastrointestinal Endoscopy." *Gastrointestinal Endoscopy* 37 (1991): 27–56.

Edmonson, James, and Patsy Gersner. *The Instruments of Gastrointestinal Endoscopy: An Interactive History* (CD-ROM). Ann Arbor, MI: Historical Center for the Health Sciences, University of Michigan, 1999. CD-ROM.

Eliot, Llewellyn. "A Case of Hysterical Dysphagia." Read at a Meeting of the Medical Society, Washington, DC, Nov. 17, 1897.

Equen, Murdock. "Clinical Negligence in the Labeling of Lye." *Journal of the Medical Association of Georgia* 13, no. 7 (July 1924).

Evening Bulletin (Philadelphia), "Foul Play Ruled Out in Case of Mystery Bones." May 17, 1974.

Evening Public Ledger (Philadelphia), "Dr. Jackson First Wooed Muse of Art." 1929.

———, "Dr. Jackson Hurt in Crash; Goes on With His Duties," October 23, 1933.

Fanon, Frantz. "The Fact of Blackness." In *Black Skin, White Masks,* tr. Charles Lam Markmann. New York: Grove Press, 1967.

Ferenzci, Sandor. "Materialization in Globus Hystericus." In *Further Contributions to the Theory and Technique of Psychoanalysis.* New York: Basic Books, 1952.

———. "The Phenomena of Hysterical Materialization (Thoughts on the Conception of Hysterical Conversion and Symbolism)." In *Further Contributions to the Theory and Technique of Psychoanalysis.* New York: Basic Books, 1952.

Fishbain, David A., and Dean J. Rotondo. "Foreign Body Ingestion Associated with Delusional Beliefs." *Journal of Nervous and Mental Disease* 171, no. 5 (May 1983): 321–22.

Foer, Jonathan Safran, ed. *A Convergence of Birds: Original Fiction and Poetry Inspired by the Work of Joseph Cornell.* New York: Distributed Art Publishers, 2001.

Forth, Christopher E., and Ana Carden-Coyne, *Cultures of the Abdomen: Diet, Digestion, and Fat in the Modern World.* New York: Palgrave, 2005.

Frazer, John E. "Don't Swallow a Nail!" *Philadelphia Magazine,* Jan. 1950.

Freedgood, Elaine. "That People Might Be like Things and Live." Presentation, University of Rhode Island, Mar. 12, 2009.

French, Thomas R. "Two Voices and a Double Epiglottis." *British Medical Journal* 2, no. 1025 (Aug. 21, 1880): 311–12.

Freese, Arthur S. "Medical Magician: Doctor, Artist, and Technician." *Today's Health,* Dec. 1968.

Freud, Sigmund. "A Child Is Being Beaten," tr. Joan Rivere. *Collected Papers of Sigmund Freud.* New York: Basic Books, 1959.

Friedman, E.M. "Caustic Ingestions and Foreign Body Aspirations: An Overlooked Form of Child Abuse." *Annals of Otology, Rhinology, and Laryngology* 96 (1987): 709–12.

Gilchrist, Brian F., Evans P. Valerie, Mihn Nguyen, Charles Coren, Donald Klotz, and Max L. Ramenofsky. "Pearls and Perils in the Management of Prolonged, Peculiar, Penetrating Esophageal Foreign Bodies in Children." *Journal of Pediatric Surgery* 32, no. 10 (2003): 1429–31.

Gitlin, David F., Jason P. Caplan, Malcolm P. Rogers, Orit Avni-Barron, Ilana Braun, and Arthur J. Barsky. "Foreign-Body Ingestion in Patients with Personality Disorders." *Psychosomatics: Journal of Consultation Liaison Psychiatry* 48, no. 2 (Mar./Apr. 2007): 162–66.

Gonzalez-Crussi, F. *Suspended Animation: Six Essays on the Preservation of Bodily Parts.* Photographs by Rosamond Purcell. New York: Harcourt Brace, 1995.

Greenblatt, Stephen. *Marvelous Possessions: The Wonder of the New World.* Chicago: University of Chicago Press, 1991.

Greer, Hilton R. "Chevalier Jackson, Who Couldn't Be Tough," *Dallas Morning News,* July 6, 1938.

Gross, Samuel D. *Autobiography of Samuel D. Gross, M.D., with Sketches of His Contemporaries.* Philadelphia: George Barrie, 1887.

Gudger, E.W. "Live Fishes Impacted in Food and Air Passages of Man." *Archives of Pathology and Laboratory Medicine* 2 (Sept. 1926): 355–75.

Hacking, Ian. *Mad Travelers: Reflections on the Reality of Transient Mental Illness.* Charlottesville: University Press of Virginia, 1998.

———. *The Social Construction of What.* Cambridge, MA: Harvard University Press, 1999.

Hall, Gayland C. "Esophagoscopy and Bronchoscopy." *Kentucky Medical Journal* 19 (Aug. 1921): 482–91.

Hamdy, Shaheen. *Adult Neurogenic Dysphagia: Disorders and Conditions That Disrupt Swallowing.* International Foundation for Functional Gastrointestinal Disorders, 2007.

Hansell, Peter, and Jean Hansell. *Dovecotes.* Bucks, UK: Shire Publications, 2001.

Harrison, Victoria L. "Chevalier Jackson, M.D.," with lyrics to "Poor Mary," presented at 17th annual meeting, Atlantic City, NJ, June 1–3, 1911. *The President's Book: A Brief History of the Triological Society,* presented at the 100th annual meeting, Scottsdale, AZ, May 12–14, 1997.

Hartford Daily Times, "Doctor Battles Deadly Swallowed Safety Pin," Mar. 8, 1927.

Hartigan, Lynda Roscoe, Richard Vine, and Robert Lehrman. *Joseph Cornell: Shadowplay Eterniday.* New York: Thames and Hudson, 2003.

Hays, Isaac. "Instruments for Illuminating Dark Cavities." *Philadelphia Journal of the Medical and Physical Sciences* 14 (1827): 409.

Hays, Samuel P., ed. *City at the Point: Essays on the Social History of Pittsburgh.* University of Pittsburgh Press, 1989.

"Here's My Story." *Popular Science,* Jan. 1941.

Heimlich, Henry J. "The Heimlich Manoeuvre." *British Medical Journal* 286 (Apr. 1983): 1349–50.

Hopkins, George G. "Foreign Bodies in the Stomach; Gastrotomy; Specimens; Illustration." *Brooklyn Medical Journal* 14 (1900): 990–92.

Howard, John Tilden. "The Gospel of Gastroscopy in the United States." *Gastrointestinal Endoscopy* 17 (1970): 19–22.

Huizenga, Eelco. "On Esophagoscopy and Sword Swallowing." *Annals of Otology* 78 (1969): 32–39.

Hutchison, Percy. "Doctor! Baby's Swallowed a Pin." *New York Times Book Review,* June 26, 1938.

"Illustrations of Tumors Among the Chinese," *Boston Medical and Surgical Journal* 32, no. 16 (May 21, 1845): 316–18.

Jackson, Chevalier. "Address Upon Accepting the Philadelphia Award." *Philadelphia Forum Magazine,* Mar. 1927.

———. "The Bacillus of Leprosy: A Microscopical Study of Its Morphological Characteristics." *Proceedings of the American Society of Microscopists* 10 (1888): 119–27.

———. "Bacteria in Ice, Especially in Their Relation to Typhoid Fever." *Proceedings of the American Society of Microscopists* 11 (1889): 70–84.

———. "Benign Laryngeal Lesions Producing Hoarseness (Diagnosis and Treatment)." *Transactions of the American Laryngological, Rhinological, and Otological Society* 41 (1935): 128–40.

———. *Bronchoscopy and Esophagoscopy; A Manual of Peroral Endoscopy and Laryngeal Surgery.* Philadelphia: W.B. Saunders, 1922.

———. "Direct Methods of Examination of the Larynx, Trachea, Bronchi, Oesophagus, and Stomach." Lecture, Kings County Medical Society, Brooklyn, NY, Dec. 19, 1911; rep. *International Clinics* 2, 211–18. Philadelphia: JB Lippincott, 1912.

———. "Discussion on Overlooked Cases of Foreign Body in the Air and Food Passages." *British Medical Journal* 2, no. 3381 (Oct. 17, 1925): 686–98.

———. *Diseases of the Air and Food Passages of Foreign-Body Origin.* Philadelphia: W.B. Saunders, 1936.

———. "Fishing in Food and Air Passages." *Hygeia* 11 (1933): 46–49.

———. "Gastroscopy: Report of Additional Cases." *Journal of the American Medical Association* 49, no. 17 (Oct. 26, 1907): 1425–28.

———. *Foreign Bodies in the Air and Food Passages (Charted Experience in Cases from No. 631 to No. 1155). Transactions of the American Laryngological, Rhinological and Otological Society.* New Bedford, CT: Reynolds the Printer, 1924.

———. "Laryngeal, Bronchial, and Esophageal Endoscopy: The Drowning of the Patient in His Own Secretions." *Laryngoscope* 21, no. 12 (Dec. 1911): 1183–85.

———. "Laryngeal, Bronchial, and Esophageal Endoscopy." *Laryngoscope* 23, no. 9 (Sept. 1913): 955–57.

———. *The Larynx and Its Diseases.* Philadelphia: W.B. Saunders, 1937.

———. "The Larynx and the Voice: An Abstract of an Address by the Most Distinguished of Throat Specialists Which Is Here Given Its First Publication." *Etude* 55, no. 8 (Aug. 1937): 501.

———. *The Life of Chevalier Jackson.* New York: Macmillan, 1938.

———. "Medical Education of Women as an Education." *Club Woman's Journal,* Nov. 1936, 8.

———. "New Mechanical Problems in the Bronchoscopic Extraction of Foreign Bodies from the Lungs and Esophagus." *Transactions of the American Laryngological, Rhinological, and Otological Society* 27 (1921): 52–94.

———. "New Mechanical Problems in the Bronchoscopic Extraction of Foreign Bodies from the Lungs and Oesophagus." *Annals of Surgery* 75, no. 1 (Jan. 1922): 1–30.

———. "Original Memoirs: Tracheo-Bronchoscopy (with report of cases)." *Annals of Surgery* 47, no. 3 (Mar. 1908): 321–31.

———. *Peroral Endoscopy and Laryngeal Surgery.* St. Louis: Laryngoscope Company, 1915.

———. "Psychosomatic Aphonia and Ephemeral Adductor Paralysis." *Laryngoscope* 59, no. 12 (Dec. 1949): 1287–98.

———. "Statistics of Seventy Cases of Gastroscopy." *American Journal of the Medical Sciences* 136 (July 1908): 1–7.

———. "The Symptomatology and Diagnosis of Foreign Bodies in the Air and Food Passages. Based Upon a Study of 789 Cases." *American Journal of the Medical Sciences* 161, no. 5 (May 1921): 625–61.

———. "Total Abstinence. An excerpt from *The Life of Chevalier Jackson: An Autobiography.*" *United Presbyterian,* Oct. 27, 1938, 12.

———. "Voluntary Aspiration of a Foreign Body into the Bronchi, Removal by Bronchoscopy." *Laryngoscope* 19, no. 12 (Dec. 1909): 1–4.

———. "What 2,000 Children Have Taught Me." *American Success Stories,* Jan. 1927, 13.

———. "What Does Your Baby Put in His Mouth?" *Hygeia,* 1937, 1–22.

———. "What Does Your Baby Put in His Mouth?" *Hygeia,* Dec. 1923, 561–64.

———. "Why Does Not the Thoracic Surgeon Cure Cancer of the Esophagus?" *Archives of Surgery* 12 (1926): 236–40.

Jackson, Chevalier, and Chevalier L. Jackson. *Bronchoscopy, Esophagoscopy and Gastroscopy: A Manual of Peroral Endoscopy and Laryngeal Surgery.* Philadelphia: W.B. Saunders, 1934.

———. *Diseases of the Nose, Throat, and Ear.* Philadelphia: W.B. Saunders, 1959.

———. *Foreign Body in Air and Food Passages: Roentgenologically Considered.* Annals of Roentgenology 16. New York: Paul B. Hoeber, 1934.

———. "Tracheotomy." *American Journal of Surgery* 46, no. 3 (1939): 519–31.

———. "Your Voice." *Hygeia,* Feb. 1939, 1–10.

Impey, Oliver, and Arthur Macgregor, eds. *The Origins of Museums: The Cabinet of Curiosities in Sixteenth- and Seventeenth-Century Europe.* Oxford: Clarendon Press, 1985.

"Iron Rations: Fakirs Swallow Swords, but Amateurs Take Cake Lunching on Hardware." *Literary Digest,* 1937, 17–18.

Jarman, Rufus. "Kids Will Swallow Anything." *Saturday Evening Post*, Oct. 22, 1949.

Jay, Ricky. "Stones, Swords, Snakes, and Other Entrees." In *Learned Pigs and Fireproof Women*. New York: Villard Books, 1987.

Jha, Alok. "It's Official: Swallowing Swords Hurts Your Throat." *The Guardian*, Oct. 5, 2007.

Kahrilas, Peter J. "The Anatomy and Physiology of Dysphagia." *Dysphagia*, 1989: 11–28.

————. "Motility of the Oropharynx and Proximal Esophagus." In *Motor Disorders of the Gastrointestinal Tract: What's New and What to Do*, ed. Robert Stephen Fisher and Benjamin Krevsky, 29–35. New York: Academy Professional Information Services, 1993.

Keels, Thomas H. *Philadelphia Graveyards and Cemeteries*. Charleston, SC: Arcadia, 2003.

Keller, Marjorie. "Joseph Cornell: The Symbolic Equation." In *The Untutored Eye*. Rutherford, NJ: Fairleigh Dickinson University Press, 1986.

Kenseth, Joy, ed. *The Age of the Marvelous*. Hanover, NH: Dartmouth College, 1991.

Knisely, William H. "Adrien Barrere and His Caricatures of the Medical Faculty of the University of Paris: 'The Nude Lady.' "*Journal of Child Neurology* 4 (Jan. 1989): 50.

Knox, Helen. "Dr. Chevalier Jackson—His Life," *Pittsburgh Sun-Telegraph*, Sept. 5, 1958.

Kurzweil, Allen. *A Case of Curiosities*. New York: Harcourt Brace Jovanovich, 1992.

Lake, Talbot. "Dr. Jackson Writes of Fishing for Junk," *Post Star*, June 29, 1938.

"Le Grand Chevalier." *Physician* 4, no. 1 (June 1946): 14–16.

Lees, Hanna. "Take a Look Inside." *Collier's*, Nov. 7, 1936, 71.

Lindgren, Laura, ed. *Mütter Museum: Historic Medical Photographs (The College of Physicians of Philadelphia)*. New York: Blast Books, 2007.

"Literary Surgeons." *British Medical Journal* 1, no. 4512 (June 28, 1947): 939.

Los Angeles Times, "Safety Pins Made His Fame," July 3, 1938.

MacDonald, Helen. *Human Remains: Dissection and Its Histories*. New Haven CT: Yale University Press, 2005.

Major, A.R. "History of the Stomach Tube." *Annals of Medical History* 6 (1934): 500–509.

Margolin, David A., and Jeffrey M. Marks. "History of Endoscopic Surgery." In *Minimally Invasive Surgery: Principles and Outcomes*, ed. Charles H. Andrus, John M. Cosgrove, and Walter E. Longo. Harwood Academic Publishers, 1998.

Martin, G. Ewart. "A Plea for Better Endoscopic Training." *British Medical Journal* 2, no. 4118 (Dec. 9, 1939): 1138–39.

Mason, Jennifer. *Civilized Creatures: Urban Animals, Sentimental Culture, and American Literature, 1850–1900*. Baltimore: Johns Hopkins University Press, 2005.

Moore, Irwin. "A Historical Survey of Peroral Endoscopy from Its Origin to the Present Day." *British Medical Journal* 1, no. 3398 (Feb. 13, 1926): 278–82.

Morgenstern, Leon. "Endoscopist and Artist: Chevalier Jackson, MD." *Surgical Innovation* 14, no. 3 (Sept. 2007): 149–52.

———. "From the Sword to Schindler: A Saga of Gastroscopy." *Surgical Innovation* 16, no. 2 (June 2009): 93–96.

Muth, D., and R.W. Schafermeyer. "All That Wheezes." *Pediatric Emergency Care* 6 (1990): 110–12.

Myers, Eugene N. "The Evolution of Head and Neck Surgery." *Laryngoscope* 106, no. 8 (Aug. 1996): 929–34.

Myers, Jay Arthur. "Chevalier Jackson and the Bronchoscope." *Hygeia*, 1944, 576–77.

Myerson, Mervin C. "Bronchoscopic Observations on the Cough Reflex in Tonsillectomy under General Anesthesia." *Laryngoscope* 34, no. 1 (Jan. 1924): 3–8.

———. "Esophagoscopy." *New York Medical Journal and Medical Record* 116 (July 19, 1922): 82–85.

Natov, Roni. "The Power of the Tale." *Children's Literature* 13 (1985): 199–203.

Naylor, Douglas. "The Four Corners of Pittsburgh," *Pittsburgh Press*, Apr. 11, 1932.

Negus, V.E. "The Course of Endoscopy in Chevalier Jackson's Service." *Journal of Laryngology and Otolaryngology* 34 (1924): 145–49.

———. "The Simplification of Technique in Peroral Endoscopy." *British Medical Journal* 2, no. 4120 (Dec. 23, 1939): 1223–24.

Nelson, Marilyn. *Fortune's Bones: The Manumission Requiem.* Asheville, North Carolina: Front Street, 2004.

"A New Bronchoscope and Bronchoscopic Technique." *British Medical Journal* 1, no. 3869 (Mar. 2, 1935): 420.

New York Herald Tribune, "Modern Equivalent of a Saint," July 24, 1938.

———, "What America is Reading," July 17, 1938.

New York Times, "Baby Flies to Clinic: She Travels 1,800 Miles with Open Safety Pin in Throat," Nov. 19, 1942.

———, "Baby, Nail in Lung, in from Australia," June 25, 1936.

———, "Boy, 5, Flies from South Africa to Be Treated for Throat Ailment," Aug. 18, 1945, 16.

———, "Boy Ends 10,000-Mile Trip," May 27, 1946.

———, "Boy Who Journeyed to Philadelphia Recovering—Operation Takes Four Minutes," Jan. 21, 1924.

———, "Boy Who Swallowed Nail Coming to U.S. Surgeon," Mar. 13, 1936.

———, "Bronchoscope Clinic Keeps Realistic Record of Work," Sept. 18, 1927.

———, "Can Opener Removed After Child Is Flown to Philadelphia," Aug. 11, 1942.

———, "Child in Race Against Death," Aug. 16, 1942.

———, "Corn Kernel from Child's Lung," Apr. 12, 1931.

———, "Doctor Treats Lung Abscess Through Tube; Frenchman Also Removes Foreign Objects," Oct. 20, 1930.

———, "Dr. Jackson Quits Active Practice," June 10, 1938.

———, "Football Cheers Punish Larynx, Says Dr. Jackson," Dec. 30, 1938.

———, "Former Miss Biddle of Philadelphia, Suffering from Poisoning, Is Believed Out of Danger," Mar. 22, 1925.

———, "France Honors Dr. Chevalier Jackson," June 20, 1929.

———, "Mercy Operation for Boy," July 17, 1945.

———, "Nail in His Lung, Boy, 3, Undaunted," June 14, 1936.

———, "Nail in Lung Gone, Boy, 3, Tours City," July 31, 1936.

———, "Opera Troupe Elects Head," Dec. 23, 1949.

———, "Razor Blade Is Taken from Boy's Stomach," June 13, 1931.

———, "Swallows False Teeth," July 13, 1931.

———, "Trip to Save Boy's Life: South Africa Raises Fund to Fly Child, 5, to Philadelphia," June 27, 1945, 15.

News and Observer, "Monument to Doctors and Scientists," Oct. 23, 1938.

Nixon, George W. "Foley Catheter Method of Esophageal Foreign Body Removal: Extension of Applications." *American Roentgen Ray Society*, Mar. 1979, 441–42.

Norris, Charles M. "Dr. Chevalier Jackson, A Pupil's Esteem." *Temple University Medical Center Bulletin* 5, no. 2 (Dec. 1958): 5.

Norristown Times Herald. "Jackson, the Genius," Jan. 7, 1932.

Norton, Richard F. "The Modern Miracle Man." *Grit*, Feb. 12, 1928.

Nuland, Sherwin. *The Mysteries Within: A Surgeon Reflects on Medical Myths*. New York: Simon & Schuster, 2000.

———. "A Voyage Through the Gut." In *How We Live*, 280–325. New York: Random House, 1998.

O'Keefe, John J. "The Development of Bronchoscopy at Jefferson." *Transactions and Studies of the College of Physicians of Philadelphia* 32, no. 4 (Apr. 1965): 171–74.

Ono, J. "Sir William Osler and Chevalier Jackson." *Annals of Otology, Rhinology, and Laryngology* 81, no. 6 (Dec. 1972): 770–71.

"Operation: Dr. Jackson Draws a 'Nyle' Out of Kelvin Rodgers." *Newsweek*, July 4, 1936.

Palta, Renee, Amandeep Sahota, Ali Bemarki, Paul Salama, Nicole Simpson, and Loren Laine. "Foreign-Body Ingestion: Characteristics and Outcomes in a Lower Socioeconomic Population with Predominantly Intentional Ingestion." *Gastrointestinal Endoscopy* 69, no. 3 (Mar. 2009): 426–33.

Parkinson, William N. "Chevalier Jackson (1865–1958): A Tribute." *Temple University Medical Center Bulletin* 5, no. 2 (Dec. 1958): 3–4.

Patterson, Ada. "Strange Things Folks Swallow." *Popular Science*, May 1925.

Peña, Carolyn Thomas de la. "The Machine-Built Body." In *The Body Electric: How Strange Machines Built the Modern America*. New York University Press, 2003.

Pennsylvania Gazette, "Dr. Jackson Resigns," Feb. 3, 1930.

Philadelphia Record, "Dr. Jackson's New Device Surpasses Bronchoscope," Mar. 10, 1932.

————, "Dr. Jackson Hurt in Crash: Bronchoscopic Expert Gives Self First Aid," Oct. 24, 1933.

Philadelphia Sunday Record, "The Man Who Saved a Thousand Lives," Sept. 24, 1939.

Phillips, Adam. *Winnicott.* Cambridge, MA: Harvard University Press, 1988.

————. *The Beast in the Nursery: On Curiosity and Other Appetites.* New York: Pantheon, 1998.

————. *On Kissing, Tickling, and Being Bored: Psychoanalytic Essays on the Unexamined Life.* Cambridge, MA: Harvard University Press, 1994.

Pinchin, A.J. Scott, and H.V. Morlock, "The Bronchoscope in the Diagnosis and Treatment of Pulmonary Diseases." *Postgraduate Medical Journal* 8 (1932): 337–41.

Pittsburgh Press, "Bronchoscope Removes Pin Swallowed by Schoolgirl: Medical Science Comes to Aid of Millvale Child After Unusual Classroom Accident," Feb. 17, 1938.

Podolsky, Edward. "Chevalier Jackson and the Blocked Passages." *New Physician*, Sept. 1963, 366–68.

Pontalis, J.B. *Windows*, tr. Anne Quinney. Lincoln: University of Nebraska Press, 2003.

Porter, Fairfield. "Joseph Cornell." In *Art in Its Own Terms: Selected Criticism 1935–1975.* Boston: MFA Publications, 2008.

Pottstown Mercury. "Pottstown Mourns Dr. Jackson, Man of Mercy and Medical Genius," Aug. 18, 1958.

Pottstown News. "Tack Added to Dr. Jackson's Exhibit," Jan. 26, 1924.

"Pouched Throats," *Time*, Mar. 21, 1932.

Poulet, Alfred. *A Treatise on Foreign Bodies in Surgical Practice*, 2 vols. New York: William Wood, 1881.

Proust, Marcel. *Swann's Way*, tr. Lydia Davis, ed. Christopher Prendergast. New York: Viking, 2003.

Public Ledger (Philadelphia), "Baby Flown Here from Kansas, Has Corn in Her Lung," Aug. 10, 1938.

Purcell, Rosamond. *Special Cases: Natural Anomalies and Historical Monsters.* San Francisco: Chronicle Books, 1997.

Purcell, Rosamond, and Stephen J. Gould. *Illuminations.* New York: Norton, 1986.

Raffel, Dawn. *In the Year of Long Division.* New York: Alfred A. Knopf, 1994.

Ravich, William J., Lynn Norwitz, and Anthony N. Kalloo. "Swallowing Disorders." *Johns Hopkins Gastroenterology and Hepatology Resource Center*, 1–31, http://hopkins-gi.org/?SS=&CurrentUDV=31 (accessed Feb. 2007).

Ravich, William J., Ron S. Wilson, Bronwyn Jones, and Martin W. Donner. "Psychogenic Dysphagia and Globus: Reevaluation of 23 Patients." *Dysphagia* 4, no. 1 (Mar. 1989): 35–38.

Richards, Annette. "Automatic Genius: Mozart and the Mechanical Sublime." *Music & Letters* 80, no. 3 (Aug. 1999): 366–89.

Richardson, Ruth. *Death, Dissection and the Destitute.* New York: Routledge, 1987.

Rodriguez, Barbara. "NC Doctor Removes Plastic Fragment Lodged in Lung," *San Francisco Gate,* Sept. 17, 2009.

Ross, Alexander. *Arcana Microcosmi; or, the Hid Secrets of Man's Body Discovered* (1652, bk. 2, ch. 8, pp. 138–44, http://penelope.uchicago.edu/ross/index.html (accessed June 2009).

Rothman, Lily. "The Aye Has It: One Woman's Extraordinary Journey from Bulimic to Sword Swallower." *Bust,* Dec. 2009–Jan. 2010.

Rush, Agnes. *Russell H. Conwell and His Work; or, One Man's Interpretation of Life.* John C. Winston, 1926.

Salisbury, Laura. "Gagging, Peristalsis and Compulsion in the Trilogy" (forthcoming).

Sappol, Michael. *Dream Anatomy.* U.S. Department of Health and Human Services, National Library of Medicine, 2003.

Sastry, A., P.D. Kargos, S. Leong, and S. Hampal. "Bulimia and Oesophageal Foreign Bodies." *Journal of Laryngology and Otology* 122, no. 16 (2008).

Saunders, Barry F. *CT Suite: The Work of Diagnosis in the Age of Noninvasive Cutting.* Durham, NC: Duke University Press, 2008.

Sawday, Jonathan. *The Body Emblazoned: Dissection and the Human Body in Renaissance Culture.* New York: Routledge, 1995.

Saxena, Amulya K., Ursula Seebacher, Philipp Baumann, and Michael Kristler. "Introduction of the Euro: The Change Is Easily Swallowed at a Young Age." *European Journal of Pediatrics* 167 (Feb. 2008): 243–44.

Savitt, D.L., and S. Watson. "Delayed Diagnosis of Coin Ingestion in Children." *American Journal of Emergency Medicine* 6 (1988): 378–81.

Savitt, Todd L. *Medicine and Slavery: The Diseases and Health Care of Blacks in Antebellum Virginia.* Chicago: University of Illinois Press, 1978.

Schindler, Rudolf. "Gastroscopy with a Flexible Gastroscope (with Discussants Chevalier Jackson and William A. Swalm)." *American Journal of Digestive Diseases and Nutrition* 2, no. 11 (Nov. 1935): 656–63.

Sedgwick, Eve Kosofsky. "A Poem Is Being Written." In *Tendencies.* Durham, NC: Duke University Press, 1993.

Serlin, David. "Producing Surgery on the Internet: Is the Rectum a Cinema?" *Cabinet: A Quarterly Magazine of Art and Culture* 1 (Winter 2000).

Shapiro, S.L. "Chevalier Jackson: A Notable Centenary." *Eye, Ear, Nose, Throat Monthly,* Nov. 1965, 100.

Solomon, Deborah. *Utopia Parkway: The Life and Work of Joseph Cornell.* New York: Noonday Press, 1997.

Sontag, Susan. *Illness as Metaphor.* New York: Vintage Books, 1979.

Southard, E.E. "Non-dementia non-praecox: Note on the Advantages to Mental Hygiene of Extirpating a Term" (1919). *History of Psychiatry* 18 (2007): 483–502.

Stiegler, Lillian N. "Understanding Pica Behavior: A Review for Clinical and Education Professionals." *Focus on Autism and Other Developmental Disabilities* 20, no. 1 (Spring 2005): 27–38.

Stenn, Frederick. "The Need for a Comprehensive Medical Audio-Visual Aid Center." *Science* 118, no. 3077 (Dec. 18, 1953): 753–55.

Stevenson, Robert Scott, *Morell Mackenzie: The Story of a Victorian Tragedy.* London: William Heinemann Medical Books, 1946.

Suita, S., H. Ohgami, and A. Nagasaki. "Management of Pediatric Patients Who Have Swallowed Foreign Objects." *American Surgery* 55 (1989): 585–90.

Sunday Bulletin (Philadelphia). "Chevalier Jackson Is Dead at Age 92; Famed Doctor's Clinic Saved Thousands," Aug. 17, 1958.

Sunday Star, "Specialist Reveals Rare Zeal," Sept. 4, 1938.

Sword Swallowers Association International. "Sword Swallower's Hall of Fame," www.swordswallow.com/halloffame.php (accessed Mar. 23, 2007).

Terpak, Frances. "Objects and Contexts." In *Devices of Wonder: From the World in a Box to Images on a Screen*, ed. Barbara Maria Stafford and Frances Terpak. Los Angeles: Getty Research Institute, 2001.

Thompson, Ralph, "Books of the Times," *New York Times*, June 15, 1938.

Thompson, Virgil. "Voice Forum," *New York Herald Tribune*, Nov. 17, 1946.

———. "Voice Forum," *New York Herald Tribune*, Dec. 1, 1946.

Toliver, Ramone. "Airway Foreign Body." *eMedicine*, July 28, 2005, www.emedicine .com (accessed Feb. 2007).

"Trip to Surgeon Spans 9,000 Miles." *Literary Digest* 121 (Apr. 1936): 45.

Tsai, Shih-Jen. "Foreign Body Ingestion in Psychiatric Inpatients." *International Medical Journal* 4, no. 4 (Dec. 1977): 309–11.

Tucker, John A. "Presidential Remarks." American Laryngological Association, www.alahns.org (accessed Nov. 3, 2008).

van Dijck, José. "Fantastic Voyages in the Age of Endoscopy." In *The Transparent Body: A Cultural Analysis of Medical Imaging.* Seattle: University of Washington Press, 2005.

van Loon, Emily Lois. "Dr. Chevalier Jackson: President of the Woman's Medical College of Pennsylvania, 1935–1941." *Transactions and Studies of the College of Physicians of Philadelphia* 33 (1965): 49–51.

van Manen, Max. "The Pathic Nature of Inquiry and Nursing." In *Nursing and the Experience of Illness: Phenomenology in Practice*, ed. Irena Walton and Jo Ann Walton, pp. 17–35. London: Routledge, 1999.

Vilardell, Francisco. *Digestive Endoscopy in the Second Millenium: From the Lichtleiter to Echoendoscopy.* Stuttgart, Germany: Thieme, 2006.

Virginian-Pilot and the Portsmouth Star, "Dr. Jackson Looked Down Human Wells," Aug. 24, 1958.

"Visual Examination of Air Passages and the Stomach." Review of *Tracheo-bronchoscopy, Esophagoscopy and Gastroscopy* by Chevalier Jackson. *British Medical Journal* 1, no. 2473 (May 23, 1908): 1236–37.

Waddell, Louis M. "Against All Odds: Chevalier Jackson, Physician and Painter." *Pennsylvania Heritage* 18, no. 3 (Summer 1992): 17–23.

Wain, Harry. *The Story Behind the Word: Some Interesting Origins of Medical Terms.* Springfield, IL: Charles C Thomas, 1958.

Walk, L. "The History of Gastroscopy." *Clio Medica* 1 (1966): 209–22.

Wallace, Emily Duane. "Dr. Chevalier Jackson and the Bronchoscope." *Scientific Monthly* 51 (Nov. 1940): 487–88.

Warner, John Harley. *Dissection: Photographs of a Rite of Passage in American Medicine: 1880–1030.* New York: Blast Books, 2009.

Weintraub, Barbara. "A Case of Airway Obstruction: A Rubber Ball in a Baby's Throat Didn't Get There on Its Own." *American Journal of Nursing* 106, no. 8 (Aug. 2006): 35–38.

Weschler, Lawrence. *Mr. Wilson's Cabinet of Wonder.* New York: Vintage Books, 1995.

White, David R., Miguel Bravo, Shyan Vijayasekaran, Michael J. Rutter, Robin T. Cotton, and Ravindhra G. Elluru. "Laryngotracheoplasty as an Alternative to Tracheotomy in Infants Younger Than 6 Months." *Archive of Otolaryngology Head and Neck Surgery* 135, no. 9 (May 2009): 445–47.

Wilson, Elizabeth A. "Gut Feminism." *differences: A Journal of Feminist Cultural Studies* 15, no. 3 (200): 66–93.

Williams, William Carlos. "The Use of Force." In *The Doctor Stories.* New York: New Directions, 1962.

Witcombe, Brian, and Dan Meyer. "Sword Swallowing and Its Side Effects." *British Medical Journal* 333 (Dec. 2006): 1285–87.

Wood, Lisa. *The Swallowing Plates: Objects Swallowed and Recovered from the Human Body.* Blurb, 2007, www.blurb.com (accessed May 8, 2010).

Woodson, Gayle E. "The History of Laryngology in the United States." *Laryngoscope* 106, no. 6 (June 1996): 677–79.

Woolf, S.J. "Science with Long Fingers." *Rotarian* 59 (1941): 28–31.

Worden, Gretchen. *Mütter Museum of the College of Physicians of Philadelphia.* New York: Blast Books, 2002.

Zipes, Jack. "A Second Gaze at Little Red Riding Hood's Trials and Tribulations." *Lion and the Unicorn* 7–8 (1983–84): 78–109.

Zufall, Nora L. "Endoscopy: A Description of the Technics Used at the Jackson Bronchoscopic Clinics, Philadelphia." *American Journal of Nursing* 29, no. 10 (Oct. 1929): 1209–16.

———. "Endoscopy: Part II." *American Journal of Nursing* 29, no. 11 (Nov. 1929): 1289–95.

———. "Endoscopy: Part III—Operating Room Technic." *American Journal of Nursing* 29, no. 12 (Dec. 1929): 1407–14.

ACKNOWLEDGMENTS

Swallow was made possible by the beneficent guidance of numerous outstanding archivists and the collections in their care. I am especially grateful to F. Michael Angelo, University Archivist at Thomas Jefferson University, Scott Memorial Library, for his knowledge, expertise, and on-going correspondence, for his warmth, and for his enthusiasm for this project. F. Michael Angelo introduced me to the gastroenterologist, Dr. V. Alin Botoman, whose generous conversation, instruction, and collaboration grace some of the pages of this book. Dan Super did a fabulous job with photographic reproductions from Jefferson's collections, and M.M. Alice Haworth's firsthand account of Idlewood in the Jefferson University Archives, "Some Recollections of Idlewood," brought that place alive for me and provided me with a living history from which I could draw.

Anna N. Dhody, Curator of the Mütter Museum, The College of Physicians of Philadelphia, welcomed me from the start, and I wish to thank her especially for enriching my understanding of the possible significances of the bones found in Jackson's attic as well as for entrusting me with the important work ahead: the co-curation of the newly improved Chevalier Jackson fbdy collection display. Laurel K. Weller, former Museum Educator, Mütter Museum, graciously introduced me to Margaret Derryberry, and Brandon Zimmerman, former Administrative Coordinator and Designer, Mütter Museum, shared excitement for this project as well as helpful stories about the history of the fbdy collection while tracking down X-rays and other bits of material culture that form a context for the collection. Andrea Kenyon, Director of the Library, and Joan R. McKenzie, Technical Services Librarian of the College of Physicians of Philadelphia, helped me to mine the resources at their disposal and even found traces of work I myself had carried out in the library decades ago that I would have otherwise forgotten.

Stephen J. Greenberg, Coordinator of Public Services, History of Medicine Division, National Library of Medicine, National Institutes of Health, Department of Health and Human Services, and James Labosier, Associate Curator of Manuscripts at the National Library of Medicine, responded to my research queries, in person and from afar, thoroughly and with aplomb. James Labosier's impeccable reproductions of so many valuable traces of Jackson's medical legacy were unsurpassed, and the library and History of Medicine Reading Room is such an endlessly rich resource, I think I could easily live there.

I spent a wonderful afternoon poring over Jacksoniana with Eric W. Jentsch, Associate Curator, Division of Medicine and Science, National Museum of American History, Smithsonian Institution, and I thank him and his colleagues at the

Smithsonian's Archives Center, the Behring Center, for their generous attention and time: David Haberstitch, Associate Curator of Photography; Reuben Jackson, Associate Curator; Wendy Shay, Deputy Chair; and, Kay Peterson, Customer Service Representative.

Sarah Elder, Curator of Collections, Glore Psychiatric Museum, and Scott Clarke, the museum's former curator, filled in important blanks relative to the history of the stomach contents display, and Duane Chandler of Kings County Hospital, Brooklyn, helped me to search for traces of the case of hardware swallower, Miss Mabel Wolfe. I thank Franklin Institute Curator, John Alviti, for his engagement with me and for his swift re-discovery and documentation of the Jackson fbdy display that was built for the museum and on view at the Institute in the 1930s. I am indebted to his staff: Erin Johnson, Research Assistant; Cheryl Desmond, Curatorial Department, Collections Manager; Charles Penniman, Institute volunteer; and Susannah Carroll, part-time Curatorial Associate, all of whom provided me with photographs and other material relative to the exhibit.

Temple University Special Collections Head, Thomas M. Whitehead, enabled me access to the Chevalier Jackson Postcard Collection; Gail Binderup of the American Triological Association was extremely helpful in locating sources for the Triological songbook; and, Jacqueline M. DeGroff, Curator, The Drexel Collection, graciously tracked down a reproduction of a portrait of Chevalier Jackson by S. George Phillips that hangs in the auditorium of Drexel University's Queen Lane Campus.

Carl Klase, Assistant Administrator, Pennypacker Mills, was a sensitive, informative, and generous guide to the Old Sunrise Mills property and new materials discovered in Jackson's barn. I thank him, additionally, for the magical presentation of Chevalier Jackson's coat.

My earliest archival experience relative to the life and work of Chevalier Jackson takes precedence in my memory and in the genesis of this book. I am grateful to Tracy L. Sullivan, former Director, The John Q. Adams Center for the History of Otolaryngology—Head and Neck Surgery (AAO-HNS), American Academy of Otolaryngology (Alexandria, Virginia), and Brooke Hinrichs, former Librarian and Archivist there. This repository contains the most replete collection of medical illustrations, chalk drawings, and paintings in oil by Chevalier Jackson; thus, it was with tremendous regret that I learned of the library's closing. I refer the reader, and any student of medicine and of medical humanities to this archive in the event of its re-opening should they wish to see the images to which my descriptions in chapter one refer, especially Jackson's magnificent illustrations of the normal stomach and the normal larynx.

I am greatly indebted to Louis Waddell, historian, Pennsylvania Historic and Museum Commission, for his generous feedback on my book prospectus, for recollections of his meeting with Chevalier Jackson's granddaughter, Joan Jackson Bugbee, and her husband, Frank Bugbee, and for writing what I consider the single most important essay on Chevalier Jackson's life and work, "Against All Odds: Chevalier Jackson, Physician and Painter."

I am awed by the new communities forged and friendships made as a result of my writing and research on Jackson's fbdy collection. For trusting me with their stories and breathing life into this project, for sharing their memories with me, and painting a vivid landscape of the past that my words can only approximate, I thank Sallie Harwood Norris, widow of Dr. Charles Norris, close colleague and friend of Chevalier Jackson, and Sallie Harwood Norris' sons, Steve Norris and Dr. Carl Norris; Margaret Derryberry and her daughter, Peggy Derryberry Gould; Arlene Maloney, widow of Dr. Walter H. Maloney, close colleague and friend of Chevalier Jackson; Arlene's son, Dr. Hugh Maloney, and her daughter-in-law, mover and shaker, Carol Maloney, who made our meeting possible. Nothing can compare to corresponding with the living descendents of Chevalier Jackson, and I am grateful for their opening the door of their lives to me: Chevalier Jackson's great-grandson, Frank Bugbee, Jr.; Frank's partner, Jennifer Peters; Jackson's great-granddaughter, Susan Bugbee Ruby; Frank Jr.'s daughter, Kristine Bugbee; and Frank Bugbee, Sr., husband of the late Joan Jackson Bugbee, daughter of Chevalier L. Jackson.

My companion in curiosa, the San Francisco-based artist, Lisa Wood, creator of the beautiful *Swallowing Plates* (http://www.lisawoodcuriosities.com) has been a source of inspiration and shared intrigue. Sword swallower Dan Meyer has been extremely kind in reading and responding to the chapter in which my interpretation of his work appears, and I look forward to collaborative presentations with both of these colleagues. A gathering to mark Arlene Maloney's donation to the Mütter Museum of a group of Jackson's medical illustrations led to my meeting book designer and publisher of Blast Books, Laura Lindgren, whose generosity, erudition, expertise, and friendly correspondence have helped *Swallow* along at various strategic points in its conception and composition. I am grateful to Laura for putting me in touch with Rosamond Purcell—whose photographs and writing on natural history and nature's anomalies were already an inspiration for *Swallow*, and I am additionally honored by Rosamond Purcell's allowing The New Press to use two of her photographs of the fbdy collection in this book. Laura also put me in touch with James Edmonson, medical historian and Chief Curator, Dittrick Medical History Center and Museum, Case Western Reserve University. James Edmonson's swift and generous response to my queries were invaluable, and his research, including an interactive CD that he shared with me *gratis*, "The Instruments of Gastrointestinal Endoscopy," was an indispensable resource.

To work on any of the Mütter Museum's collections is to enter the sphere of influence created by curator Gretchen Worden's singular legacy. Though I did not have the chance to meet Gretchen Worden before she died, I composed *Swallow* in the spirit of her life and work as glimpsed through the essays she wrote, books she collaborated on, and radio and documentary appearances that she made in which one finds a person who was not only learned, good-humored, and appropriately quirky for the work entailed by the Mütter Museum's curation, but someone whose spirited disquisitions on the Mütter's specimens lent a warmth to the collections, and someone who maintained a genuine interest in the lives of people whose bodies, or parts of bodies, resided there. I am grateful for the imaginative reach and unusual intellection that distinguished Gretchen Worden's work, and I hope she would find delight and kinship in the approach that I have taken here.

At the University of Rhode Island, my intellectual, creative, and pedagogic home since 1991, I had the good fortune of working with three dedicated librarians, Barbara Gavin, Tawanda Rand, and Marilyn Jamagocian who went above and beyond the call of duty in tracking down hard to find items and keeping on top of my daily library orders. I am especially indebted to them for their collective advice on how to treat inflammation of the thumb joint brought on by my overuse of a microfilm machine on which I attempted to read the entire run of Philadelphia's *Public Ledger* for 1926 across the course of two afternoons. The English Department's Administrative Assistant, Michelle Caraccia, provided me with clerical assistance and moral support, and I am grateful to a gifted cadre of research assistants from among the University of Rhode Island's undergraduate and graduate student body: Lia Ottaviano, Kara Lafferty, and Erin Vachon, each of whose felicitous relationship to language helped to inspire my own. URI alum Jillian Tomaino gave me the wonderful line, "all things are secretly edible" when instructed in my poetry workshop to riff on Ashbery's "all things are secretly bored," and Jennifer Cochran's writing on thirst was something I aspired to. A very special community of graduate students in my seminar in creative nonfiction let me test out passages on them late into the season's weekly Tuesday nights and took risks with form that gave me courage—Nancy Abeshaus, Bo Allen, Theo Greenblatt, Jeremy Hawkins, Linda Langlois, Cathryn Molloy, Max Orsini, Lia Ottaviano, and Jennifer Sullivan. Claire Roche's work on collections and collecting also spurred me on.

My colleagues in the English Department at the University of Rhode Island teach me daily, and their own challenging and original work is in many ways a model for my own. I am grateful to Martha Elena Rojas for apprizing my partner, Jean Walton, and me, of the Mütter Museum's giant bowel and suggesting that we go there in the first place; J. Jennifer Jones for guiding me on an excursion into a passage from Samuel Taylor Coleridge on forms that pass into and out of oneself; and, Travis Williams for making me aware of relevant passages from Dickens. Peter Covino and Dr. Tim Cavanaugh listened to excerpts from the book-in-progress, engaged me with questions, appreciated the poetry of these pages, and discussed the implications of the book's material at length. Carolyn Betensky helped me to understand the psychoanalytic subtleties of my material; Naomi Mandel made me realize I was dealing with an extreme art; and Erik Sklar listened with the ear of a scientist. Friend and colleague Stephen Barber introduced me to the biographical model of Neil Bartlett's book on Oscar Wilde (*Who Was That Man?*), brought me passages from Virginia Woolf to consider, and showed passionate interest in my descriptions of this project; as Department Chair, Professor Barber provided me with the conditions of possibility for bringing this book to completion.

I am grateful to Professor Galen Johnson, Director of the Center for the Humanities at the University of Rhode Island, to the Center's Executive Committee, and to Dean Winifred Brownell, Dean of the College of Arts and Sciences, for providing me with the institutional support that made my writing possible. The Richard Beaupre Faculty Subvention Grant in the Humanities, and a Richard Beaupre Faculty Research Fellowship in the Humanities supported my travel to archives as well as costs for rights and reproductions.

Soon after starting work on this book, I was interrupted by a cancer diagnosis that took me off course while at the same time deepening my relationship to this material. Throughout my cancer ordeal, my agent, Malaga Baldi, helped me to believe that I would live past my treatment and write the books I still had in me. Malaga's inimitable insight, publishing savvy, her presence at my readings, her drive and her push, her humor and her subtlety, mean the world to me. "Swallow" was her title for this book from the get-go. People who helped me through the course of cancer treatment and who have helped me to stay well since are too many to mention. I include here only a handful of trusted readers, writers, and editors; friends who were okay with my passing images of swallowed objects around the dinner table, or whose respective fascination with and repulsion toward this material helped me to understand the stakes of this writing; people who shared their swallowing tales with me, and those who shared their knowledge of medicine: Jack M. Payson, Dr. Maureen Chung, Deidre Pope, Arthur Riss, Nina Markov, Divya Epstein-Lubow, Laura Doan, Sheri Wills, Marie Christine Aquarone, Monica Allen, Derek Walls, Penelope Cray, Sarah Higley, Dr. Joe DiMase, Barbara Morris, Rebecca Allan, Amy Hoffman, Colby Adams, Jerry and Eileen Spinelli, John Gennari, Emily Bernard, Stephen Corey, Bill Thomas, Dr. Noah Rosenberg and Deb Rosenberg, my literary nonfiction-writing cohorts—Edi Giunta, Barrie Jean Borich, David Lazar, David Shields, Patrick Madden, and Sara Greenslit; Dr. Thomas Duffy, Director, Program for Humanities in Medicine, Yale University School of Medicine; and, my editor at Alyson Books, Don Weise, who gave my writing on cancer a home.

I am blessed with a group of intellectual companions and writer-friends to whom I entrust everything I write first and last, and whose own writing is the sonorous envelope for what I compose: James Morrison, Karen Carr, Russell Potter, and Jean Walton read or listened to multiple versions of these pages as my most serious interlocutors, and Russell aided my searches for everything from the cover photo for this book to the coordinates of Chevalier Jackson's descendants. I owe special thanks to Jennifer Manlowe who insisted I read the first 150 pages to her aloud on a drive from Providence to Maine and who provided me with examples and with confidence in the singularity of this project. The nature of *Swallow*'s adventurous meditations are very much indebted to the work of British psycho-analyst, Adam Phillips. My admiration for the model he provides as practitioner, essayist, and public intellectual runs deep, and I am grateful for his enduring interest in my work.

Sarah Fan, my extremely hard-working editor at The New Press, greatly aided in the clearing of *Swallow*'s throat. By asking me to return to what I thought I knew well, she helped me to know it even better, to revisit and revise. Sarah Fan's dedicated close reading and the keen review of the manuscript by Gary Stimeling, copyeditor, were uncommonly illuminating, thorough, and smart.

The constant admonitions of my father, Joseph Salvatore Cappello, that all parts of the object world were potential swallowing hazards no doubt has some-thing to do with my excursion into swallowing's underbelly. I am thankful for hav-ing learned to turn what he would otherwise have us fear into something worthy of my interest and understanding. My mother, the poet Rosemary Petracca Cappello, has read and supported me even when the subjects I choose to write about have given her pause. Having taught me to love and even court the strangeness in the world, and in myself, she laid the groundwork for my work on Chevalier Jackson.

Jeannie Walton, with whom I've eaten breakfast, sometimes lunch, and always dinner for the past twenty years, who taught this Catholic girl the pleasures of im-bibement, first caught sight of the fbdy collection and enjoined me to "look." Her own edgy and elegant work on peristalsis, or what goes out, tempted me to think about the meanings attached to what goes in.

Last but not least, I am immensely grateful to Dr. Chevalier Quixote Jackson for living a life that could inspire my best poetic efforts and analyses. I have tried neither to get him right nor to offer a definitive account of his life and times, but only to open the cabinet of curiosity he made, to read his books and the countless case histories of his patients with care, and with the hope that more books, poems, films, and other forms of attention will emerge from the inexhaustible treasure trove that is the Chevalier Jackson Foreign Body Collection of the College of Phy-sicians of Philadelphia.

INDEX

Note: *Page numbers in italics indicate photographs and illustrations.*